DREAMWORKING

Photo by Andrew Johnson

About the Author

Dr. Christopher Sowton (Toronto, Ontario) holds a B.A. from the University of Toronto and a Doctor of Naturopathic Medicine (N.D.) from the Canadian College of Naturopathic Medicine. He is also licensed as a Registered Psychotherapist (RP) in the Province of Ontario. Christopher runs a private health care practice, specializing in naturopathy, homeopathy, and counseling. He also teaches dreamwork seminars for health care practitioners.

To Write to the Author

If you wish to contact the author or would like more information about this book, please write to the author in care of Llewellyn Worldwide, and we will forward your request. Both the author and the publisher appreciate hearing from you and learning of your enjoyment of this book and how it has helped you. Llewellyn Worldwide cannot guarantee that every letter written to the author can be answered, but all will be forwarded. Please write to:

Dr. Christopher Sowton, ND
℅ Llewellyn Worldwide
2143 Wooddale Drive
Woodbury, MN 55125-2989

Please enclose a self-addressed stamped envelope for reply,
or $1.00 to cover costs. If outside the USA, enclose
an international postal reply coupon.

Many of Llewellyn's authors have websites with additional information and resources. For more information, please visit www.llewellyn.com.

DREAMWORKING

How to Listen to the Inner
Guidance of Your Dreams

Dr. Christopher Sowton, ND

Llewellyn Publications
Woodbury, Minnesota

First Edition
First Printing, 2017

Book design by Bob Gaul
Cover design by Kevin R. Brown
Editing by Laura Graves
Interior flow chart by Llewellyn art department

Llewellyn Publications is a registered trademark of Llewellyn Worldwide Ltd.

Library of Congress Cataloging-in-Publication Data (Pending)
ISBN: 978-0-7387-5013-2

Llewellyn Publications
A Division of Llewellyn Worldwide Ltd.
2143 Wooddale Drive
Woodbury, MN 55125-2989
www.llewellyn.com

Printed in the United States of America

Disclaimer

This book is a general guide and should not be used as a substitute for consulting a qualified health care professional. The author and publishers are not responsible for any adverse effects or consequences resulting from the use of the information in this book. It is the responsibility of the reader to consult a health care professional regarding any serious issues with his or her health, emotional life, or psychological status.

Acknowledgments and Thanks

Thanks to all the dreamers who have shared their dreams with me over the years. Upon this dream material everything in my work is built.

Special thanks to the many dreamers who have allowed their dreams to be videotaped, transcribed, and included as part of this publication.

Thanks to all the members of the Dream Team Inner Circle who have supported me and my work over the years as these ideas have developed and gestated.

Thanks to my parents, Ian and Fran, for all their love, help, and support throughout the whole long journey.

Thanks to Terry and Jo-Ann for all the many ways they have helped out over the years.

Thanks to Ian Sowton for his careful proofreading and comments.

Special thanks to Jennifer for her dream sharing, her insights and reflections, her steadfast support for this endeavor, and her love.

Contents

Part 3: Common Dream Motifs

Introduction

Alice was a 29-year-old woman who came to me for help with anxiety and lack of confidence. She wrote this nutshell description of herself on the intake form: "I've always found it difficult to be okay with the unknown. When faced with a new or challenging situation, I crawl back into myself, to protect myself." She told me the following dream:

> I'm in a meadow. A 3- to 5-year-old girl is there, a cute little blonde girl. A female deer is there too, bigger than a fawn but not fully grown. All three of us are playing together in the meadow. They lead me to the edge of the meadow, where there's a forest, and a path leading into the forest. All of a sudden we stop playing. They start walking onto the path. They notice that I'm not coming with them, so they turn around. They're both looking at me. They say, "C'mon, follow us." I just freeze. I want to follow them but I can't. I want more than anything to go with them... but it's like I can't move...

While discussing the dream, we both find it striking that she cannot move. But why not? What is stopping her? It appears that nothing is stopping her except an unseen and very powerful force—the presence of a limiting fear that exists somewhere inside her. This is the same fear that causes her to crawl back into herself when faced with a new or challenging situation; she knows it all too well but she cannot remove it or fix it. The beauty of this short and simple dream is that it depicts a limiting mindset in a clear and nonthreatening way; it asks of her: what might you be able to do about this? This dream, like so many, highlights a crucial problem and calls out for some creative solution to be brought forward.

Dreams can be sacred, they can be scary, they can be fascinating, they can be funny, they can be erotic, they can be exhausting and chaotic—in fact they can be anything! And they can also be communicative—they can have a lot to tell us if we care to listen, and a lot to ask of us. They can depict our stuck points and limitations, they can speak about what makes us ill, what stresses us, how we may be behaving dangerously, how we are trying to change, and what is blocking us from changing—all issues that most of us agree are critically important. Yet most of us do not take our dreams seriously, and practitioners within the helping professions do not regularly address their clients' dream lives. Why not?

What if you were Alice? What would you make of your dream? Would you take the time to think about it? Would you want to understand how it is related to your life and your current situation? And what if Alice was your friend or your client and she asked you to help her understand the dream better. Would you dive in confidently and try to help her? If the answer to this question is no, would you like to be able to dive in? Is it possible that you are one of those people who would enjoy working with dreams? Perhaps you can become a dreamworker!

What will you need to become a dreamworker?

First, you will need to have some familiarity with the world of the dream; to become conversant with the language used in the dream world, which is essentially a language of feelings, metaphor, and the playing of parts (in other words you will need to learn how to speak Dreamish!) Second, you will need to learn and practice some method of working with dreams; a method that is not too involved and complex yet adaptable enough to handle the almost infinite variety that will be encountered in the dreams you explore. Third, you will need to be able to recognize certain universal dream motifs, especially those that have that special message-bearing quality, that seem to want to tell something or ask for something. Dreamwork done without this kind of recognition can certainly be fascinating and rewarding, but it also tends to be unfocused and lengthy. Certain dreams are like urgent telegrams asking to be read, understood, and acted upon. These are the ones the we can learn to recognize and engage without a huge investment of time.

Alice was able to experience a resonant connection between the dream scene and her life situation—in both was a desire to change thwarted by a paralyzing fear of the unknown. Once this connection was clearly understood, we were able to move to the next phase of the work, the response phase: what can she do about this problem? We began to work on the problem with a simple visual exercise. I asked Alice to imagine that she is back in the meadow. I asked her to picture the deer and the child starting to head down the path; to feel her desire to join them, and also to feel her fear of joining them. Now we are at what I call the change point. I asked her to become aware that she can introduce a new choice into the scenario right at this precise point. "What would you like to do differently?" I asked her. "I would like to join them on the path" she replied without any hesitation. So I had her visualize walking over to join the deer and the girl, and walking a few steps with them along the path. I asked her how this felt. "It's wonderful," she said, "it feels so good."

During this simple exercise, requiring only a few minutes and the use of the visual imagination (a faculty which we all possess), a very important change has taken place. A long-standing pattern of fear and paralysis has been recognized, challenged, and changed. This change is very new and fragile, that is true. It must be strengthened and reinforced through practice, but nevertheless the blueprint for the change has now been established within her imagination. This is the kind of benefit that dreamwork can bring us—dreams can plant the seeds for desired life changes. Someone must notice the seeds, recognize their importance, and help nurture them so they can grow. That someone could be called the dreamworker.

How I became a dreamworker

My own experience as a dreamworker began in the mid 1980s when I was a student in Naturopathic College. I had already immersed myself in the study of Jungian psychology and needed no convincing regarding the validity and power of dreams. But things moved to a new level when I had a life-changing dream in January of 1985. I call this dream *Three Wolves in the Water:*

> *I am walking along a path that follows the edge of a lake. I am with my companion, a female animal that seems to be both dog-like and duck-like. She is running about 30 yards ahead of me along the path. Suddenly I notice three very large dark gray wolves emerging from a cave on my left. They move toward the water and block the way between me and my companion. I am starting to feel that they could be dangerous. Will they come at me? I move cautiously into the water. The wolves also move into the water. Suddenly, I realize that they might be dark animal aspects of myself and I should swim toward them rather than trying to get away from them. So I start to swim directly at the first wolf. As we meet, the face of the first wolf dissolves into a kaleidoscopic blur of black and white lines. I swim straight at the second wolf and the same thing happens. Then the third, and this time the collision is followed by a powerful sensation of swooping up into a bright yellow light. All this time I am aware of my dog-duck companion waiting for me farther along the path ready to resume our journey together. I wake up.*

When I awoke from this dream I felt different; I sensed that some-thing had happened in the dream that changed me. I didn't even need to do anything to receive the gift of the dream, it had already happened. That morning I knew with certainty that I would become a dreamworker; I would not only work with my own personal dreams, but I would learn how to help other people work with their dreams. The dream of the three wolves, which some would call a shamanic dream or an initiation dream, had delivered to me my vocation. I was tested within the dream and I passed the test, now it was time to get back on the path with my compan-ion and resume the journey.

Resuming the journey meant seeking out further training and expe-rience in working with dreams. In the decade following my wolf dream (concurrent with finishing my studies, graduating, becoming licensed as a naturopathic doctor, and establishing my practice), I sought out an ad-vanced education in dreamworking. I cannot quite say that I traveled to the four corners of the earth, but looking back on this period of my life I am struck by the realization that I found four valuable teachings in four very different places and cooked them together to get what I needed.

Within the rich world of Jungian psychology, I discovered a modern tradition of using dreams in the service of personal health and self-discovery. Jung and his followers took dreams very seriously, as seriously as I did, and I felt a deep sense of familiarity and kindred appreciation among Jungians. I read and studied voraciously and even entertained the possibility of becom-ing a Jungian analyst. Dog-duck and I might have taken that road but for two things—since I had just graduated as a naturopathic doctor, I felt it was time to get down to work—and I couldn't possibly afford it!

From my years of personal experience in group therapy and Gestalt therapy (both as a participant and as a group facilitator), I learned that we all have sub-personalities or parts, and that each of these parts has its own desires and its own agenda. I observed again and again how the parts of a person appear in his or her dreams, usually cloaked in the guise of a seemingly external figure. I began to appreciate how important dream role-playing is and how easily it lends itself to the pursuit of self-awareness and personal growth.

From the world of primal therapy, I experienced how the lasting imprints of our early experiences, from conception to toddlerhood, stay with us throughout life as deeply embodied feeling states. I was struck by how commonly these "primal" experiences are featured in dreams, not as words or stories (since they originated at a pre-verbal stage of life) but as body memories and pervasive feelings. How, for example, can a person go through life feeling that the world is hostile and untrustworthy all the while knowing in his or her conscious mind that things are reasonably safe and secure? How does such a dichotomy arise? I learned that it often arises from primal experience, is remembered indefinitely in the body, and appears nightly as the feeling backdrop of one's dream life.

From modern neuroscience, I have come to realize how much of the stuckness that plagues us in both our waking lives and in our dreams is rooted in brain function. The new science of neuroplasticity has shown us how it is possible to adapt and develop new neural patterns, but the converse is also true—the human brain can get mired in repetitive and dysfunctional patterns very easily, as anyone battling an addiction or a bad habit can attest. A huge category of dream motifs (what I call brain field motifs) arise from and depict this kind of hard-wired neural stuckness. These dreams (a classic example of this type would be the dream of being back in school and feeling unprepared for a test) are usually experienced as tormentingly anxious and repetitive, yet they can be a gold mine of opportunity because they give the dreamer an exaggerated snapshot of a stuck point and thus a chance to understand and change it.

By the late 1990s, I was starting to feel as though I had gathered enough training and experience to shift out of student mode and into full-on practitioner mode. I felt confident entering the world of another person's dream and helping them experience it more fully. I knew that I didn't need to provide any brilliant insights or interpretations, I just needed to help the dreamer arrive at and experience the insights for him or herself. My four teachings had cross-pollinated and coalesced sufficiently and I soon realized that I had developed my own individual dreamworking method. I have practiced this method very consistently for the last fifteen years and used it to explore (I would roughly estimate) fifteen thousand dreams. Since I was in fact becoming more and more of a therapist over the years, I decided to make it official, so in 2015 I obtained a license as a registered psychotherapist in the province of Ontario. I continue to run my private practice in Toronto as both a psychotherapist and a naturopathic doctor.

As so often happens in the healing professions, the practitioner role quickly leads into the teacher role. In the early 2000s I was beginning to feel the need to teach dreamwork in a more formal way to the many practitioners who had sought out informal teaching from me. I was getting frustrated with squeezing the dreamwork into the footnotes and tea breaks of the lectures I gave to naturopaths and homeopaths. Dreamwork is often viewed as a sideline or an adjunct in health care training (if indeed it is given any place at all), but I knew it to be a powerful medicine in its own right. In 2003, I began to teach the medicine of dreamwork, running a series of seminars and workshops that continue to this day.

My teaching career has shown me that many people are fascinated by dreams and by dream-based personal growth work. They would like to be able to do consistent and effective dreamwork, both for themselves and for others; they are only waiting to acquire the tools and the confidence. If you are one of those people, this book has been written for you. It will provide you with a reliable toolkit that you can use to enter the world of dreams; and it is a fascinating world indeed.

This book is designed to help you get more from a dream—more insight, more connection, more depth, more richness—whether it is your own dream or the dream of another person. The book puts you, the reader, squarely in the position of a practicing dreamworker as it coaches you through the key aspects of dream facilitation. It lays out a five-step method that you can use for yourself, for your friends and family, or for your clients. It gives you the techniques, the phrases and questions you will need to use, and the theoretical guidelines to follow as you put the theory into practice. The dreamworking tips address common issues and problems that will arise as you work with a dream, and suggest practical solutions that can be tried. The book is laid out in such a way that it can be easily consulted in mid-session if you are lost, stuck, or trying to find a better approach. If you intend to use this method to delve into your own dream, I suggest that you mentally divide yourself into two people—you the dreamer and you the dreamworker. This will help you keep some objectivity as you literally interview and facilitate yourself.

This book is *not* a dream dictionary and should not be used as such. It does not tell you what a dream of a snake means (which could be virtually anything, depending on the individual dreamer and his or her current situation). The goal of this method is not to interpret or analyze dreams—it is simply to help dreamers arrive at resonant insights about how their dreams connect to their lives, and then to support them in doing something with these insights. The book is organized into three sections—theory, method, and recognition of dream motifs. Let's start with the theory that underlies dreamworking.

Theory

When you are learning about dreams, there is no acceptable substitute for working with real dream material; you cannot make do with generalizations or the mock dreams of mock subjects. You cannot fake a dream. For this reason, every subject discussed in this book is supported and illustrated by one or more transcripts of dreams that were shared with me in my own practice; in addition, I include a few of my own personal dreams. It is with much honor and gratitude that I share these dreams with you.

I have tried to keep the theory section very trimmed down. The focus is on the whys and hows of practical dreamwork. I include the terms and concepts you will need to stay in the game as you start to work with a dream. For those who are interested in probing deeper, there are many references to other source materials that support, substantiate, and extend my theoretical model.

When using any method, it is important to keep a *goal* in mind. In this method of dreamworking there are two primary goals—the first is to create the conditions for experiencing an insight about how the dream connects to your (or the dreamer's) life. For Alice the connection happened when she re-felt the paralyzing fear in the dream and recognized it as the same fear that blocked her from undertaking new challenges in her waking life. This insight naturally led her toward the second goal—to figure out what the dream was asking her for, and attempt to respond to its request in some creative way. The first line of response in this case (and this is typical in my style of dreamwork) occurred within her imagination. Alice imagined forcing herself out of her paralyzed state and walking a few steps down the path. This new development was subsequently strengthened and reinforced with further visualizations of walking along the path (this was Alice's homework).

In this method the goal is not to make an interpretation or an analysis of the dream. Both these terms carry the post-Freudian association that only a highly trained analyst would be able to see into the depths of the dream, recognize its hidden meaning, and come up with a sophisticated analysis. In my experience, it is more useful for you to experience your own connections to your dream than to have your dream explained to you. If you do not participate in the work and resonate with the connections made, then the work may not help you much, even if you are very impressed. We attempt to facilitate with this method, not interpret.

Method

In the second section, the five steps of the method are presented. The method has the following essential characteristics:

- It is facilitative rather than interpretive. If you use this method to help another person, this facilitative quality helps to safeguard against you projecting your own theories, associations, and psychological contents onto the other person's dream (this is always a central concern in dreamworking). The method is constructed to keep the focus on the dreamer's own associations, feelings, and connections.

- It is designed to be practically useful within a limited time frame (on average 20 to 30 minutes per dream).

- It is divided into stages so if you get lost or confused (which you certainly will sooner or later), you can reorient yourself by returning to the five stage model.

- It is goal oriented. The first goal is to support an understanding of how the dream connects to your (or the dreamer's) life. The second goal is to support some real change that arises from this insight.

At first, I would encourage you to use the method in an imitative way without too much deviation. During this period of practice, the steps of the method will become more and more familiar. After some months of assimilation, the steps will become second nature; you will find yourself doing them instinctively and without conscious effort. At this point, you can forget the method, relax, and follow your own intuitions more freely.

The words you use in dreamworking are very important. Finding the right question or phrase can be key in helping to unlock a dream. You are welcome to imitate and borrow freely from the material presented in this book; try out the questions, adapt them, and develop some good ones of your own. Each phrase should be as short and as clear as possible, and always focused toward the goal of helping get the dream connected. You will need to have this material at your fingertips when you are in the middle of a dreamworking session. In Appendix 1, you will find a quick reference list of all the key questions and phrases I use for each step of the method. Consult this list next time you're working with a dream; try using the phrases verbatim. See how they sound coming out of your mouth. After you use them a few times, they will become an integrated part of your dreamworking vocabulary.

Recognition of common dream motifs

The third section of this book is devoted to dream motifs—how to recognize them and how to work with them. All the motifs we will consider are frequently encountered in dreams, and all are very relevant for our personal growth, self-knowledge, health, and well-being. Each motif will be considered from the following vantage points:

- the central message of that motif

- what that motif may be asking for

- how to recognize common variants of that motif in a dream

- the psychodynamics that give rise to that motif

- common dreamworking techniques that can be used for that motif

- dream examples of that motif

You will notice that every dream discussed in this book has been given a name. I always encourage my clients to name their dreams, for many reasons. Naming your dream will help solidify it in your long-term memory and will also confer a sense of value and "realness" upon the dream. And when you choose a name for your dream, try to reflect on the most critical aspect. Is there a central figure, a key event, a powerful emotion? This critical element can be highlighted by the name you choose. The subject of naming dreams is discussed more fully in chapter 10.

You will also notice that the dreams are reported in the present tense, not the past tense. This is also something I encourage you to practice with your own dreamwork. Keeping the dream "in the present" will help you when you re-enter the dreamscape to work with it and explore new possible directions. It fosters a sense that you are working with a living thing, a work in progress, not just a static record of something that happened in the past.

In Appendix 2, you will find a quick reference list of the distinctive features of all the common dream motifs. If you really want to boost your dreamworking skills, I suggest you look at this list carefully and start to absorb it. You will recognize several of these features right away from your own dream life. It is good to start connecting all these distinctive features to a motif category that in turn opens up a sense of what that type of dream may be asking for, which then gives you some degree of orientation. Familiarity leads to recognition. The more familiar you are with these common dream features, the more oriented and helpful you will be in the world of dreams. Another interesting benefit many people have reported after becoming familiar with these features and motifs is their dream recall improving dramatically. If you recognize something, you are more likely to appreciate its significance and therefore remember it.

Alice's dream was a simple dream. It was not earth-shatteringly intense, but nevertheless it proved to be extremely helpful for her in her personal journey. She was able to have an embodied experience of re-entering the dreamscape and "knowing" how this fear hindered her in life. She also had the experience of challenging the fear, imaginally at first, then gradually in more and more actualized ways. We have all had dreams like Alice's but we do not always make use of them. The potential of such dreams is often wasted, perhaps because no effort is made to remember or anchor the dream, perhaps because no method of working with the dream is ever tried. I encourage you to develop a fuller relationship with your dream life. Dreams come knocking at your door every night. Go to the door, open it ... and see what happens!

PART 1

Dreamworking Theory

CHAPTER 1

Why We Should Pay
Attention to Our Dreams

Why should we pay attention to our dreams? One answer is: they may want something from us. They may quite literally want us to do something, to understand something, to change something, to respond in some way. If we do not pay any attention to our dreams, we lose this opportunity to receive the internal guidance that comes to us through this very dynamic system of request-and-response.

Here is an example: Valerie was a 42-year-old woman who was struggling to find both a rewarding career and a satisfying relationship. She shared this dream with me, which she called *The Tiny Neglected Puppy:*

> *I suddenly remember that I have a puppy, but I had forgotten all about it for several days. I'm horrified! How could I have forgotten about my puppy? I run to the front door and open it. The puppy is laying there,*

a little gray puppy, very thin and disheveled. I pick it up and bring it inside. I feel terrible for forgetting about my puppy. It's still alive, I hope it will be okay…

This is a very common kind of dream that I have come across numerous times. It is a simple dream, but vitally important. These few lines tell us a great deal about Valerie, her current psychological and emotional state, and what she might do to improve her situation: First, we know that she has not been caring for herself; she has "forgotten" about herself in some critical way (the forgotten puppy). Second, we know that the problem has to do with basic self-care (the puppy is thin and disheveled). Valerie has not been giving herself enough of the basic things we all need—good food, exercise, love, affection, attention—things a puppy would need to thrive and be happy. Third, we know that the problem is relatively recent (the dream gives a time frame of "several days"), suggesting that the dreamer is usually able to care for herself but there has been a lapse recently.

We would also suspect that Valerie is dealing with the kind of depression (a dis-spiritedness) that happens when the personal spirit is suffering or traumatized. Something has happened; it was a serious blow to her spirit or she would not have forgotten about herself. The metaphor of the dream (as always) is very precise—people who are looking after puppies do not suddenly forget about them for several days unless something serious is going on. So the dream is pointing out two kinds of work that need to be done: in the immediate short term, she must reconnect with herself and start to care for herself better; in the long term, she must try to understand what has injured her spirit and start to address this issue.

Lastly, we can marvel at the way that Valerie's unconscious mind has created such a perfect dream message to mobilize her and guide her through her current predicament. It has communicated the urgency of her situation by using the image of a starving puppy (who would not be moved to immediate action by a starving puppy?), but it also reassures her by showing that the puppy is still alive and if it is loved and cared for properly, it can thrive and be happy.

Now let's look at the dream through the lens of what it is asking for—what does the dream want Valerie to do? First, it wants her to realize that she is ignoring her important self-care needs; and second, it wants her to change this situation, both the short-term and long-term situations. Two very specific and direct requests have been delivered to her in a dream. Of course she could come to the same realization in other ways. It could have come in a conversation with a friend, a suggestion from a caregiver, a synchronistic event, or a sudden epiphany. Eventually, if none of the early stage messages were picked up, a symptom or an illness might need to be manifested to deliver the message more urgently. In my experience dream messages usually arrive first. If we are attentive to them, they are typically the first line of communication in matters of health and well-being. If we do not listen to our dreams, we may miss this communication from our inner guide (I believe our inner guide function has many aspects—inner healer, inner conscience, inner reality check, inner warning system, inner mirror, to name a few).

As a health care practitioner (a naturopath and psychotherapist), I have been listening to dreams like Valerie's for many years. I find them to be endlessly fascinating, unfailingly useful and informative, and I often marvel at the brilliant insights and important warnings they contain. I cannot imagine being a health care practitioner of any kind without having dreamwork at the very center of my practice; for me, that would mean I was trying to function as an external guide without listening to the messages coming from the person's own inner guide.

But I realize that not everyone is in agreement about the relevance of dreams and the validity of using dream material in health care. Some people may need convincing. They may ask: what is the rationale behind dreamwork? What practical application does it have? What can be gained from looking at our dreams? How can dream insights benefit us in our search for better health and well-being? These are legitimate questions, so let's try to answer them. An argument for the relevance of dream material could be based on the following premises:

- *Premise 1:* We have an unconscious part of our mind.

- *Premise 2:* Our unconscious mind is larger than our conscious mind. It knows more.

- *Premise 3:* Our unconscious mind attempts to communicate with our conscious mind in various ways.

- *Premise 4:* Some of these communications are benign and potentially helpful.

- *Premise 5:* These communications often occur in the form of dreams.

Ask yourself—do you disagree with any of these premises? If you do, then you may need to be shown some proof about the validity of dreamwork. This "proof" could come from no better place than an experimental period of working with your own dreams, remembering them, recording them, and pondering their possible meaning (preferably but not necessarily with some guidance and support). After six months to a year of commitment to your own dreams, ask yourself again—does dreamwork have value? The answer will probably be yes.

The inner guide

If you already accept these five premises, then it is only a short step to the following conclusion: we all possess an inner guide that tries to help us by sending us messages in our dreams. Dream-based therapies attempt to tune in the voice of this inner guide so we can hear the messages and understand and respond to them.

Why, then, do some people find it very difficult to feel the presence of this inner guide? I think the answer to this question is largely cultural and historical—our modern society has somehow lost touch with the whole concept of the dream guide. Dreamwork is not taken seriously or taught at any level of our current education system from the nursery school to the university. Furthermore, most children were not raised in a family culture involving the regular sharing and understanding of dreams. Sadly, most of us arrive in adulthood virtually illiterate in the language of dreams.

Within the vast (almost infinite) variety of what is possible to dream about, there are certain types of dreams that are of particular importance in relation to our health—our physical, emotional, mental, and spiritual health. These are the kinds of dreams that are particularly highlighted in this book. By watching out for these dream motifs and giving them special attention, we can learn to hear the advice of our own inner guide; we can adjust self-harming behaviors, recognize what is in us that needs to be healed, and make better life choices.

Why is it important to know what is going on in our unconscious mind?

Consider the case of a person who is aware of a bad habit they have. They have been trying to change this habit for years, but have not been able to. Why? Because it may be only the conscious mind (the ego) in favor of changing the habit. Another part of them—an unconscious part—may not be in favor of the change, and this part may be more powerful. So if this person is ever going to understand what is going on, and why they are having such difficulty making this desired change, they will need to have *some* way of knowing what is going on in their unconscious mind. (My working definition of the unconscious is simply everything in ourselves of which we are not usually conscious.)

Consider the dream of a 32-year-old woman named Margo who had been wanting to get in shape for several years but had not been able to mobilize herself to exercise regularly. She titled this dream *Massaging My Classmate:*

> *I am in some kind of workshop where we have to do bodywork on our classmates. I am paired up with Jessie. She is considerably overweight and very sensitive around body issues. In real life she always managed to avoid anything that involved bodywork or touch. She is lying on her front and I am massaging her back, but she can't take it, and she tells me to stop. So I get her to turn over and I just massage her very lightly on the arms. This goes a bit better. Then I have the idea to lie down right in front of where she was lying so we can both raise our legs into the air together, connecting our tailbones. I wiggle my spine, which in turn moved Jessie's spine too. In the next part of the dream, I am a basketball player. I am in fantastic shape, with beautifully defined muscles. I am able to soar through the air, with incredible "hang time." I make a basket, and it feels familiar and great!*

Margo's ego was completely aligned with the idea of getting in shape, but there was another part of her that had a different agenda. In her dream this part is played by her overweight and over-sensitive classmate Jessie. This part of her is not interested in working on the body, it is the part of her that (like her classmate Jessie in real life) wants to avoid anything to do with the body. Probably Margo will have a great deal of difficulty gaining any traction on the getting in shape plan until she can get some kind of communication happening with her inner Jessie, and get her to make a shift. The dream gives her some clues as to how she can start to work with this part, and it ends in a very positive and encouraging way.

How do we come to know about the existence of these inner and unconscious parts? We all need a way to know ourselves better and more fully, to know what is happening in the non-ego regions of ourselves. Dreamwork is such a way.

Why is dreamwork a good way
of relating to the unconscious mind?

Human beings have devised many ways of delving into the unconscious mind and trying to fathom what is happening "in there" beneath the ego consciousness—hypnosis, psychotherapy, meditation, peer counseling, and the exploratory use of drugs, to name a few. Paying attention to dreams is one of these ways. In my view, it is the safest and most accessible way, and it can bring all the same benefits that these other methods offer. Dreamwork can allow a person to explore his or her unconscious safely in a process that includes all parts of the psyche, both ego and non-ego. It does not require the use of any external agent, drug, or procedure. It need not be hugely expensive nor require the employment of a specialist, it is something that we can all learn to do at least to some extent. It regularly and firmly challenges our ego position and our stories about who we think we are. And all this is offered to us in the most free and natural way—dreaming and dream recall is something that can happen naturally, every night, for all of us.

The benefit of ongoing dreamwork

Although much can be gained from the experience of understanding a single dream, the most effective dreamwork is done while working with an ongoing sequence of dreams tracked over time. One good metaphor for this kind of dreamwork is a path of stepping stones. Each dream insight is like a flagstone that has been laid down. One insight sets up the next insight; from the vantage point of the recently laid flagstone another one can be laid, and then another, until there emerges a sense of moving along a path. Valerie did not just have an insight about the dream of the neglected puppy, she went on to respond to this insight. The first response happened in her imagination—she visualized picking up the puppy, cuddling it, and feeding it, and making a care pact with it. Next, she carried the response into the actualized realm of making changes in her life routine that involved better and more consistent self-care. These responses were noticed by her unconscious and this set the stage for further dreams, which carried the healing progress forward.

A one-off dream insight can be fascinating and valuable, undoubtedly, but cultivating the habit of regular dreamwork gives one a practical tool to use in the lifelong process of acquiring self-knowledge. I believe it is one of the primary skills we can harness for personal growth, by which I simply mean the manifesting of our inner potential.

Evidence for the effectiveness of dreamwork

Is there empirical evidence to support the effectiveness and validity of dream-work? Yes there is. Clara Hill, a researcher at the University of Maryland, and her colleagues have developed a three-stage dreamwork method called the Hill Cognitive-Experiential Dream Model, designed for use in ongoing psychotherapy. The effectiveness of this model in practice has been studied and you can find the results of this research in chapter 12 of Dr. Hill's *Dream Work in Therapy: Facilitating Exploration, Insight, and Action.* In a review of nineteen studies, it was found that clients rated the sessions in which they worked on dreams as more valuable than their non-dream therapy sessions. These clients reported that the dream therapy sessions were "deeper," that the sessions had "more perceived power and value" than regular therapy sessions, that they gained more insight, and also that dream sessions contributed more to strengthening the alliance with the therapist.[1]

Dreamwork has been used as a helpful therapeutic tool in the treatment of several specific disorders including trauma, PTSD, and recurrent nightmares. Much of the supporting research for the validity of dreamwork in the treatment of these conditions has been gathered together and published in an excellent book edited by Kramer and Glucksman called

---

1   Clara Hill, ed., *Dream Work in Therapy: Facilitating Exploration, Insight, and Action* (Washington, DC: American Psychological Association, 2010), 251–252.

Dream Research: Contributions to Clinical Practice. (See the Recommended Resources section for more detail.)

Summary

Dreamwork is really about listening for your own inner voice. When you sense that your inner voice is speaking, make it a priority to listen. What is it trying to say? What does it want from you? Dreamwork can play a central role in therapy and counseling, and it can also be a wholly private and personal practice, something you can resolve to do both for and by yourself. In either case, it is something that must be tried with an open mind and an open inner ear. A guide can only help us to the extent that we are willing to trust and follow. Try to suspend any judgment about the legitimacy of dreamwork until you have resolved to try it for a period of time. Let your own experience be the judge.

CHAPTER 2

Where Do Dreams Come From?

How are dreams made? How do they come into existence? Who or what organizes the contents of the sleeping mind into the form of a story filled with skillfully chosen metaphors and delivers it as a message to the waking ego-self? This is in all likelihood one of those questions that can never be fully answered because it verges on the paradox that we only have our own minds to try to understand how our own minds work. These great mysteries will always be running a few steps ahead of us.

Do dreams arise from inside us or outside us?

This is one of the first questions we need to consider when we ponder the true nature of dreams. Are they in essence subjective phenomena, something generated inside our own minds while we sleep? Or are they objective phenomena, the result of being visited by something from outside of us? Some people will understand them subjectively and some objectively; others will think both are possible, and some will simply say they don't know.

To take a simple example, I recently dreamed of my grandmother who has been dead for over twenty years. Does this mean that my actual external grandmother came into my dream in some form; that her soul or spirit visited me in my sleep? Or does it mean that my sleeping brain generated a likeness of my grandmother, drawing on my own internal memories, associations, and feelings about her? How could we ever know the answer to this definitively? I don't think we can, but I think we need to have a working hypothesis if we are going to work with dreams. My working hypothesis is that the vast majority of dreams are subjective in essence; they are created within our own sleeping brains and bodies. The communication they carry is internal communication, messages are sent from one part of us to another part.

However, there are certain unusual dream experiences that do seem to involve direct contact with the outside world and with external figures. Many of these unusual types of dreams are the subject of a book titled *Extraordinary Dreams and How to Work With Them* by Stanley Krippner, Fariba Bogzaran, and Andre Percia de Carvalho. (See the Recommended Resources section for more detail.) These rare and special dreams are not the focus of this book; we are concerned here with understanding the more common nighttime fare we all experience frequently in which our unconscious mind appears to be trying to establish a dialogue with our conscious mind.

The dreammaker

For our purposes as dreamworkers, I think we must allow that there is something inside the human mind that makes dreams. Whatever it is, it is able to take the contents of the sleeping mind as its raw materials (visual contents, feeling contents, ideas, words, memories, associations, connections, everything in there) it can select from them, filter them, organize them, adapt them, and render them into what I call a coherent dream (see chapter 6 for a discussion of what makes a dream coherent). I call this something the dreammaker.

The dreammaker is able to generate a phenomenon within the sleeping mind that features the dream ego having experiences it believes to be "real." Later, on waking, as we cross over the bridge between the sleep state and the waking state, our dream ego transforms back into the waking ego, and as it does it can often bring back some memory of the dream experience. As our conscious waking mind reboots itself, it is usually able to make a distinction between what was in the dream and what is "real" (i.e., pertaining to waking reality). When we recall and mull over the memory of these dream experiences, we often have a sense of amazement and a feeling that we have been given a message.

A fascinating type of dream, commonly known as a lucid dream, is an exception to this usual form of dream. In lucid dreams the dream ego is aware that he or she is in a dream and is often able to influence the content of the dream significantly. See the Recommended Resources section for further discussion of lucid dreaming.

The dream ego

The dream ego can be defined as the sense of "I" we have in a dream. In most dreams we have some sense of who we are, that "I am me, I am in this setting and I am experiencing this." The dream ego shares many subjective traits with the waking ego; most (but not all) of the time it is the same gender, the same species, roughly the same age, speaking the same language(s) as when awake, with similar thought patterns and a similar feeling of self-awareness. The dream ego seems to maintain a relatively stable sense of itself in many dreams (especially coherent dreams, the most valuable type for dreamwork).

Also the waking ego and dream ego tend to share the same concerns—we tend to dream about the things that concern and affect us in our waking lives; this is often referred to in dream circles as the continuity hypothesis.

If something is really on our mind in waking life we will probably dream about it, with a different spin usually, but the concern is similar.

The good side of weakened ego control in dreams—anything can happen!

The grip of our self-conscious ego, so tight in waking life, is greatly weakened in our dream life. The "I" we are in dreams is far more labile and more uncritically accepting of whatever may happen. In dreams we find ourselves doing things, thinking things, and feeling things that we never would in waking life. And the external surroundings are also much more unpredictable and changeable—when we dream, we are presented with a huge variety of bizarre events and sudden morphings. It is a far greater variety of experience than our waking ego must contend with. For some people, this unpredictability and changeability of the dream world is frightening and chaotic. Many people feel alienated from their own inner dream life because it is so bewildering and they have so little control over what is happening in it.

In addition, there is typically a lowering of self-awareness in dreams— our dream egos do not seem to be very concerned with reflecting on what is happening around them (with the important exception of lucid dreaming). For many people this is a negative feature of the dream world—we are so uncritical and so accepting when we are asleep that we are subjected to the most ludicrous and incoherent ramblings, and the defenses of our rational mind are not on hand to tell us that such things are not possible.

But what if we turn this on its head and see it not as a deficiency of the dreaming mind, but rather a marvelous potential? Because our self-awareness function is dialed down every night in our dreams, we can be much more open to new ideas, experiences, and possibilities than we typically are in waking life. This noncritical quality of the dream ego is what makes it possible for us to visit a world where new and different things can happen very readily.

The dreaming mind has vast creative potential because more of everything is possible—more people, more animals, more vision, more ability, more liberties with the laws of physics, more desires, more knowledge, more crudeness, more sex, more divinity, more wisdom, more intelligence, more emotion, more insight, more geography, more kinesthetic awareness, more impulse, more cruelty, more tenderness, more pain, more attraction, more opportunity, more talent—more everything! This is why there is a much higher potential for the generation of new insights and new solutions when we have access to our dream life. The storehouse of raw material that the dreammaker can draw from to make a dream is virtually infinite.

The dreammaker is responsive to being responded to

Anyone who has done dreamwork will know that the dreammaker is very responsive to being responded to. This is simply one manifestation of a universal human trait—we all like to be listened to attentively; we all like it when the other person really hears us and responds sensitively. In the case of our dreams, if we receive a dream and take it seriously, our dreammaker will "appreciate" this and we will be rewarded by another dream that carries the conversation further.

This means that people who do regular dreamwork (meaning that they take their dream life seriously, make an effort to catch and understand their dreams, and respond to their dreams by making life changes based on dream insights) enter into a dialogue with their dreammaker. It is a dyadic relationship; each party is listening to the other and responding to what they hear. We could say that such people are cultivating a relationship with their own unconscious mind.

Characteristics of the dreammaker

In summary, the study of dreams reveals the existence of some function within the human psyche that is able to generate dreams and has the following characteristics:

- It can draw its raw material from anywhere, but is capable of selecting and presenting that material in a way that makes it relevant and meaningful to the waking self

- It takes advantage of the reduced self-consciousness and critical thinking characteristic of the sleeping mind to generate dream contents that have almost infinite variety and possibility

- It shares many of the concerns of the waking self, and is capable of presenting a bigger perspective on those concerns than the waking self is normally able to access

- It shares the same familiar feeling complexes as the waking self, or can readily access them to be featured in a dream

- It is capable of delivering messages to the waking self, even very specific and detailed messages

- It is responsive to efforts made by the waking self to relate to it

- It relies heavily on metaphor and the playing of parts in the making of dreams

- It has the ability to generate and present solutions for problems that the waking self is unable to solve

- It can challenge the values and positions held by the waking self

Here is a dream I had a few years ago that highlights many of these characteristics of the dreammaker. I call it *The First Woman to Run for President:*

It is the mid 1800s, nearing the end of a presidential campaign. I am a woman who is running for president (I am a man in waking life). A large crowd had gathered to await the final tally of votes and the announcement of who the next president elect will be. We are sitting outside in a large outdoor auditorium, several hundred, perhaps a thousand

people. The men are all dressed in black suits, looking like Abe Lin-
coln. Myself and the other women are in long period dresses, with wide
brimmed hats, shawls, and parasols. I have a feeling that I have run a
very good campaign, and have received quite a lot of support, mostly from
other women who have just recently become enfranchised. Nevertheless I
feel pretty sure that I will lose this election because I am a woman. The
establishment and the powers that be are too entrenched to allow such
a radical thing to happen. I don't feel discouraged or bitter about this
though, I feel like I did the best that I could. Another woman asks me if
I would like to move to a seat near the aisle so it will be easy for me to
go up to the stage and give my speech. I think it will almost certainly be
an acknowledgment of defeat speech, not an acceptance speech, so this is
what I am mentally and emotionally preparing myself for. I accept her
kind offer and move to an empty seat near the central aisle. Sitting right
there beside me is Barack Obama. We greet each other warmly. He says
it's wonderful that I could run for president as a woman, since he could
not as a black man. I feel a wave of deep emotion and exhaustion; I lean
forward in my chair and start to sob. Two people put their hands kindly
on my back to comfort me. I'm crying so hard that I have to take a deep
breath … and this wakes me up.

This dream came at a time in my life when I was wondering if all my
hard work to establish myself as a dreamwork educator was ultimately
going to be successful or not. The feeling complex in the dream of "having run a good campaign" and "done the best I can," yet being aware that
the campaign would probably not be successful and I would not win the
election was a very apt representation of what I was experiencing at that
time. The feeling of grief and exhaustion at the end of the dream was an
exaggerated yet very accurate depiction of the sadness and disappointment I often feel about the fact that dreams may never find acceptance
within our mainstream establishment (or perhaps not within my lifetime
anyway). I feel exactly like a woman fighting so that women of the future

may find their way into the structures of power, or a black person fighting so the black people of the future will achieve acceptance and full enfranchisement. The presence of Barack Obama in the dream was greatly encouraging; it made me feel that the long fight is worth fighting and that someday dreams will find their rightful place in our society and in our healing traditions, even if I am not around to celebrate it.

I don't think the waking human imagination could possibly have fabricated such an unlikely story line (certainly not mine anyway); its elements, including the gender shift, are too far-fetched to be generated by the rational waking mind. Yet it is incredibly accurate in its oddness, and its message was so helpful and encouraging that I was yet again left dumfounded by the intelligence of the dreaming mind, and by its willingness to communicate with me in such a supportive and encouraging way. Clearly I had been sent a message by an entity that is creative, intelligent, wise, caring, and responsive—I don't see how anyone could possibly dispute that.

Summary

If you would like to explore further into the nature of dreaming and the different possible types of dreaming see the Recommended Resources section at the end of this book. Questions about the nature and source of dreaming will always be with us. Along with consciousness, dreaming is one of our great human mysteries and it will always elude full comprehension. Fortunately to work with our dreams we do not require a complete understanding of how dreams are actually generated. But we do need to have some familiarity with the language of dreams; let's now take a look at the characteristic elements the dreaming mind uses to craft its nightly messages.

CHAPTER 3

The Language of Dreams

I do not believe, as Freud did, that dream information is usually disguised or latent, repressed, or taboo. In Freud's writing there is often a sense that the true meaning of the dream is hiding itself from the dreamer; it is there, but it requires the analyst to see through its disguise, analyze it, and explain it to the dreamer. This is certainly not my experience; I believe the dream tries to communicate with the dreamer as clearly as it possibly can.

Why then are most dreams not more straightforward in what they are trying to say? Many people wonder: "If a dream wants to give me a message, why doesn't it just come right out and give me the message, clearly and literally?" I believe the dreammaker is indeed trying to be clear and direct but speaking in its own native language—the language used in the land of the sleeping dreaming mind. Those of us who want to understand dreams must become familiar with this language.

Do you speak Dreamish?

If you want to become a dreamworker, you must dedicate a good chunk of time to learning the language. The amount of time required is probably roughly equivalent to the time required to learn spoken languages—it will take you months to learn how to get by and years to become fluent, but it will be well worth it! There are five key aspects to the language of dreams:

- Dreams use figures to "play parts" (these may be parts of the dreamer's psyche or important figures and features of the dreamer's life)

- Dreams use metaphor

- Dreams contain feelings and emotions that correspond to the feelings and emotions we experience in our waking lives

- Dreams often employ exaggeration and heightened urgency

- Dreams use figures of speech, idioms, puns, and wordplay

The use of figures to play parts

Most dreams typically feature the dream ego (the "I" in the dream) and one or more other key figures or entities. One of the most important skills of dreamwork involves being able to determine who these figures are representing. Are they representing parts of the dreamer? They may be, but not always. It is an often-repeated misconception that everything in our dream is a part of us. This is most certainly not true—we can dream about anything, and we often dream about people and things external to us.

Lyra, a 58-year-old woman, was struggling to free herself from a strong web of enmeshment with her family of origin. She felt manipulated and repeatedly disappointed by her father, yet still longed for his love and hoped that he would finally do the right thing and become the father that she wanted. Her dream *George, Brittany, Tony, and Me* features a dream ego and three other figures, and it illustrates how crucial it is to get clear on which figure is playing which part.

> *George Clooney is a killer. He is going to kill two people—Brittany Murphy and Tony Soprano. But I know about this and I grab him. I hold him upside down over a balcony, threatening to drop him. In the end I decide not to drop him.*

Clearly these three famous actors are not representing themselves here, Lyra's psyche has enlisted them to play parts in her dream. Famous people are used in dreams all the time because they have clear and exaggerated attributes. Lyra described George Clooney as "handsome and charming, but can be a killer." Her associations for Brittany Murphy were "powerless, sensitive, fragile, like a lamb to the slaughter." Tony Soprano was "strong, selfish, brutal, but also wounded."

Now we needed to figure out who these actors are representing in the dream. As we worked on the dream, it soon became clear that George Clooney was playing the role of Lyra's father (a very charming and seductive figure in waking life). George Clooney's intent to kill the two other figures at the beginning of the dream represented two ways that Lyra felt her father was harming her. First, he was harming her sensitive and fragile Brittany Murphy–like part, constantly raising her expectations and then wounding her with disappointment and grief. Second, he was harming her strong and self-assertive Tony Soprano–like part, a part of her that was able to function very well in most areas of her life but was weakened and wounded when it came to her father.

Through hard personal work, Lyra has recently come to understand that she must protect herself from her father's repeated pattern of seducing then harming. This is depicted in the dream as her (the dream ego's) ability to grab the father and hang him upside down over the balcony. Lyra's dream is showing her that she is now stronger than he is (or we could say, she is now stronger in relation to her father complex, which had not been the case previously). The dream is also posing a very important question—should she drop him? This would mean, metaphorically and psychologically, that she would be "killing" her susceptibility to being repeatedly taken in and hurt by her father through closing off some inner door she still keeps open for him in hopes that he will finally come through as the good father she longs for.

So, in this dream we have four players on stage: the dream ego, one figure playing an outer part, and two figures playing inner parts. A dream like this cannot be understood and connected to the dreamer's life in a satisfactory way until all the role-playing is clarified. For example, if we were to take George Clooney as an inner figure, a part of Lyra, it would lead us to considering her own seductive nature and the possible damage that it was doing to other parts of herself. We could try this on, but if it does not resonate as true with the dreamer (and with the facilitator) it will get confusing and eventually bog down and end up going nowhere in particular. When this happens (which it often does in dreamwork) simply use the Inner/Outer guideline—switch your orientation from inner to outer and try again. (See chapter 12, "Orienting through inner and outer.")

Tip: Write down two or three associations for each key figure in the dream

When a dream features a famous figure or someone the dreamer knows, ask the dreamer to quickly list off two or three descriptive words or associations that they would connect to that person (e.g., "handsome, charming, can be a killer"). Write them down and be prepared to quote them back to the dreamer as he or she tries to make the connections. This will help both of you identify what part that figure is playing in the dream.

The use of metaphor

As dreamworkers we must always be on the lookout for metaphor, for anything that may stand for something else. Almost everything in a dream that is not realistic (i.e., a seemingly realistic depiction of someone or something in the dreamer's waking reality) is likely to be making an appearance as a metaphor. For example, if we dream about an elephant it will almost always be appearing as a metaphor for something. If we recently saw an elephant at the zoo (or if we are an elephant keeper who actually works with elephants), we could be dreaming about a "real" (non-metaphorical) elephant whose plight we may be concerned about. But in most instances our dreammaker will be "using" the elephant to stand for something in us or in our world.

Having surmised that the dream elephant is a metaphor for something, we still do not know if the metaphor is pointing inward (standing for an aspect of the dreamer that is elephant-like) or outward (standing for something or someone in the dreamer's life that is elephant-like). Thus the dreamworker must perform a quick mental operation for every key figure that appears in the dream that goes something like this:

- Is the elephant referring to a real elephant, or is it a metaphor? Or might it be functioning as both?

- If it is a metaphor, is it an inward-pointing metaphor, standing for an aspect of the dreamer?

- Or is it an outward-pointing metaphor, standing for someone or something in the dreamer's life?

- Or might it have both an inner and an outer aspect?

The dream metaphor is precisely chosen for its qualities and associations

The dream object or figure that is functioning as a metaphor is not chosen randomly. The dreammaker will make its choice for a very precise reason that has to do with the outstanding qualities of that object or figure. An elephant, for most people, would carry associations of great size and power, but also gentleness, dignity, and wisdom. Of course it is always the dreamer's associations that are most relevant, and the facilitator must ask what those associations are for every key dream figure if they are not spontaneously given.

Domenica, a 35-year-old woman, was overworked, exhausted, and close to a health crisis. She felt that she was giving far too much of herself to her work and not getting much satisfaction in return, yet she could not seem to change the situation. In her second appointment with me, she told me a dream of a big loon (a duck-like water bird of the northern lake country). We called the dream *The Big Loon:*

> *I'm driving in my car, and I notice something off with the steering. I try to turn left, and it's going right and it's almost like there's no proper steering connection; there's something not right. So I decide to park the car. I don't bump into anything. I'm safe. I'm able to park. Then I get out of the car and this older woman comes running down the road, and she says to me that I can't park there. She says it's blocking her driveway and there's no way I can park. So then I notice this younger woman who's next to my car, who's being a little more cooperative. We exchange numbers and I tell her I'll be back for the car. I just have to make sure it's safe before I get into it again. Then I see a lake and there's a loon, an oversized loon. It's definitely a loon but it's huge. I think, "Wow, it's beautiful!" It's looking at me, trying to get my attention somehow. I don't know what it wants. All I know is I feel overwhelmed by the beauty of it, the size of it, the colors, the rich colors, the calmness of it, the grace of it. It was so graceful and so big.*

This is a wonderful dream. It is a good example of an Inspiring Contact dream in which the dreammaker presents a numinous image to the dreamer that has the power to move and inspire. In this case, the dream seems to be saying that if Domenica can slow down the dangerous pace of her life and "park" herself for a moment she will experience something very special. She will experience something very large, very rich, very colorful, very beautiful; something peaceful, calm, and graceful.

If we look at this dream through a metaphor-exposing lens, we see that there are multiple metaphors at work here, as there are in almost every coherent dream:

- *The car* is a metaphor for how Domenica exercises control over where her life is going.

- *The problem with her car's steering* is a metaphor for the fact that she is not in control of where her life is going at this time; therefore, it is not a time to be driving.

- *Parking* is a metaphor for being able to slow down and stop herself.

- *The old woman* who tells her she cannot park there is a metaphor for an old (long-standing) part of her that believes she cannot slow down and stop.

- *The younger, more cooperative woman* is a metaphor for a newer part of Domenica that has recently learned how to be more internally self-caring and self-supporting, making it possible for her to stop, at least for a short time.

- *Exchanging numbers* is a metaphor for being in better communication with this new part of herself.

- *The loon* is a metaphor (here we could call it a symbol) for the wondrous part of her that she will encounter if she can slow down and stop over-working.

- *The over-sized stature of the loon* is a metaphor for its huge importance in her psyche.

None of these metaphors are hidden, or disguised, locked, or buried; they are fully exposed and open for viewing, requiring only some effort of recognition and translation. The facilitator has three tasks in working with this dream: first, to recognize the loon metaphor; second, to help the dreamer consider that this dream is speaking about an emerging aspect of herself; and third, to stress the importance of this development. To use the language of the dream, this would mean encouraging Domenica to park her car as soon as possible and make the encounter with the loon her top priority. Previous experience working with such dreams tells us that if she can encounter the loon and incorporate it with her sense of who she is and what she is like, she may experience a very positive change.

The use of feelings and emotions

Dreams are typically laden with feelings and emotions. Strangely, the feeling content is often the first aspect of the dream that is forgotten upon waking in the morning. Many people will report a dream as if they are telling a story to which they have no emotional attachment; they remember the events and the characters but they have forgotten the feelings. This is why it is so important to encourage your clients (and yourself) to make a special point to remember and record the feeling tones that were present in every part of the dream. The correspondence between the feeling tones of the dream and the feeling tones of that person's waking life is often very close; so much so that one of the most effective ways to help a person connect a dream to their life is through the feeling tones (see "Connecting through feeling tones" in chapter 13). We dream about what concerns us, worries us, what moves us, what frightens us, what saddens us—the concerns and experiences of our emotional body are shared by the waking ego and the dream ego.

Here is an example of a series of dreams where there is a close correspondence between the feelings of the dream and the feelings of waking life. Carrie, a 34-year-old woman, is struggling with serious health concerns. Her family is very supportive, but she often feels they are over-supportive, too close, too quick to offer help, and too much in her life.

Carrie had the following sequence of dreams, which she titled *Can't Find a Private Bathroom to Use!*:

> *I had four dreams in a row about toilets! What the heck does that mean? I need to pee in my dream, so I'm looking for a toilet to use. I find some, but I can never use them because there is no privacy. They are out in the open. In one dream I am holding two cracked eggs in my hands, trying to get into a toilet. I have to make sure I don't drip the egg on the floor. When I finally find the bathroom, someone goes in right before me! She is just standing there the whole time by the door, then when she sees me coming she goes in. I get so angry at her that I start to hit her!*

Carrie made the connection that the inability to find a private toilet had the very same feeling that she often felt with her family, particularly her mother. When she needed some personal space to explore and express difficult emotions her family members would often jump in and offer to help at the very time when she most needed to be alone. She found it intrusive but felt she couldn't tell them to back off because they were, after all, trying to be helpful. The dream helped Carrie realize just how angry she had become about this issue, and she resolved to address it in a more proactive way.

The use of exaggeration and heightened urgency

There is often a sense in a dream that the unconscious is exaggerating the urgency of its message, in order to try to get the attention of the ego and make sure that it takes the dream message seriously. This is particularly the case when a dream theme has been repeating for a while. Subsequent variations on the repeating theme tend to become more and more urgent, as if to say, "Why are you not getting this message? Okay then! If you refuse to listen I will send the message in an even more urgent way!"

Joan was caught up in a relationship in which she had been repeatedly lied to, cheated on, and deeply hurt. She was aware that she should try to leave the relationship; many friends had urged her to get out, but she was unable to. Joan kept hoping that her partner, Eddie, would finally realize what he was doing, change his ways, redeem himself, and that everything would be okay. She had the following dream, *Eddie Shooting Me Again and Again*:

> *I'm in our kitchen with Eddie. He is across the room shooting me, again and again. I can feel the pain of the bullets going in to me. I'm bleeding from everywhere, dozens of bullet wounds. I don't think it will kill me, although I am very badly hurt. I keep thinking that this will be the last shot. He will stop soon, I'll go to hospital and get patched up, and I'll recover.*

This dream gave a stark and accurate depiction of Joan's situation, clearly very exaggerated, but accurate nevertheless. The dream delivered a clear, simple, unambiguous and urgent message to her: you must get out of this situation; there is no sign that it is going to get any better and you cannot keep exposing yourself to this. Joan finally got the message and ended the relationship shortly after having this dream.

The use of figures of speech, idioms, puns, and wordplay

The dreammaker will stop at nothing to get its message across. It will stoop to using the most outrageous puns and double meanings. Figures of speech and colloquialisms are used constantly; they are so much a part of dream language that they are often completely overlooked. The dreamworker should be constantly on the lookout for this kind of thing, because it can crack open the meaning of a dream in an instant when a figure of speech or a play on words is spotted (see "Connecting through spotting a figure of speech" in chapter 13).

Here's a little quiz for you—see if you can spot the figure of speech in the following three dreams. The answers are given at the end of the chapter, though keep in mind there may be more than one answer; the answers given here are the figures of speech that, once recognized by the dreamer, helped them to arrive at a resonant understanding of the dream message.

Spot the figure of speech quiz

1. *"Face Down in the Pool"*

There was a couple (a man and a woman) in a pool, and they were floating on top of the water. They were facing down. I was looking at them. The guy's arm was around the woman. I realized that they cannot possibly be breathing... not in a conventional way. I noticed the way they were breathing—at least the guy—he stuck the sole of his foot out of the water, facing the ceiling (she gestures palm upwards), and I thought that was the way he was breathing. I thought—"oh, how unconventional! That must be a breathing technique I didn't know about." Then I looked over and I realized that the girl was not doing the same thing. Then I had the horrible feeling that he's pulled her into this position, and he's holding her there and she's actually suffocating... she was actually dying. I woke up, and I knew right away that was a reference to my relationship.

2. *"Flying Paper Ride"*

In the dream, my partner M and I are on two pieces of paper, just big enough for a person to be sitting on with our legs folded and we're floating along, a couple of inches off the ground. We're moving with pretty good velocity and we're traveling down a road in a pastoral setting, there are beautiful rolling hills and nice properties. It's a beautiful summer day and we're just enjoying the scenery as it goes by..."(dream continues)

Hint: the dreamer and his partner have recently experienced a great strain on their relationship, in part due to the fact that one of them started to feel the desire to have children and the other was not so keen.

3. *"Pit Bull Kills My Cat"*

In the dream I have a cat and a pit bull (in real life I just have a cat). The cat is at the top of the stairs; it's looking at the pit bull, kind of apprehensive. The pit bull is starting to shake with energy and jingle its collar, looking at the cat. Suddenly the cat gets scared and runs down the stairs. In a flash the pit bull is after it, catches it and bites its head off. I'm stunned and feel completely helpless. My dog just killed my cat. It was so fast I couldn't do anything…

Summary

Learning any language requires both study and practice. The language of dreams is no exception to this rule. The study part involves learning about how the language works. The practice part simply involves working through dozens and dozens of dreams until things start to feel familiar, and repeating motifs and patterns become readily recognizable.

Answers to quiz

Dream 1: ***Her soul cannot breathe*** in her current relationship—the sole/soul wordplay is quite common in dreams. Always consider it whenever a dream features either the bottom of a foot or the bottom of a shoe.

Dream 2: ***Not on the same page***—the dream points out that even in the early halcyon days of their relationship when things were rolling along nicely the dreamer and his partner were not on the same page about some key issues.

Dream 3: ***Biting someone's head off***—this dreamer had a great deal of trouble controlling his temper and his intense need to convince other people of his point of view. The dream was pointing out to him that he had a pit bull–like part of his personality that, when unleashed, would make people want to defend themselves and say: "Don't bite my head off!" This dream contained another wordplay—the dreamer's girlfriend at the time, the most frequent victim of his pit bull attacks, was a woman named Catherine or Cat for short. As is usually the case, the dreamer did not notice either of these wordplays until they were pointed out for him to consider.

Once they were pointed out, they seemed blatantly obvious and he could not believe he had missed them; they also immediately and poignantly helped him understand the message of the dream.

CHAPTER 4

Why Do People Shy Away
From Doing Dreamwork?

A few years ago, one of my student dreamworkers in training described the following experience at one of our workshops:

I was working with a patient at the clinic last week; she had a dream that she was in a house and couldn't leave because there was a small dead furry animal in the doorway. I asked her the feeling and it was frustration, she just refused to step over a dead animal. I then asked her what it would feel like to be the dead animal... and she responded: "But then I'd be dead!" And then I panicked. I didn't know what would happen if I asked her to be dead. I stopped the dreamwork at this point and we went on to something else.

Sarah was using the Be the Part technique in this case (see chapter 12), as it was a good direction to go and probably would have yielded interesting results if she had stayed with it. Unfortunately, she lost her nerve because she feared it might harm her client's psyche to have her imagine being dead.

A group discussion followed that was very helpful for all of us in attendance. A number of interesting points were raised:

- In the language of dreams, when a figure is "dead" it usually does not refer to death in the literal physical sense, especially in cases where the figure is functioning as an inward-pointing metaphor. Rather it could mean that something is not very alive, not animated, not currently active, dormant, or repressed. "Dead" things in dreams can often come back to life.

- The use of the imagination is a powerful tool and it is the primary tool of dreamworking. There are very few (are there any?) limits to what we can imagine—we can indeed imagine that we are dead without making ourselves physically dead, just as we can imagine ourselves flying or breathing underwater or a whole host of things that are not physically possible in waking life.

- If the dreamwork runs into difficulty, the best strategy is often to rephrase the same question with a slightly different emphasis. A possible rephrasing here would be: Do you think that the animal might represent a part of you that is not currently very alive?

- We must not forget to ask the Inner/Outer question, if only in the back of our minds. This dead animal is most likely to be an inner dead animal (i.e., a part of the dreamer that needs to be more animated and alive). But it could also be pointing outward; for example, it could be referring to someone in the dreamer's life who has died, and the repercussions of this death are keeping her from venturing out into the world. (See "Orienting through inner and outer" in chapter 12.)

After this workshop, Sarah was able to revisit *The Dead Animal on the Doorstep* dream with more confidence, and she was soon able to help the dreamer arrive at an important connection that led to a significant change of attitude. Sarah's experience got me thinking about all the reasons why people who want to work with dreams have trouble translating this desire into actuality. In our collective attitude toward dreams, there is clearly a strong attraction, but there is also something that keeps us away. This same paradox exists among people in the helping professions. On the one hand, they often express interest in the idea of working with their clients' dreams, yet they rarely if ever actually do any kind of focused dreamwork. Why? Why do so many interested people shy away from dreams? There are probably thousands of good answers to this question, but I would like to put forward five possible answers, the stumbling blocks I encounter most frequently in my work:

- Negative and paradoxical attitudes toward dreams

- Difficulty perceiving metaphor

- Fear of causing harm

- Feeling lost in the dreamscape

- Resistance to acknowledging the uncomfortable truths that dreams offer

Negative and paradoxical attitudes toward dreams

The ambiguity of our collective attitude toward dreams can be highlighted in an interesting way by asking a number of people what the purpose of a dreamcatcher (the spiderweb-like Ojibwe craft now widely adopted by many other Native American peoples) is. Some will say that a dreamcatcher's job is to intercept dreams and hold them so they cannot come into the sleeping person's head (rather like hanging garlic to ward off vampires). Others will say its purpose is to catch onto the dream as it flies by and deliver it into the sleeping person's head (more like a fishing net). Still others will say that a dreamcatcher has the ability to distinguish between good and bad dreams. It captures the bad dreams and holds them fast in the webbed area, but if the dream is a good one it is allowed to slide down the feathers into the sleeper's head (this way of thinking is problematic from the dreamworker's point of view, since dreams that most people would consider bad often bring with them the greatest potential for growth and change). Are some dreams in essence "good" and others "bad"? There is a huge spectrum of different attitudes among people, many of them negative. They are often partly unconscious and may need to be flushed out into consciousness so they can be addressed and debated. Below are some of the dream disses I often hear, and some quick counterarguments that you may want to have ready.

Negative perceptions about dreams and how to counter them

Negative perception: Dreams are random and chaotic. Counter-argument: It is true that some dreams appear random and chaotic, but others clearly exhibit evidence of coherence and even great intelligence. Most people would agree that they have had at least a few dreams that made them feel that someone or something was trying to deliver a message. Even if only these occasional "message dreams" are taken seriously, a great deal can be learned.

Negative perception: Dreams are merely the regurgitation and replaying of recent events and stimuli. Counter-argument: Dreams certainly do make use of the events and stimuli of the previous few days (this is often dismissively referred to as "day residue"). But the dreammaker is capable of selecting from all these elements, borrowing them for very precise reasons and putting them to use as metaphors and backdrops within the larger context of the whole dream.

Negative perception: Dreams may contain communication but the communication is not clear and straightforward, so they are in most cases not decipherable. Counter-argument: The communication that comes in dreams is not usually literal and straightforward, true. It is as if our dreammaker is using a different language to communicate with us. This puts the onus on us to make the effort to learn the language of dreams. Dream language is primarily based on metaphor. Once we have become conversant with this language, things become much easier and more enjoyable.

Negative perception: In dreams we are not able to distinguish between what is "real" and what is unreal, absurd, and impossible. Why should we place any value on the absurdities that typically occur in dreams? Counter-argument: Because our self-awareness function is dialed down every night in our dreams, we can be much more open to new ideas, experiences, and possibilities than we typically are in waking life. This non-critical quality of the dream ego makes it possible for us to visit a world where new and different things can happen very readily.

Negative perception: Dreams disturb the sleep; we would be better rested without them. Counter-argument: In the normal sleep cycle, the periods of deep restorative sleep are different from the dreaming periods. The primary purpose of the dreaming periods (on average five per night) is something other than rest; it seems to have something to do with insight, communication, and guidance.

If these two critical functions of sleep, rest, and dreaming cannot coexist in a healthy way, then something is awry and it needs to be addressed. Ignoring or suppressing one's dream life is not the answer.

Negative perception: Dreams can be frightening and tormenting; why would we want to expose ourselves to even more negativity by remembering them and retelling them? Counter-argument: Dreams can indeed be tormenting and frightening. Many such dreams can be viewed as urgent messages that require a response. If they are not received and responded to, then the frightening messages must be delivered again and again, prolonging the suffering indefinitely. If we can learn to be proactive in response to our "bad" dreams, they will begin to change for the better in almost all cases. It is often the "bad" dreams that carry the greatest potential for growth, but they must be faced.

Negative perception: The unconscious is meant to be unconscious, and whatever is in it should just stay in it, including dreams. Counter-argument: If the unconscious were intended to remain completely unconscious, it would be difficult to account for the whole realm of human experience that involves contact between conscious and unconscious. This realm does not just include dreams; it also includes intuition, sudden insight, precognition, instinctual gut feeling reactions, synchronicities and premonitions, not to mention the whole area of so-called paranormal experiences. It seems clear that in the normal state of psychological health, there is an axis of communication that operates between the unconscious and conscious minds, and that a substantial part of this communication occurs in dreams.

Having these arguments at the ready may also prove useful for the practitioner who is trying to sell the validity of dreamwork to a patient or client.

When I am feeling out a particular client to get a sense of whether or not they might be interested in dreamwork, I will usually ask them questions like: "How do you feel about your dreams? Do you think they are important? Do you think they have something to say? Have you worked with them before? If not, why not?" This kind of questioning will often bring forth a variety of reservations and negative attitudes about dreams that can then be addressed and debated.

Difficulty perceiving metaphor

Our culture is in many ways extroverted, materialistic, and literalistic. Many people are not accustomed to working with metaphors and symbols; they are not naturally good at perceiving metaphor and they have not been trained to do it. Such people do not easily accept that a dream elephant is likely to be a depiction of something elephant-like inside them or affecting them. Since metaphor comprises the primary meaning-containing element of dreams, metaphor-resistant people usually find dreamwork quite laborious and even absurd. They often simply don't "get it" and therefore are not likely to believe in its relevance. A few years back, I experienced a frustrating dreamwork session with a 66-year-old man named William who told me this dream, called *Knocking Out the Two Monkeys:*

> *I hear two monkeys at the end of my bed. I take each one and knocked them out… and wake up totally shocked that I would ever have a dream like that. I'm not a violent person, and yet it was a particularly violent confrontation.*

William and I worked together on this dream for about thirty minutes with me trying various different approaches to get the dreamer to consider the monkeys as a metaphor for something that was disturbing him, but he remained insistent that they were literal monkeys and that was that. Therefore, the dream was absurd because he would never do violent harm to monkeys. For myself, it was (to use another metaphor) like pulling teeth. Because William was not getting anything out of the process, it did not engage him and soon started to fatigue and irritate him; after a while there seemed to be no point in continuing.

Fear of causing harm

One of the fears that prevents potential dreamworkers from delving into a dream is the fear of causing harm or doing some damage to another person's psyche by somehow mishandling or misinterpreting his or her dream. The previously mentioned dreamwork session with *The Dead Animal on the Doorstep* shows how a well-intentioned dream facilitator can be stopped in her tracks by the fear of doing harm. There is some potential for harm in dreamwork—this is certainly true. Dreamwork is a form of counseling and as such comes with potential risks and dangers. The safeguards that help reduce the risk of causing harm with dreamwork are similar to those in other forms of counseling (see "Ethical considerations in dreamwork" in chapter 5). Yet I have observed many times that practitioners who will readily engage in other forms of psychotherapy and counseling will shy away from doing dreamwork, even when their client is asking them for help with a specific dream. This reluctance may arise from a natural respect for the dream, awareness that a dream is a door opening into the depths of a person's unconscious mind; therefore, if we are going to cross through that door we must be cautious and respectful.

Do the contents of the unconscious want to be exposed?

A number of years ago, I was engaged in an internal debate on this question, and some related questions: are there some dreams that should not be subjected to any kind of scrutiny? Are there some people who should not work with their dreams? Are there some regions of the unconscious that should just be left alone? Then I had a dream that seemed to have something to say about these matters; I call it *The Angry Seals:*

I'm on a working holiday retreat, renting a house near the beach in Malibu, California. I have just arrived and I'm eager to get down to the beach and explore it. I head down to the beach with my dog. When we get there I find that it's not really a beach, but has large concrete steps going down into the water. The water is a beautiful turquoise color, very inviting. When my dog goes down to stick his paw in the water, a man standing nearby gives him a very disapproving look; I wonder—are dogs not allowed here? Then a seal stands up in the water about twenty feet away from us. He's holding a large rock. Then he throws it in our direction! I call my dog over to me, to keep him away from the water's edge. Then a second seal, bigger than the first, stands up and faces us, holding an even bigger rock. He throws it right at us, almost hitting us! I leash my dog and back away… this seems very serious… I don't want to mess with these seals…

Upon waking I had a strong sense that this dream was about dreamwork, and more specifically about how dreamwork was viewed from the perspective of the unconscious mind. It would appear that the seals (inhabitants of the ocean/the unconscious) had some resistance to me and my dog exploring the water's edge (the area of contact between conscious and unconscious). Did they not want us to be poking around in the water? The dream had the very familiar pattern (which I believe is both archetypal and psychodynamic) of an escalation of intensity through a series of three encounters—first the disapproving bystander, then the first angry seal, then the second seal, who was bigger, angrier, and more accurate with his rock throwing! The dream seems to be saying that the unconscious wants to defend itself from certain unwanted intrusions. The seals were very clear in their communication: "Get away from the water's edge!"

A beach or shoreline in a dream often serves as a metaphor for the liminal area that straddles both consciousness and unconsciousness and sets a stage for the many phenomena that happen there, including dream recall. Before this angry seal dream, my own shoreline dreams had usually been inviting and mysterious. I usually felt that I could explore the ocean, venture in deeper and deeper if I wanted; it was only my own fear and stuckness that would stop me. But now two native ocean dwellers were stopping me, seemingly acting as guardians of the deep. A client's words from a session years earlier were echoing through the dream image: *What if the unconscious just wants to be left unconscious?* I began to feel like a commercial whaler found guilty of over-fishing the oceans, pulling out content that would be better left alone and not harassed. I decided that I had to accept this as an ego check dream, one that offers compensation and mirroring to an imbalanced or lopsided ego position.

Could this mean that I was being too aggressive or invasive in my approach to dreams? Was there some way in which I was not being respectful of the natural integrity of the unconscious? Was I being too "California" in my approach to dreams, since the dream was set in Malibu (for me "California" could mean the anybody-can-take-a-workshop-and-be-a-spiritual-expert mindset). Could it be reminding me that there are some people who should not do dreamwork? Or that there are some circumstances in which dreamwork could be harmful or contraindicated?

I set out to have a direct experiential encounter with a key element of the dream to get more clarity on the dream message. This is an *imaginal response,* happening within my own imagination while awake, and using the exact setting and characters given by the dream. It occurred to me that it might be the presence of my dog that was upsetting the seals. This particular dog is a mixed breed that included some border collie, so it definitely had the instinct to chase, herd, and nip at the heels. This might represent an over-zealous attitude of wanting to "herd" dreams and dreamers toward my desired goal of extracting meaningful messages from them (something that could have been a fair criticism of my work at the time, hopefully less so now). I decided to try the following visualization as a response to the dream:

I leash my dog and take him back to the beach house. Then I walk back to the waterfront alone and stand at the edge. The disapproving man is no longer there. I wait for a while. The seals do not appear. I take this to mean that they are not so strongly opposed to my presence when I approach without the dog. I venture down the concrete steps and into the water, slowly, one step at a time. Still the seals do not appear. I swim into the water, staying close to shore at first but submerging my head to scan around for the seals. I see them in the distance, lots of them. I focus on one of them (I think he is the big one from the other dream). He approaches me. He has a big seal frown on his face. He seems a bit irritable but not hostile or aggressive. We come face to face under the water. I tell him that I am aware that this is his world and I am a visitor. I explain that I have great respect (even reverence) for the creatures of the deep. He grunts: "Just make sure you keep the dog away." I promise that I will. He turns away. As he brushes by me I can feel the immense power in his body. I return to the land.

Since this time, I have tried to keep the energy of the sheep-herding dog out of my dreamwork as much as possible. This has often been difficult for me because I have a great fascination for dreams, it is often hard for me to keep things in the passionate-but-not-over-zealous range. I still get impatient with people who can't muster up the energy to remember and record a dream properly. At these times, I glance up at the picture of a seal poking its head above water that hangs on my office wall (I call him "Guardian of the Unconscious" and hung it there in response to this dream). It reminds me that perhaps a client's seeming laziness may be a way of protecting his or her unconscious from being overfished. I have more respect now for the naturally occurring defenses and avoidances of the unconscious. I'm more subtle in the way I ask for dream material and I have been well rewarded by receiving more and more of it. I still believe that the unconscious wants to communicate through dreams much of the time. We only need to remember that seals are *not* sheep.

If we believe that a dream may be an attempt to communicate, it is a pity that so many of these attempts do not get through to anyone because of fear. In my experience, when we get lost or bogged down in working with a dream it does not usually lead to any harm being done; it typically leads to a sense of incompletion and uncertainty, a feeling that the message has not been fully understood. Perhaps it is confusion, but it is not harm.

Feeling lost in the dreamscape

Perhaps the most common reason why people shy away from dreamwork is that they have had the experience of trying to work with a dream only to feel completely lost. Since we are able to dream about *anything* in the universe, real and unreal, possible and impossible, past, present, and future—it follows that in working with a dream there is a very great potential for getting lost.

Yet experienced dreamworkers have ways of finding their bearings, of getting oriented within the dreamscape. How do they do this? I suspect that many dreamworkers orient themselves using educated intuition; through experience they are able to recognize features in the dream that they have come across before, and this starts to shape the questions they use for further facilitation. They may not be using a formal technique or method but there is a method operating beneath the surface. The method taught in this book places a lot of emphasis on orientation. You will learn and practice seven reliable ways of getting oriented; all these are discussed in detail in "Getting oriented" in chapter 12.

Resistance to acknowledging the uncomfortable truths that dreams offer

I suspect that the biggest reason that many people steadfastly ignore their own personal dream life is a simple one: they don't want to look in the mirror. They would rather not have to face the difficult and challenging truths their dreams point at. Dreams are constantly giving us feedback on our behavior and on the accuracy of our beliefs and perceptions. What if we don't want this feedback? Then we had better turn our back on our dream life because it will be working overtime to show us our ego stance in the hopes that we might recognize the need to change. The kind of dream motif that offers us feedback, reflection, and reality checks (which I call the ego check motif) is a very important and very common one.

Summary

Ask yourself: What is it that stops me from working with my dreams more often and more deeply? Perhaps your reticence is related to one of the issues discussed above. Or perhaps you may feel that you simply don't have enough background knowledge about dreams and dreamwork. If that is the case, take a look at the recommended resources at the back of this book, where you will find my reading list for a crash course in dreams. Whatever it is that may be holding you back, perhaps now is the time to challenge your resistance and invigorate your relationship with your dream life.

CHAPTER 5

The Goals of Dreamwork

What are the goals of dreamwork? What are we trying to do? What exactly is it that can be helpful when we work on a dream? Where is the medicine? Presumably we are aiming for some kind of understanding of the dream, but "understanding" can mean different things, so I think it's very important to be clear about what our desired goal is when we work with a client's dream. Is our goal to interpret the dream? To analyze it? What exactly do these terms mean anyway? Let's briefly consider both terms and think about their connotations and associations:

- **Dream analysis:** *Analysis* is derived from a Greek word for "loosening" or "untying," carrying with it a meaning of scrutinizing something very complex so it can be separated into its constituent elements. The word also carries strong associations from Freudian psychoanalysis that I believe are counterproductive, particularly the notion that a dream is so complex and its true meaning so disguised that it requires a trained analyst to decode its hidden messages.

- *Dream interpretation: Interpretation* is derived from a Latin word meaning to "translate" or "explain." In my view, this term is much better than "analysis" because there is a sort of translation needed in dreamwork—the translation between the metaphorical language of the dream and the more ego-centered language of the dreamer's waking understanding. However, the term "interpretation" still carries the unfortunate connotation that an expert authority with a vast background of knowledge is needed to explain the dream to the person who dreamed it.

In my view, both of these terms are problematic as they tend to take the dream too far away from the dreamer. The dream can only be really understood by/with the dreamer, since it arose from his or her life. I wholeheartedly agree with the writers of the ethics statement of the International Association for the Study of Dreams when they say: "systems of dreamwork that assign authority or knowledge of the dream's meanings to someone other than the dreamer can be misleading, incorrect, and harmful." [2]

The first goal: Connecting the dream to your life

What if we put aside both analysis and interpretation and aim for a different target? In my experience, the most positive and effective thing we can do with a dream is to help the dreamer connect the dream to his or her life. Facilitating the understanding of a connection is much simpler and more straightforward than analysis or interpretation. It may contain elements of analysis and interpretation but in essence it is neither of these. Above all it must be done by/with the dreamer, and it must resonate with the dreamer.

---

2 "Dreamwork Ethics Statement" prepared by the IASD Ethics Committee, Carol Warner, Chair. 1997. www.asdreams.org/ethics-and-confidentiality/.

To help clarify the concept of connection, let's use one of my own dreams as an example. I had this dream while writing this book, and I call it *Blowing on the Fire*:

> *I am at a campfire, trying to get a big log to ignite. There are many other people seated nearby. It seems that they are watching me but not help-ing me with the fire. I have the feeling that it is up to me and me alone to get the fire going. I spend a long time building little hot areas around the main log and blowing on it, and blowing and blowing as hard as I could… trying to get it to go. Several times I feel waves of frustration and bewilderment—it should be hot enough. Why isn't it catching? Finally it bursts into flame! The whole scene is suddenly bathed in warmth and light, and everyone who is looking on cheers. I feel fantastic!*

When I awoke I immediately felt that this was an important dream. It was vividly remembered and had strong feeling tones. And it had a clear sense of *coherence* (the feeling that some inner intelligence is try-ing to deliver a message). But what was the message? So—as my own facilitator—I set about to ask myself: "How does this dream connect to my life?" I wanted to set up a question that would help me make the con-nection. Since the dream is full of strong feelings, it was a good bet that a connection could be made through these feelings. I used the following construct—I reiterated the feelings that were present in the dream, then I asked myself where these feelings existed in my life. I feel I must put in a lot of sustained effort and energy into getting something to happen in the dream; there are others present and interested in what I am doing, but I feel I must do it on my own. I am frustrated and bewildered that it is taking so long. Where in my life do I have this combination of feelings?

With the help of this setup, I was able to make a resonant connec-tion quite quickly—I had this combination of feelings about my efforts to write and publish this book! It was taking a frustratingly long time and required an enormous effort and input of energy, and I felt that while many other people are interested in it, they could not really help me with it. Encouragingly, the dream seemed to be saying that the project would eventually catch fire. Arriving at this insight was very helpful for me; I still think of the dream when I feel discouraged or worn down about my creative work. But what kind of dreamwork was done here? Can we call this an analysis or an interpretation? Perhaps it has some overlap with these, but essentially it is simply a technique designed to lead toward the understanding of a connection.

Connection can be an elusive and unpredictable thing; sometimes it happens spontaneously, sometimes by lucky accident; sometimes you will have already made a resonant connection and don't need any help, sometimes it never happens. But in the majority of cases you will benefit from using a structured technique. Are there reliable, straightforward, and learnable techniques that can be used to help you arrive at a resonant connection? Yes! I have described the three primary connecting techniques that I use every day in my practice in chapter 13: Connecting the Dream to Your Life.

The double resonance test

How do you know when you have made a good connection between the dream and your life? The simple answer is resonance; there is a resonant feeling of true-ness that happens. And when one person is helping another with a dream, a double resonance can occur, whereby the connection resonates with both the dreamer and the facilitator, rather like two tuning forks that start to vibrate together. (It may seem vague and whimsical but when it happens it is quite distinct and unmistakable.) Both dreamer and dreamworker simultaneously have an Aha! experience; "yes, that's it! That's where it connects!"—mission accomplished. The resonance is felt in the emotional body and has an excitement to it, an unmistakable thrill. If the connection seems to happen on the mental level alone, without this characteristic emotional reaction, I have found it to be far less reliable. For me it is this embodied feeling—the exciting feeling that I have perceived a connection between the dream and my life—this is what I am aiming for; this is the first goal of dreamwork.

The second goal: Responding to the dream

Once this has happened, a second goal can take center stage—"what am I going to do now that I have understood this connection?" In my experience, every dream that has been resonantly connected and understood can be seen as a request for change. Having understood a dream, we can always frame the question, "What does this dream want from me?" We certainly do not *need* to look at the dream in this way (there are always a myriad of ways to look at a dream), but we *can* look at it in this way. If we do, we are drawing the message of the dream into the service of our personal growth. We are now using its guidance. Now a different kind of benefit starts to happen that does not necessarily happen when we ask only "what does the dream mean?" If we can shift the question to what the dream wants, we are in a much more dynamic position, albeit one that requires some dedicated effort and follow-through. This will be discussed more fully in "Responding to the dream" in chapter 14.

Ethical considerations in dreamwork

Are you interested in becoming a dreamworker? Perhaps you already work in the helping profession in some capacity and you would like to incorporate dreamwork into your practice. If so, you must be mindful of the ethical considerations that will need to be in place. These are similar to the ethical considerations underlying other forms of therapy and counseling. Dreamwork does not have a clear identity in the world of the helping professions, and it often falls between the cracks when it comes to formal definitions regarding scope of practice. Is it a form of psychotherapy? Is it counseling? Does it constitute a therapeutic intervention?

If the most powerful tools of dreamworking are utilized, then some form of therapeutic intervention is indeed happening—if you move to the level of responding to the dream, you are suggesting or supporting a specific life change that the dreamer will attempt to make based on the insight obtained from the dream. This means that you are suggesting an intervention, something that in my view means you are in the realm of counseling at the very least; some would argue that this puts you into the realm of psychotherapy.

The Dreamwork Ethics statement of the International Association for the Study of Dreams succinctly covers the key ethical considerations concerning dreamwork I think should be considered by anyone contemplating adding a dreamworking component to their practice. I would encourage you to read it in full on the IASD website.[3] Here is an excerpt:

> IASD celebrates the many benefits of dreamwork, yet recognizes that there are potential risks. IASD supports an approach to dreamwork and dream sharing that respects the dreamer's dignity and integrity, and which recognizes the dreamer as the decision-maker regarding the significance of the dream. Systems of dreamwork that assign authority or knowledge of the dream's meanings to someone other than the dreamer can be misleading, incorrect, and harmful. Dreamwork outside a clinical setting is not a substitute for psychotherapy, or other professional treatment, and should not be used as such.

Informed consent

If you already have some kind of health care or counseling practice, you will probably already have a procedure in place to obtain informed consent to treatment from your clients. If not, you need to get such a procedure in place if you are planning to do dreamwork.

---

3   "Dreamwork Ethics Statement."

The key element of informed consent is communication; before something is done in a health care appointment, the client has been told about it. They will not feel blindsided by something happening that they were not expecting, and they have a chance to say no once they fully understand what is being proposed. In the case of dreamwork, I think this communication should cover the following key points:

- the dreams discussed in session will be treated with full confidentiality (unless otherwise agreed upon, e.g., using transcripts for teaching or publishing purposes; discussing a specific dream with a spouse or significant other)

- the client is aware that the dreams may open up very powerful or personal material

- the client is aware that they have the right to discontinue the dreamwork at any time without jeopardizing the other forms of treatment that have been agreed upon

- any recorded forms of the dreams brought to a session (emails, case notes, video recordings, etc.) will be kept as part of the client's case records, and the privacy, safety, and confidentiality of these records will be the responsibility of the practitioner

Dreamwork can go very deep very quickly, even when it happens spontaneously in an informal setting, talking with a friend, or discussing our dreams at a party. A person who is sharing a dream may suddenly feel they are in the middle of something deeply personal and uncomfortably exposing. For this reason, dreamwork—even if informal—should always be done with sensitivity and respect. But don't let this caveat discourage you from doing it.

Summary

Next time you have a dream that catches your attention, try looking at it from the perspective of these two goals: how does it connect to my life and what is it asking me for? Does this feel different from the way you usually think about your dreams? You may find that you feel engaged in a different way, as if you are in a conversation with someone that could continue and evolve over time. Indeed, you *are* conversing with someone—your own inner self. You are not only trying to perceive the meaning of an event now past (which I would call dream interpretation), you are engaged in an ongoing process that is alive in the present and moves into the future. This is dreamwork.

CHAPTER 6

Choosing a Good Dream to Work With

Brenda, a 60-year-old woman, is a regular dreamwork client of mine. A few years ago we were about two-thirds of the way through our session when I asked her if she had a dream to share. She replied, "Well, I do but I'm not sure if its anything we can really work with. It's just a short snippet of a much longer dream, so I'm sorry I can't remember the rest of it." She seemed reluctant, almost as if she wanted to avoid talking about this dream. In my experience when someone introduces a dream with a disclaimer like this, I know that I am about to hear something very important, something that will yield valuable insight when worked with. Here is Brenda's dream snippet, which we called *Big Man Sticking Me With Pins:*

> *I'm in a corner. A big man with blonde hair and an overcoat is sticking me all over with pins. He's jabbing them in and out, really fast. I'm terrified. I'm just hunching over trying to make myself small…*

As we started to work with the dream, it quickly became obvious that we were exploring a gold mine. This dream fragment showed Brenda (with the exaggeration and heightened urgency that dreams so often employ to get their message across) that she was cowering in a masochistic position and allowing herself to be repeatedly hurt. But where in her life was this happening? Often the best way to find out is to re-enter the dreamscape and experience the emotional impact of the dream again.

Tip: First figure out what the dream is asking for within the dream scenario itself, then translate this insight into waking life

I encouraged Brenda to go back into the dream. How would she like to change this scenario? She could not think of anything; her imagination seemed to be stuck in the same cowering and cornered position depicted in the dream; she literally could not think of any better options. When this kind of paralysis of the imagination occurs, it is a time for active facilitation; someone needs to put a few possibilities onto the table for the dreamer to consider and try on. I asked Brenda, "Would you like to fight back? Would you like to run away? Would you like to call out for help?" She considered all these for a few moments, then said: "I want to fight back." I noticed as she said this that her voice seemed stronger, there was a new feeling of resolve and strength that had not been there before. Next I asked her to imagine moving out of the hunched and cowering posture, to stand up and face the attacker with the pins. She did this. "What would you like to do next?" I asked. Her imagination was now fully unstuck; she no longer needed prompting. "I'm pushing him back," she said. "The bastard! I'm screaming at him, 'How dare you do that to me?'"

This emotionally charged moment brought forth a fully resonant connection—Brenda now understood that the man in the dream was playing the role of her father, someone she passively allowed to wound her again and again. This brief imaginal experience also made it very clear that she needed to move out of her masochistic posture and stand up to him and push back if need be.

Now she knew what the dream was asking for: firm self-defensive action to prevent her father from continuing to hurt her. She arrived at this knowing by working imaginally within the terms and setting given in the dreamscape. Now we tackled the next question: how could she initiate an analogous change in her waking life with her actual father? I advised Brenda to practice and rehearse for a few days on the imaginal level before launching into any external action. In this case, I suggested revisiting the dream scenario once a day for three days. I have found that this kind of interior work brings more clarity and resolve about what may eventually need to be done in the exterior realm. Following the IRA guideline (Imaginal-Ritual-Actual, fully explored in chapter 14), I suggested this imaginal homework first; to be followed up with a ritual unsent letter to her father, and finally, when she felt clear and ready, an actual confrontation with him.

Brenda had almost discarded her short dream snippet on grounds that it was not a whole dream, merely a fragment of one. Yet it turned out to be one of her most valuable dreams because it was so clear and easy to work with (on all three levels). I include Brenda's example because it illustrates several important facets of what makes a dream workable. First lesson: Never dismiss a dream because of brevity. Second lesson: You do not need the whole if you have a standalone part. Third lesson: If somebody tries to downplay the value of a dream by introducing it with "it's just a ... " you are probably about to hear something very important. Fourth and finally: Any dream or dream fragment with a strong emotional charge is likely to yield good results in dreamwork.

Qualities of a good working dream

Clearly some dreams are better candidates for focused dreamwork than others. We cannot work on all our dreams so we must do some kind of prioritizing when we choose which dream to invest our time and energy in. I propose that when we make an assessment of a dream's working potential, we can consider all the following qualities:

- *Coherence:* Some dreams have a message-like quality; they seem to have been created by an intelligent part of the psyche, and contain information that is organized in a communicative or narrative way. The dreamer will feel that they have been shown or told something after having a coherent dream; they have been "spoken to."

- *Oddness:* Some dreams have a striking quality of oddness, weirdness, or peculiarity. The dreamer is struck upon waking, "Why on earth would I dream about *that*? What a bizarre thing!" These dreams will characteristically yield interesting results in a dreamwork session. They are relatively easy to work with because they have a natural focal point— the weird part.

- *Urgency:* Some dreams have a striking intensity of feeling, as if they are depicting a state of affairs that is of great concern and requires urgent attention. This urgency is often communicated through the unusual vividness of the dreamscape and the high emotional voltage of the dream. These dreams tend to stay longer in the memory because their vividness makes them difficult to forget (indeed for many people this is the only kind of dream they can remember).

- *Repetitiveness:* If a person's dreams are repeating, or have a repeating theme in them, this may indicate a stuckness or blockage calling out for attention. The unconscious may be saying, "Here is where we are stuck, and we cannot move on until this problem is addressed." For tips on making the distinction between functional repetitiveness and dysfunctional repetitiveness, please see chapter 12.

- *Universality:* If you can recognize the presence of a familiar or universal motif in a dream (especially one of those described in part 3's universal motifs), the chances of being able to do helpful facilitation are greatly enhanced. This is because of the orientation that comes through recognizing the underlying psychodynamic issue that produced the dream.

- *Staying Power:* If a dream has stayed in the dreamer's mind for some reason (even from long ago, including from childhood), it is probably of great significance, and may be worth revisiting.

Most of these qualities are, I believe, self-explanatory. Universality is dealt with at length in part 3, which is concerned with motif recognition. The first two qualities, coherence and oddness, may need a bit of clarification.

Coherence

Coherence is perhaps the most important quality to have in a good working dream, but it is hard to define and describe. It is perhaps best described as a sense that a message has been delivered. The dreamer may not understand the message, but they feel they have been given a message. The dreammaker seems to have selected and organized the contents and rendered them into some kind of story with a message.

Dreams do not always have this message-like quality. Some dreams seem highly chaotic and disorganized, even if they have been well caught and anchored. They seem like the randomly displayed contents of the unconscious, fascinating perhaps, often very vivid, but not rendered into a coherent form. The less coherent a dream is, the harder it will be to remember. This is very often true of dreams that occur in deeper sleep during the early part of the night—the waking mind typically finds them so strange and chaotic that it cannot grasp hold of anything long enough to make any sense of it. It is also characteristic of dreams produced by the mind suffering through an acute illness or a fever, which are often vivid and tormentingly repetitive yet utterly chaotic and nonsensical at the same time.

Some people claim that their dreams are *always* chaotic and nonsensical. Is it possible that some people never have coherent dreams? My experience is that there is a significant variation in dream coherence from person to person, just as there is a significant variation in the ability to remember dreams (indeed these two may be related, since it is much easier to remember a coherent dream story than it is to remember unrelated excerpts of mental contents).

Nevertheless, though some individuals may be challenged in the area of coherence, I do think it is something that can be improved through practice (as is also the case with dream recall). It is helpful to cultivate the notion of dreams as messages, because if you have the attitude of wanting to receive a message from your dreammaker, the dreammaker will respond accordingly by sending more relevant and coherent messages.

Poorly remembered dreams and long rambling dreams

The poorly remembered dream and the long rambling dream are the dreamworker's two worst enemies. If a dream is poorly remembered (not well caught and anchored), this may be contributing to the lack of coherence. If you feel that the client's reporting of the dream is incomplete or out of order in some critical way, then you may be better off not attempting to work with it as a whole integral dream. At this point, you have two main options—you can leave that dream altogether and try to find another one to work with, or you can work with one part of the dream.

Tip: If you can't handle the whole dream, work with one part of it

Long rambling dreams can be very difficult to work with. Coherence suffers because there is too much material. In these cases, try to divide up the dream and extract a coherent segment that seems to have its own integral form (its own beginning, middle, and end). It's much better to make a helpful connection with one small part of a dream than get lost and muddled in a whole dream that is too much to handle. If your intuition is drawing you to a certain part of the dream, trust it and choose that part to work with.

Remember, you can't do helpful dream facilitation without some degree of orientation. If you find yourself listening to someone's dream and it seems too long or too much to get a handle on, just work with one part of it. Choose the part of the dream that you feel most oriented in and most comfortable with. It's fine to say to your client or yourself: "Let's just work with the part of the dream where … "

Picking out the odd part of a dream

If a dream contains something that stands out as being odd or out of place, this makes it a good candidate for dreamwork. It is as if the dreammaker is shining a spotlight on one particular thing in the dream to call attention to it and say "The key to understanding this dream is in this odd part right here." This kind of dream is usually relatively easy to work with because it has a natural focal point—the odd part. Ellen, a 58-year-old woman, lost her husband three years earlier and was grieving the loss, finding his death impossible to accept. She related a long dream with many segments. I chose to work with the following segment (fully coherent in itself) which features something very odd and out of place. We called the dream *The Big Grasshopper:*

> *My husband and I are in our home. It is nice but not like a real home. My husband is present in body with me but strangely devoid of emotion*

and social understanding. His blankness scares and saddens me greatly.
My former brother-in-law appears. This bothers me even more because I
want only time with my husband. Our former small white dog follows us
around the house making sounds of movement (this startles us because we
expect only quietness). My brother-in-law and a baboon are outside the
door waiting—they are just sitting waiting on the stairs in a stupor. We
close the door to keep them out. Then, to our surprise, a big grasshopper
appears inside the room.

At first glance there would appear to be two things in this dream that are very odd and out of place—a baboon and a grasshopper. But Ellen was not surprised by the presence of the baboon in connection with her brother-in-law; she found her brother-in-law to be rather baboonlike and often felt that he was an unwelcome presence. The imagery made sense to her and did not feel odd or out of place. The grasshopper, meanwhile, *did* feel odd and out of place to her, both within the dream and upon recalling it in the waking state. Why would there be a large grasshopper inside the house? Grasshoppers don't belong inside the house—they belong outside. This strange quality makes the grasshopper very important—the dream-maker has put a grasshopper in the spotlight. Why? It must be there for an important reason. We don't know the reason yet, but we sense that the grasshopper may be part of the solution to the problem presented in the first part of the dream segment (the problem of her husband being present but not present, a metaphor for her inability to fully accept and process the fact of his death). As so often happens in dreams, it is the oddness that catches our attention.

Many of the mysterious oddities that appear in dreams are not fully understood at first; understanding may not come until much later, months or even years after the dreaming. But they should not be glossed over and forgotten. In this case I assigned a kind of response homework for Ellen designed to keep the image alive and relevant in her mind and invite her dreammaker to say more about it. I asked Ellen to think about the grasshopper, using her visual imagination to picture it in the room, and repeating this several times a day until the next session. This kind of response sends a powerful message back to the dreammaker: "I'm interested in the grasshopper, please tell me more about it." It is a version of a technique often referred to as dream incubation; asking for further dream input on a particular subject. Ellen's dreammaker responded by sending her another fascinating dream that featured a grasshopper some months later (see *The Traveling Minstrel Grasshopper Show* in chapter 14).

Tip: A quick checklist for selecting a good dream to work with

If someone were to ask you (or if you're wondering yourself), "I have lots and lots of dreams; which one(s) should I choose to work on?" here are some good suggestions to guide the choice:

- Do you have any with a repeating theme?

- Do you have any that have stayed with you for a long time?

- Do you have any that strike you as odd or mysterious?

- Do you have any that seem to be strikingly vivid or emotionally intense?

Summary

If you are a prolific dreamer, you will certainly have to do some selection and prioritizing about which of your many dreams you will choose to devote time and energy to. Working with a dream *does* take up some time, and most of us are pretty busy already. Follow your intuition. If you're intuition is not giving you a clear answer, try using these guidelines we have discussed—they have all proved very reliable for my students and myself.

CHAPTER 7

Fixed Meanings in Dreams

Tara, a woman of Sri Lankan background, had a dream of a crow with glowing eyes appearing at her window. Partly because of her cultural background, she has many negative associations about crows, including that they are common and dirty. She is also somewhat influenced by a very widespread belief that a bird trying to enter the house is a bad omen, particularly a black bird. In addition, Tara associates the crow with a particular movie in which a woman saw a crow and her lover died shortly after. Three layers of negative association, yet the crow in her dream had remarkable glowing eyes and seemed to be trying to communicate with her. As she told me the dream, I felt strongly that the crow might be something potentially very important and positive for Tara. But would she be open to seeing the crow in a positive light? Here is a verbatim transcript of Tara and I discussing her dream, *The Crow With the Glowing Eyes:*

It's nighttime. I'm in a house, and it's dark outside, spooky. The wind is howling. There's a moon. I send my dog out and then I'm waiting for him to come back. I expect him to come back but he's not coming back. I see a crow at the window. The window is sort of tilting outwards so he can't fly directly in, but he's outside the window and he has glowing white eyes … a black crow. Then he manages to get in through the window. I can't really remember what he says but it's in some kind of cooing language. He doesn't sound like a crow. More a humming or cooing, like a dove … He tells me something different or if it was worried too about the dog not returning. Why is the dog not coming back? I don't remember what it told me exactly.

Dreamworker: How did you feel about this crow being inside with you?

I was okay. At first when it was at the window it was sort of scary, with the eyes, and trying to get in … once it was in I felt it had something to tell me … so I was feeling okay about it; not threatened. I wasn't scared. At first I was a bit alarmed, but then I was okay with it being inside.

DW: Does the crow itself have a bad connotation for you?

It's common. And associated with dirt. So I'm wondering why I dreamed of a crow particularly—it's sort of common but then the eyes make it uncommon … from another world.

DW: Do you think you can be the crow? Just imagine that you're the crow.

Okay … it's very different … scary because it's powerful, because of what it knows, the message it's bringing. It's almost too spiritual and full of energy to be it. (long pause) *I don't know what the crow is saying.*

DW: But just imagine the feeling of what it's like to be the crow.

Expansiveness and power … and everything … just a great expansion of unlimitedness.

DW: Do you like that?

Yes. Positive, and powerful… scary that it's powerful.

Some focused work had to be done to help Tara open herself up to the suspected positive qualities of the crow and step outside the box of her prior associations. By the end of our session, the crow had become a very positive image for Tara, another example of an inspiring contact motif (see chapter 25). As in the case of the dream of *The Big Loon* discussed in chapter 3, the crow is the symbol of a new set of potentials opening up in the dreamer. The pattern of the disappearance of the old dog followed by the appearance of the crow seems to represent an important inner transformation—the old and familiar replaced by the new and mysterious.

When we work with a key figure or object that has appeared in a dream, it is important to stay open to all possible meanings and associations the figure may carry. For example, a snake in a dream does not have one fixed meaning; it can have literally thousands of different meanings and associations that are unique and individual to a particular person and the current situation the dream is addressing. I have found that the problem of fixed meanings and interpretations tend to creep into the picture in three ways:

- Fixed associations with certain dream figures that the dreamer has inherited from their culture. For example, I have worked with several people of east European background who believe that if a bird enters the house, it *always* means that the dreamer will soon get the news that someone has died.

- Fixed or simplistic associations that are taken from books, dream dictionaries, dream websites, etc. For example, a current website of dream animal interpretation tells us that to dream of a monkey "symbolizes deceit."

- Freudian clichés that have survived from the early days of psychoanalysis, and are still tenaciously rooted in some people's minds. Here is an example of Freud's obsessive dogmatism regarding what he believed were sexual elements in dreams: "All elongated objects such as sticks, tree trunks, and umbrellas (the opening of these last being comparable to an erection) may stand for the male organ—as well as all long sharp weapons, such as knives, daggers and pikes. Boxes, cases, chests, cupboards, and ovens represent the uterus, and also hollow objects, ships and vessels of all kinds. Rooms in dreams are usually women; if the various ways in and out of them are represented, this interpretation is scarcely open to doubt. There is no need to name explicitly the key that unlocks the room."[4] The problem with all of these is simply that they limit the field of possibility and lock us into a system where only one meaning is possible.

What to do when the dreamer is attached to a single fixed meaning

There will probably be times when you feel that your dream figure *must* be XYZ because figures like that in dreams are *always* XYZ. When this happens, stop for a moment and consider—am I overly attached to one fixed meaning or association? Might there be other possibilities? This is often a good time to try being the figure. Through identifying directly with your dream figure, you will often be able to step outside the limiting box of prior associations and you may be able to experience a whole new set of associations. It's not about right or wrong, it's about not limiting yourself.

---

4   Sigmund Freud, *The Interpretation of Dreams* (New York: Avon Books, 1965), 389.

Patricia Garfield, in her book *The Universal Dream Key—The 12 Most Common Dream Themes Around the World,* includes a section on cultural influences for each of the common dream themes she discusses. She notes: "Whatever you were taught and experienced as a child is likely to persist in your dream fears." [5] Be mindful of this cultural and familial level whenever you are dealing with associations to dream figures. These inherited associations may of course be "real" and valid but they can also be restrictive and limiting. We dreamworkers must be on the lookout for them and prepared to question them when they arise.

Tip: Include and expand

If you are helping someone with a dream and they say something like: "In my culture when you have a dream about an X, it means _____" or "My grandmother used to say it means _____ when you dream about Y" you might be dealing with a fixed meaning problem. Do not challenge or negate the dreamer's association, even if you sense it is doing the dream a great injustice. Use a phrase that includes and expands, such as: "Okay good, we have that possibility. Now let's see if there can be another possible meaning as well." Then, if you think they are open to it, ask them to *be* X, and see if they can experience some new identification with it. If, after exploring a few new possibilities in good faith, the dreamer comes back to the original association learned from her grandmother or her culture, and feels that this is the most true and resonant point of connection, then that is fine; you have done your due dream diligence!

Summary

Dream figures, images, and symbols can be very rich and multifaceted. Tara's crow can only be Tara's crow. Your crow would be a different crow carrying

---

5   Patricia Garfield, *The Universal Dream Key: The 12 Most Common Dream Themes Around the World* (San Francisco: Harper San Francisco, 2001), 4.

a different message and asking for a different response, and mine would be different as well. For this reason we should avoid making any general statements about crows in dreams. Certainly when you recognize a familiar motif, you may have a suspicion that you might be dealing with a familiar issue and that's fine. Indeed it would be hard to do effective dreamwork without having such suspicions. But remember: don't lock the dream crow in a cage of single meaning; let it be whatever it may be.

CHAPTER 8

What Do Our Dreams Want?

Have you ever had a dream of being bitten by a cat or dog? If so, did you consider that the dream animal may have wanted something from you? As it turns out, dreams of being bitten by animals are surprisingly common. I am amazed by how frequently they occur and how often they follow this pattern: an animal engages with the dream ego in a focused and intense way; the dreamer is typically not terrified but there is an anxious concern that the encounter could become more dangerous; the dreamer wants to stop the encounter but the animal persists; the dreamer tries not to show fear; the animal almost always bites or threatens to bite the dreamer (most commonly on the hand or arm); the urgency of the encounter tends to ramp up, often leading to a panicky awakening. What is this kind of dream trying to say? What does it want from the dreamer?

Here's an example told to me recently by Paul, a 32-year-old man. Paul is a father of two young boys and is working hard to get ahead in his career; in short, he is a very busy man, living with high stress levels on several fronts. Paul's dream of *The Big Gray Dog* was the second in a series; he'd had another biting dog dream a few months earlier:

I'm in some kind of space with a woman who has a big dog. The dog is very tall, with long light gray hair. The dog wants to interact with me, to play, with its open mouth, play-biting but not really biting, pushing on my hands and arms as I'm trying to push it away. I feel that if I don't go along with the game and do the right thing, it will escalate and it might really bite me. I feel it's pushing me to do something I don't want to do, and I also feel like it's testing me somehow. But I do not want to play this game, I just want to get away. There is a risky feeling, like this could quickly get out of control. I wake up.

As we discussed the dream, I suspected that the dog was trying to tell Paul something, or better yet—trying to get him to do something. When a dreamer is close to being able to identify with a figure in his dream but cannot quite do it, I will usually ask him to Be the Part. So I asked Paul to be the dog. "Okay ... I am the dog," he said. "What do you want Paul to do?" I asked. This is what the dream dog said:

I want Paul to show me that he can handle me without being intimidated. I don't want him to be frightened or intimidated. I want to test him and force him to find a way to handle me firmly, without panicking. He needs to be calm in a difficult and tense situation and prove that he can deal with it.

At this point Paul was starting to feel a resonant connection between the dream message and his life. The dog's message seemed to fit well with his financial and career situations, which were currently difficult and tense. He knew in some way that he needed to be firmer and more assertive, yet he found this difficult because he wasn't "that kind of person."

Now that the dream was well connected, we could move on to a response. We started with the first level of response—the imaginal level. I asked Paul to try standing above the dog (in his visual imagination) and give him a solid command to sit. Paul had some resistance to doing this; he said: "I do not want to either receive or give commands." This was another very resonant moment. It felt like we were face to face with something in Paul's nature that did not believe in being firm and commanding. I felt strongly that this is why the dream dog needed to come to him—to help him find and develop the commanding part of his nature he wished to disown.

I persisted. I asked Paul again to stand up and give the "sit" command. At first it did not sound convincing, a bit better the second time, but the third time there was that magical change that happens in fairy tales and old stories. The feeling in the scene shifted completely. The dog was now sitting and looking up at him attentively. Paul's feeling about the dog also transformed—he no longer wanted to stop the encounter and get away from the dog. He wanted the dog to be with him.

Now if we step back from the scene and look at it psychodynamically, we can see that a wonderful thing is happening here. An animal ally has appeared; it *wants* Paul to adopt and develop a new set of behaviors. Because Paul is resistant to owning such behaviors in himself the encounter is tense and threatening at first. But if the meeting is allowed to move forward then the animal's teaching can be received and tried on, and the characteristic positive shift occurs. This dream type falls within the larger category of the shadow dream in which a true part of self that has been held at arm's length appears and demands to be accepted and integrated.

Three advantages of considering what the dream wants

The more I work with dreams, the more I find that taking the perspective of considering what the dream wants consistently brings the most dynamic and useful results. It is not the only way to look at a dream, of course, but it is one good way. It has three significant advantages: first—it speeds things up; it tends to bring insight much faster than thinking about what the dream might mean. This makes it very well suited for doing dreamwork within a limited time frame.

Second, it creates a natural gradient that flows through understanding and insight toward action and change; it is not content to stay with understanding alone. This gradient sets up a very dynamic rhythm of positive intra-psychic feedback that does not necessarily happen if we only seek an understanding of the dream. It is as if our subconscious says, "I see you got my message, and you really did something about it. I appreciate that! So here's my next message..." This makes it particularly well suited for people who are interested in personal growth because it trains them to listen to their own inner guide and respond to its suggestions.

Third, it keeps the burden of understanding the dream where it should be—with the dreamer. Only the dreamer can know with any certainty what the dream is asking for. I could make an educated guess about what the big gray dog wanted from Paul, but only Paul could really know with the kind of knowing that happens in the emotional body as well as the intellect. Anyone who takes on the task of figuring out what a dream *means* has put himself in the position of the interpreter/analyst, and this is not an easy position to hold. It requires great sophistication and long years of training and experience to be a good dream interpreter. It is a much simpler task to hold the question: what does this dream want? Yet this simple question can lead quickly and surely to the goal.

What if it is not clear what the dream is asking for?

In many instances it is not obvious what the dream wants to happen, even when there is a good sense of orientation. In these cases, it is usually best to re-enter the dreamscape and do some imaginal work designed to clarify what the dream is asking for. Here's an example: Rosalie had recently moved to a new part of the country and was struggling to get her health care practice established in a new place with different regulations and different client expectations. She had a dream that she titled *Gordon Ramsay and the Giant Sushi Rolls:*

> *I'm a contestant on* MasterChef *(the cooking competition show starring the famous chef and TV personality Gordon Ramsay; I actually do watch this show in waking life). I walk into a kitchen. In front of me there are three giant sushi rolls, the size of logs. They're not made out of rice and fish, they're made out of sandwich materials. We contestants are expected to use these giant sushi rolls as our inspiration to create our own sushi rolls. The clock starts. We start cooking as fast as we can. I'm putting together the first roll, which has duck in it. The way I roll it is all wrong and when I go to slice it, it falls apart. Oh no! There's no time to fix it though, I have to move on to the next two rolls and get them completed before the clock runs out.*
>
> *At this point Gordon Ramsay comes to look at my work. He looks at the duck roll and says, "What happened here? This is a mess!" I say, "Don't even look at that roll, I'm not even going to put it on the plate, I'm moving onto the next two rolls." He says, "All right, tell me about your next two rolls." I reply that my next roll will be a "meat lover's delight." He seems to be okay with that, and asks me about my third roll. I reply that it will be vegetarian. He frowns; he is not pleased with this idea. He says, "You should just smile . . . because you're done!" He walks away. I'm frantic. Now I'm second-guessing my third roll. Maybe I should forget my vegetarian idea and use some of the fish; maybe I could do a fish and cream cheese roll. The clock is running out! I've got to work fast!*

Rosalie and I worked with the dream and were able to get it connected to her life fairly quickly using a setup with the feeling tones: "In the dream you feel like you are competing, you are judged, stressed, frantic, under time pressure, and second-guessing yourself; where in your life do you have those feelings?" She connected it to her career as a health care practitioner. Rosalie had recently moved to a new part of the country and was trying to cope with the stresses and demands of establishing herself in this new environment. The feelings of being judged, under time pressure, and second-guessing herself all fit this part of her life.

I asked her to describe how she felt about the giant sushi rolls. "I don't like them," she replied. "The idea of making a giant sushi roll is insane. It makes no sense to me. It's not something I could be passionate about. It's not the way I would want to do it. I would want to make the smaller traditional sushi rolls." This also connected to Rosalie's new health care practice; there were many aspects of it that were feeling unnatural and wrong for her. She did not feel passionate about these elements of her work although she felt obliged to continue them because they were generating business for her.

The dream felt satisfyingly connected to Rosalie's life now, but we still didn't know what it is asking her to do. Is it asking her to continue to strive under these very stressful conditions where she feels as if she is in a competition, being judged, on the clock, and is second-guessing herself all the time? Or is it asking her to walk away from the whole thing, to leave this scene and find a place where she can do what feels right for her, making a more modest-sized and traditional kind of sushi roll? Only the dreamer could know the answer, and Rosalie was not yet clear about the answer. I presented both of these options to her, and they both seemed to have their pros and cons. How can we move this situation forward so that the dreamer knows what she is aiming for in devising a response to this dream?

Re-enter and explore

What I do at times like this is something I call "re-enter and explore." Help the dreamer (or yourself) re-enter the dreamscape and explore the different possible action scenarios that could move things in a good new direction. I asked Rosalie to go back into the dream, at a point near the end where the stress and time pressure are at their peak. I waited a few moments as she went back into the set of *MasterChef*. For this technique to work well, she must be re-experiencing the emotions of the dream, not just remembering the storyline and the visuals. Then I asked her to catch herself and become aware that she could now change the situation. How would she like to change it? I reiterated the key choice point that the dream seemed to be highlighting: should she stay on set and continue to do her best, or should she walk away from the whole frantic scene? "Let's try both," I said (this is important because it signals to her that she can fully explore both paths without committing and being locked into the wrong choice). I asked Rosalie which scenario she would like to try first; she elected to begin with the walking away option.

The job of the facilitator here is to help establish the permission and the pace for the new imaginal experience to happen, very similar to what would be done in guided visualization exercises, but always beginning with the conditions and emotions that were given in the dream:

> *All right then. There you are, you're running out of time. You have two sushi rolls to complete... now you catch yourself. You become aware that you can now change the situation, and you decide to leave the competition and walk away. You find the door... open it and walk outside, closing it behind you. You walk away from the building; you're leaving* MasterChef *behind and moving on to something else. How does it feel?*

Rosalie let herself feel this new feeling for a few moments. "It doesn't feel right," she said, "I feel a relief from the pressure, but there's also an empty feeling. I also feel like I'm giving up too soon. I want to prove to myself that I can get these next two rolls!" I then suggested we try the other option. So we went back onto the *MasterChef* set, only this time when she caught herself and gave herself space for something new to emerge a very different creative possibility appeared: "First of all, I want to give myself more time. I'm going to slow everything down so I have a whole hour. Then, I don't have to keep trying to imitate these oversized sushi rolls. I'm going to make a smaller traditional roll, the way I know how." I asked Rosalie to play out this scenario fully in her imagination, culminating with

Gordon Ramsay coming over to judge her new rolls. How does this scenario feel? "It feels good," she said. "Gordon Ramsay and the other judges are very impressed. And I feel like I've done something that is true to me."

Find a good response within the dreamscape, then translate this into waking life

Now that we have found and developed a satisfying response within the dreamscape, we can think about what this might look like in Rosalie's waking life. "What would this mean for your actual practice?" I asked her. She replied: "It would mean bringing more elements into my practice that are true for me, going back to the basic traditional healing values. I've done too much conforming to the new trends that are happening here in order to stay competitive and relevant. The role I've taken on is too big (here the dreamer noticed the "role/roll" wordplay and laughed). It's a source of income, but it's not what I really want to be doing." Here we had arrived at a resonant sense of what the dream was asking her to do in her life, and what made this possible was the imaginal reentry and intra-dream exploration of the possibilities.

Summary

When we work from the vantage point of what the dream is asking for, we are placing ourselves right on the cusp of creating change. Often we begin to manifest this change while we are still at work within the dreamscape. I have been asked a number of times—is it legitimate to change the dream like this? My answer is yes! Many dreams like this one that end in a horrible impasse are pointing out a critical failure of the imagination. The dreamer's imagination literally cannot generate a creative solution (either dreaming or awake) to an important life problem. The dream provides us a quintessential depiction of the problem and thus gives us the best place to look for a good solution. This is the medicine of dreamwork.

PART 2

A Method of Dreamworking

CHAPTER 9

Overview of the Method

There are many ways to work with a dream, and there are many excellent dreamworking methods in use today. What distinguishes this method from other dreamworking methods? Here's my answer—its strong orientation toward change and personal growth. The whole method orbits around the central question: What is the dream asking for? The dreamer is naturally led toward the cusp of a potential life change, and for this reason it is well-suited for use by therapists, counselors, life coaches, health care workers, and anyone who is in the business of helping other people change. But above all it is well-suited for anyone who dreams and who wants to listen for and act upon the guidance that can come through dreams. This method has five steps. Often they overlap and interpenetrate, but it is helpful to try to delineate them in your mind.

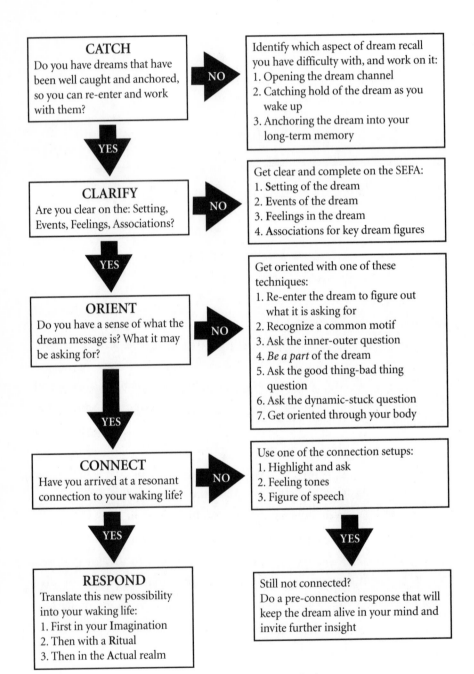

CATCH
Do you have dreams that have been well caught and anchored, so you can re-enter and work with them?

NO → Identify which aspect of dream recall you have difficulty with, and work on it:
1. Opening the dream channel
2. Catching hold of the dream as you wake up
3. Anchoring the dream into your long-term memory

YES ↓

CLARIFY
Are you clear on the: Setting, Events, Feelings, Associations?

NO → Get clear and complete on the SEFA:
1. Setting of the dream
2. Events of the dream
3. Feelings in the dream
4. Associations for key dream figures

YES ↓

ORIENT
Do you have a sense of what the dream message is? What it may be asking for?

NO → Get oriented with one of these techniques:
1. Re-enter the dream to figure out what it is asking for
2. Recognize a common motif
3. Ask the inner-outer question
4. *Be a part* of the dream
5. Ask the good thing-bad thing question
6. Ask the dynamic-stuck question
7. Get oriented through your body

YES ↓

CONNECT
Have you arrived at a resonant connection to your waking life?

NO → Use one of the connection setups:
1. Highlight and ask
2. Feeling tones
3. Figure of speech

YES ↓   **YES** ↓

RESPOND
Translate this new possibility into your waking life:
1. First in your Imagination
2. Then with a Ritual
3. Then in the Actual realm

Still not connected?
Do a pre-connection response that will keep the dream alive in your mind and invite further insight

Flowchart illustrating the Dream Method in action.

1. Catching the dream

2. Clarifying the dream

3. Orienting yourself within the dream

4. Connecting the dream to your life

5. Responding to the dream

We can easily illustrate the whole method condensed into one flow chart. (See facing page for example.)

Tip: In dreamwork, keep your questions clear, short, and simple

Choosing the right words is very important in dream facilitation. The phrases and questions that work best are clear, brief, and uncomplicated. This is equally true whether you are facilitating yourself or another person. I have often observed that people who are new to dreamwork tend to formulate long multi-part questions that leave the dreamer confused as to what part of the question he or she should be responding to. A good rule is when asking a question in dream facilitation, ask one short simple question and then wait for the dreamer's response. Don't ask multi-part questions; if there are two things you need to know the answer to, ask one at a time.

Ask questions appropriate for the step of the method you are working at

Keep in mind when you are crafting questions for yourself or for the person you are facilitating—staging is critical. If you do not yet have any sense of what the dream is saying, you should be asking open and neutral clarification questions that will gather more information for you. Once you feel you have gathered up most of what can be gathered, you should be proceeding to an orienting question, something that is designed to help you get a sense of what your client's dreammaker is trying to communicate.

Once you yourself are feeling oriented within the dream, you should move on to a connecting question, the kind of question that will help set up the dreamer to experience some insight about how the dream connects to his or her life. Once you both feel you have understood the connection, you should think about a responding question to help initiate some real life change based on the insight obtained from the dream.

Suggested questions and phrases for dream facilitation

The following is a sampling of questions and phrases distilled from my experience as a dream facilitator. I have used questions like these hundreds of times and they have all proved very valuable. If you are starting out as a dream facilitator, I recommend using phrases and questions similar to these, or even copying parts of them verbatim at first. Later, as you become more experienced, you will trust your own intuitive choice of words more and more as you develop your own unique style of facilitation.

Because of the importance of staging in dream facilitation, I have divided the questions into four categories: clarification questions, orientation questions, connecting questions, and responding questions. Each can be used according to which step of the method you are using. And to make the questions more grounded in a real experience of dreamwork, let's consider the following short dream related by one of my clients. Wendy, a 27-year-old woman, told me the dream of *The Bug-Bird* on her first consultation:

> *I'm walking somewhere. There is a relentless buzzing bug that keeps bugging me. It's buzzing nonstop, right in my ear. Finally I swat it, catch it, and smash it. But it changes into a bird, a grayish black bird, medium-sized. It is completely defenseless, and I had smashed it. I am afraid it is dead. I feel very guilty, very disturbed. When I smashed it, there was a feeling like a soul escaping…*

Clarification questions

Clarification questions are to be used early on in the dreamwork when you have not yet got much of a sense of what the dream is about. *They are simply intended to get more information*—to get clear on the setting of the dream, the events in the dream, the feeling tones that were present in each part of the dream, and to bring out the dreamer's associations with key parts of the dream. These early questions should be wide open, neutral, nonleading, and noninterpretive:

- *"You say that at the beginning you are walking somewhere— any sense of where that is?"* The setting is often important in a dream, and often glossed over in the recounting; this question gives the dreamer a chance to consider the opening setting. If Wendy does not come up with anything definite here, then it is probably not relevant to the dream message; just leave it and go on.

- *"What is the feeling of the bug buzzing in your ear?"* This will give Wendy a chance to re-visit and get clear on the feeling tones in this part of the dream.

- *"When did the bug change into a bird?"* Simply asking for clarification of the order of events.

- *"What did you feel when you realized that you may have killed the bird?"* Allowing Wendy to fully re-experience the feeling tones at this critical moment even though she has already described some feelings that were present.

- *"What do you associate with that kind of bird?"* Often the dreamer's associations with a key dream figure will be surprisingly different from yours; make sure you ask.

- *"You said: 'there was a feeling of a soul escaping'… what do you mean?"* Further clarification and exploration of this statement because it has a sense of being mysterious and very important.

Tip: Keep SEFA in mind
(Setting-Events-Feelings-Associations)

When you are working in the clarification phase, keep in mind that you need all four of these components to have a good clear picture of the dream. Most people are naturally good at remembering and reporting the events of a dream, but they will often leave out the setting and the feeling tones. The associations are usually not given spontaneously either, you will have to make a point of asking, and if it's your own dream you're working on you may need to stop and think for a moment—if your friend Dave appeared in a dream, ask yourself, "What do I associate with Dave?" A good quick trick is to jot down the first three descriptive words that pop into your mind when you think of Dave. Once you have a good sense of all four SEFA components, you should be clear and complete enough to move on to the next step.

Orienting questions

Once you have heard the full story of the dream, complete with feelings and associations, you can shift to a different type of question. Orienting questions have a specific purpose—they are designed not just to gather information but also to help with recognition. They help you *recognize* the essence of the dream. What type of dream is it? What is it trying to say? What is it asking for? Wendy may already have some thoughts and insights about the dream, so your first orienting question will often be some version of:

- *"What have you made of the dream so far?"* or *"What does the dream mean to you?"* This will sometimes open up a promising path into the dream, and may even lead directly to a resonant connection. In these cases, the facilitator doesn't need to do much in the way of finding orientation, it is provided by the dreamer. But in most cases the dreamer will respond either by saying: "I don't know" or will make associations and connections that do not feel complete and resonant. This was the case with Wendy's bug-bird dream; she knew it felt important but she was mystified. So now you can pull out the kind of questions that will help both parties get oriented:

- *"What do you think this dream is asking for?"* This question often leads to an immediate sense of both orientation and connection. For example if Wendy were to reply, "I think the dream is asking me to stop trying to get rid of the bug and to listen to it instead" then we are not only oriented but we have made a resonant connection to Wendy's life. It doesn't always work, but when it does it is the fastest route to a good insight. If the dreamer responds with "I'm not sure," simply move down the list and try another orientation strategy.

- *"Do you intuitively feel that the bug-bird is a part of you, or is it referring to something or someone in your life that is affecting you?"* This is the Inner/Outer question, very often the first orienting question you will need to ask. Often, you will find that you cannot effectively proceed without knowing the answer to this question, since you would be heading in two completely different directions depending on what the answer is. Wendy answered that she felt the bug-bird was a part of her.

- *"Do you think it is a good thing that you caught the bug and smashed it, or not a good thing?"* The deceptively simple Good Thing/Bad Thing question often quickly focuses what kind of message the dreammaker is trying to deliver. In this case, it helped Wendy realize that the smashing of the bug-bird was *not* a good thing, even though at first glance it might seem to be a good thing to rid oneself of a relentlessly buzzing pest.

- *"Can you BE the bug, buzzing in Wendy's ear? What are you trying to say to her?"* The Be the Part technique will help us explore the possibility that there may be a positive aspect to the bug buzzing in her ear. Is it trying to tell her something important?

- *"Can you BE the bird, after you have smashed it?"* How does it feel? This will help Wendy feel the full, probably urgent, impact of the dream's message.

- *"What is trying to happen in this dream?"* This last group of questions helps you get oriented by considering dynamic versus stuck—What is trying to happen? Why can't it happen? Evidently in this dream, the bug is trying to tell Wendy something, but it can't because she doesn't want to listen.

Connecting questions

Always keep in mind that our goal here is to help Wendy understand how the dream connects to her life. As a facilitator, your primary role is not to give Wendy your thoughts or interpretations; you are trying to create the conditions for her own insights and connections to appear, while holding back any insights and connections you may have. Thus the best questions are those that set dreamers up to make the connection on their own. In the case of the *Bug-Bird* dream, I felt I had a pretty good idea what this dream was trying to communicate. It was a familiar motif to me, one that I have come across many times—the killing (or near killing) of the bird pointed to a strong intolerance and suppression of a part of herself. The relentless buzzing and bugging suggested that this part of her was an aspect of her conscience, or inner voice, that was pestering her with some unwelcome truth that she did not want to acknowledge. Thus I would treat this primarily as an ego check motif. Wendy's dream is pointing out to her that she is doing something problematic.

But these were my connections, not hers. It is usually more effective for dreamers to arrive at their own insights rather than having them presented from the outside, even if the offered insights are accurate and helpful. So what we need are questions that will help set Wendy up to make her own connections. Good connecting questions often follow the highlight and ask format: you reiterate the situation or feeling depicted in the dream, then ask Wendy where this situation or feeling exists in her life:

- *"In the dream there is something that is relentlessly bugging you. What has been bugging you lately?"* You can often make a very direct connection by spotting the figure of speech that is being suggested by the dream—in this case something may be "bugging" Wendy.

- *"After you smash the bird you feel very guilty and disturbed. What have you felt guilty and disturbed about?"* Connecting through feeling tones is the easiest and most direct way for many dreamers.

- *"The bug is buzzing relentlessly in your ear. This suggests a voice persistently trying to tell you something. Do you intuitively feel it is an inner voice or an outer voice?"* This is another way of asking the Inner/Outer question, this time adapted to connection rather than orientation.

- *"Are you bothered by an inner voice that persistently tries to tell you something?"* This question is more directing and leading so you would only use a question like this if Wendy was having trouble with the more open type of questions.

- *"In the dream you put up with being bugged for a long time and then 'finally' you can't take it anymore and you smash it. This suggests that you were able to put up with this voice for a while but then, perhaps recently, you lost your tolerance and did something to silence the voice. Can you connect this to your life?"* This question attempts to set up a connection by pointing out a pattern in the dream and asking if Wendy is aware of that pattern in her waking life.

Responding questions

Once a resonant connection has been made and Wendy has a strong sense of what the dream message is, then a response can be considered. It would be ideal if Wendy came up with the response herself, but some dreamers will need suggestions. Start with a completely open question, leaving the door open for anything:

- *"Let's try to come up with some kind of response. What could you do about this?"*

- Or, if the dreamer needs a bit more direction: *"What could you do to help change this pattern of not listening to your inner voice?"*

Keep in mind that the goal of the response step is to help Wendy initiate an ongoing life change as the result of an insight obtained from her dream. The change should be one that arises from her own creative mind and something both realistic and attainable for her. You will usually want to use the real dream situation as your starting point because this is where the dreamer *is* currently. Try to craft questions suggesting modest movement in the desired direction of change; small steps, not wild leaps.

In Wendy's case, the response we worked out together involved a change in her awareness and consciousness; this was her take-home message: "When I realize that my inner conscience is pestering me, I need to stop for a moment and try to listen to it." But a response could be quite literally anything as long as it constitutes an attempt to change based on a dream insight. There are many ways to respond to a dream and different dream motifs call for different kinds of response. This is explored more fully in chapter 14: Responding to the Dream. Considering this wide range of possible responses will help you formulate your questions and make them individualized to the dreamer and the dream message.

Tip: Keep a list of good questions at your fingertips

Practice using the types of questions described above, sticking fairly close to the template at first. If you are working with your own dream, it is still a good idea to use the same questions, asking them of yourself. Better questions bring forth better answers. Try not to launch into a question without being clear about where you're going with it. Your questions should have a specific format and purpose, especially the connecting and orienting questions. For a quick checklist of the kinds of questions that can be used for each stage of dream facilitation, see Appendix 1.

What if the facilitator sees a connection but the dreamer can't see it?

There will be times in dream facilitation where the facilitator senses a critical connection and tries to set up the dreamer to make the approach, but to no avail. There are many reasons why a dreamer would miss a seemingly obvious connection point—she may be attached to an interpretation she has already made; she may be actively resisting an unwelcome truth (especially in ego check motifs); or, as was the case with Wendy's dream, she may simply not be able to get it without outside help. In cases where you as the facilitator see an important possible connection that the dreamer cannot see, you should suggest it of course, but only after you have first tried to help the dreamer find it him- or herself. As a rule, try first to set it up without any leading or suggestion; if that doesn't work, try again using more suggestive and leading phrasing. As a last resort, you may need to spell it out:

- *"I suspect that the buzzing bug may be an aspect of you, an inner voice that is trying to say something to you, perhaps something that you don't want to hear. Does that make sense?"*

After the connection point has been suggested and tried on by the dreamer it must, as always, pass the Double Resonance test—both dreamer and facilitator must feel a resonant sense of trueness. If there is no resonance at all from the dreamer (keeping in mind that strong resistance is a form of resonance), then it's back to the drawing board.

Tip: What to do when you feel lost

Here is a golden rule to think of when you feel lost in a dreamscape: come back to the clarification until you have some orientation. Continue to ask general clarifying questions until you recognize something that gives you a sense of orientation. If you still feel lost after a few minutes of clarification, skip ahead and attempt to make a connection with one of the connecting techniques. If the first one doesn't work, try another. If you have used all the possible connection techniques but you cannot make a resonant connection and you still feel lost, you may have to give up on this dream (for the time being at least).

Summary

If you want to get better at working with your dreams, I strongly urge you to adopt a method and practice it consistently. There are many good dreamworking methods in use today. The method described in this book contains many elements that you may recognize, elements that have been inspired by and adapted from other methods. In the Recommended Resources section at the end of this book you will find a brief survey of some other excellent dreamworking methods. This method, with its emphasis on connecting the dream to your life, considering what the dream is asking for, and responding accordingly, is very dynamic and change-oriented.

CHAPTER 10

Catching the Dream

Dreamwork cannot be done without remembered dreams to work with; a few dreams at least must be caught and held fast. There are effective ways of helping yourself become a good dreamer. Fortunately, dream recall is a learnable and practicable skill.

A person who says, "I have trouble remembering my dreams" may actually be having trouble with one (or more) of three different facets of dream recall:

- Opening and stimulating the dream channel

- Remembering the dream on waking

- Anchoring the dream after initially remembering it

All three of these facets need to be working well to be a good dreamer. If you are currently having trouble remembering dreams, take a moment to consider which one (or more) of these facets is not working well. There are techniques that can be used to strengthen each of these areas. Let's look at them separately.

Techniques for opening and stimulating the dream channel

Have you ever met someone who claims to never remember any dreams? I hear this claim surprisingly often. Are you currently having trouble with dream recall? People can go through periods of "oneiric constipation"— these people normally have good dream recall but periodically find themselves in a "dry spell" for some reason and would like to get things moving again. What can be done in these cases? Strategies for remembering dreams are really just variations on a theme of setting intention. It is a universal law that whatever we focus our attention on we get more of, including dream recall. Perhaps the simplest form of setting intention for dream recall is simply to focus the mind before sleep and tell ourselves that we would like to remember a dream in the morning. Having your dream journal and a pencil close at hand is an act of intention setting. If these basic steps don't work, consider one of the following techniques, all of which I have found to be helpful:

- *Read through some old dreams.* Reading through your dream journal (if you have kept one at any point in your life) is a good practice for many reasons. It reminds you that you are in an ongoing relationship with your unconscious self, and gives you a sense of the history and progress of that relationship. It also prompts your dreammaker to step up the dialogue by signaling that you are ready for the next chapter in the saga.

- *Revisit a specific dream.* If an old dream has stayed with you, its full message has probably not been fully understood and received. How far back can you go? As far as you want, even back to childhood (often these important early dreams are still very relevant). Use your visual imagination to re-enter the remembered dreamscape while awake and run through the whole dream in your mind. This is a powerful stimulus to the dream recall centers of the brain; it primes the whole system to start working again.

- *Read a good book about dreams before bed.* This will stir the dream imagination and get things moving surprisingly often.

- *Incubate a dream.* Dream incubation is a particular kind of intention setting that involves asking for a dream that will shed light on a particular concern or question. The technique essentially involves forming a question in one's mind before sleep and then considering the next morning's dream in relation to that question. Sometimes the results seem remarkably in synch with the question, other times not. Take a look at the Recommended Resources section at the back of the book for more information on this technique.

Here is an example of a dream that came in response to an incubated question. Myrna is a 35-year-old woman, a breast cancer survivor working hard to keep the disease in check. She continues to use a variety of therapies both orthodox and alternative to stay in remission, and has been very successful in doing so, outliving her original prognosis by several years. Her incubation question was, "What can I do to support my ongoing healing?" That night Myrna had the following dream that she called *Riding in the Archbishop's Car*:

> *I get the into Archbishop's car along with the Archbishop, another woman, and a driver. I sit in the passenger seat. Another woman is sitting behind me. I try to adjust my seat so I make sure there is enough room for the woman behind me. As I'm doing this somehow the back of the seat gets loose and I'm afraid it will tip over. The driver tells me how to fix it, and I do fix it. The woman behind me tells me not to worry—she has*

enough room. We were going to a church feast in another town, a kind of pilgrimage. (End of dream.)

I asked Myrna for her associations regarding this Archbishop.

I've known of him since I was a child. He was almost a magical figure to me. We used to go caroling to his place with a small children's choir. To me he always looked like Father Christmas. He is a very peace-inspiring person. He is pretty old, in his mid-eighties, and he has been very sick for a long time. When I saw him two months ago on my last visit home, I was chatting with his driver, and the driver told me that his doctors don't know what to do for him anymore—only God is keeping him alive. I think he is a symbol for somebody who can stay alive for a long time with a pretty severe illness.

Next I asked her what it felt like to be in the car with him. She answered, "It feels healing and peaceful." As we discussed this dream, we agreed that Myrna's dreammaker had responded to the incubated question with two specific suggestions—first: stay close to your spiritual center and those people and places that inspire you spiritually, because this will keep you alive for much longer than the doctors can. And second: watch out for your tendency to over-accommodate other people, because this unhinges you and makes you vulnerable to tipping over.

- *Ask for the next installment of an old dream.* Do you have any dreams from months or years ago that still seem mysterious or incomplete? There is a useful variant of dream incubation that can be used to request the "next installment" of the story. Before sleep, revisit the previous dream by running through it in your imagination, then ask your dreammaker to send another dream that will have more to say on the same topic.

Remembering the dream on waking

What happens in those all-important few moments just as we are waking up? What can be done to support our dream recall during this period? What mental drill works best for grabbing hold of a dream? In my experience this is a very individual matter—what works for one person may not work for another. Here's the drill that works for me:

- As soon as I am aware that I have had a dream, I say to myself (usually not out loud) "Oh! I just had a dream!"

- Then I go back in to the dream and run through it in my mind.

- Then I go back through it a second time. While doing this second run-through, I look around in the dreamscape for other events and details I might have missed the first time. Now I have it.

- If I sense that it is a really big dream and I want to make sure I really have a good hold on it, I may go back through it a third time.

- Now (not before I'm sure I have it in my memory) I let myself think about what it might be asking for (my go-to way of considering its message). Usually my ability to gain insight from the dream is very reduced at this early still-sleepy stage. Typically, I have little or no idea what the dream may be trying to tell me.

- Next, if possible, I tell the dream to my partner. In this sharing stage, the possible meaning of the dream often starts to come into focus, either because of some insight that she may offer, or just in the act of telling itself, which seems to fully pull the dream out of the shoreline state into full consciousness.

Tip: Don't judge your dream while you're still half asleep

When we are still standing on the shoreline, half in and half out of sleep, we often make very poor judgments about the possible significance of the dream we just had. I think there are two main reasons for this—first, the lack of a fully conscious perspective; and second, sheer sleepiness and laziness.

The weird and remarkable aspect of the dream may not become weird or remarkable until we have fully transitioned back into the waking state. Most dream content does not seem strange when we are in the dream; its strangeness only strikes us when we consider it from the waking perspective. Even in the shoreline state we may not be struck by the remarkable qualities of the dream. Many times I have said to myself once having achieved full consciousness in the morning: "Wow! I can't believe I almost let that one go!" Try not to judge and dismiss a dream until you have regained full waking perspective.

On a more mundane level, there may be a quite natural tendency to want to drop back into sleep rather than rouse ourselves sufficiently to remember a dream; at these times we might rationalize our pro-sleep choice by telling ourselves that the dream is just a rambling bit of nonsense, not worth waking up for. But what if it isn't a bit of nonsense? We wouldn't know until we make the effort.

Tip: Give yourself some shoreline time

The ideal conditions for dream recall could be likened to wading into shore on a sandy beach—you are still standing in the water of the dream feeling, but you're close enough to the land to feel your feet touching the ground of waking reality. Try to give yourself as much shoreline time as possible. Undisturbed transitional time between sleep and wakefulness creates the best conditions for most people to remember a dream. If you must use an alarm clock most mornings, then let your alarm-free mornings be your dream time mornings. On these special mornings, train yourself to go back in to the dream to retrieve further content whenever possible. You're not being lazy, you're doing dreamwork! Remember that dream recall is like any other human ability, it can be developed and improved through practice. The investment of attention will pay off sooner or later, even for those of us who are not naturally proficient with dream recall.

Tip: Watch out for water dreams

If your dream takes place on or in a large body of water it is likely saying something about your relationship to your own unconscious mind. If the dream setting is a beach or a shoreline, or any conspicuously transitional zone, it may be saying something about the way you transition and communicate between your unconscious and conscious minds. If the feeling tones of these dreams are positive, adventurous, and curious, that bodes well—it suggests you have a positive feeling about relating to your unconscious self, including doing dreamwork.

Tip: Jot down or draw one thing from the dream (capture a cue)

If you don't think re-entering the dream will work for you, here's another good trick. Have a notebook and pencil by your bedside. When you wake up with a dream but you have a powerful desire to go back to sleep or you need to get up right away, just take a few seconds (literally!) to jot down one thing from the dream; it could be one word, like "car" or the name of a figure in the dream, like "Archbishop"; or if you're a very visual person, it could be a quick sketch of something in the dream, like the car seat tipping over. *Now* you can get up and silence your alarm clock, or start your day, or roll over and go back into a nice cozy sleep. This little cue that you have captured from your dream may be enough to bring the whole thing back to you later that day or even the next day.

Anchoring the dream

Has this ever happened to you? You wake up with an amazing dream. You remember it vividly. You are absolutely certain that you will continue to remember it, so you get up and start your day. By mid-morning you say to yourself: "Oh, what was that dream I had?" You search back in your mind but nothing comes. The dream is completely gone, never to return! What about this experience? You wake up with an amazing dream and you write it down. "Now I'll remember it for sure," you think to yourself. A few days later when you read it back to yourself, it's just random words on a page. All memory of the dream has vanished.

Well, you're not alone! Both these scenarios are extremely common. Remembering a dream when we wake up in the morning is one thing. But fixing it in our long-term memory so we will remember it days later is another matter. A dream that has been written down is not necessarily an anchored dream—it may still drift away like an unmoored boat. To describe it in terms of brain function—the neural networks involved in holding the dream as a memory will be pruned away along with a lot of other unwanted memories. If you do not do something to prioritize and strengthen the specific neural network dedicated to your dream memory, it will fade and eventually disappear.

Tip: Find out what you need to do to anchor your dreams ... and do it

Dream anchoring is an individual matter—some people must speak the dream out loud to another person to anchor it securely; for some it must be written down within a certain time; for others it must be revisited in the mind to remain alive. But for most people if something is not proactively done to keep the dream alive it will usually fade away and disappear within a few days. Find out what works for you and start to cultivate it as a habit.

Good dream anchoring skills are particularly important for those of us who want to develop an ongoing practice of dreamwork. Anchoring will help give the dream a firm place within an ongoing record of dream-informed personal history and growth. Can dreamers still remember important dreams three years later? Twenty years later? They can if they anchor them properly.

Roger remembered his dream of *The Golden Cape* very clearly on the morning he dreamed it, and he even wrote it down (at my request). But it was not anchored—by the time he came to our session a few weeks later he had only the written words on the page, there were no feelings, no emotion, and no strong visual sense of the dream. Here's how Roger described his dream:

> *Presently I don't remember having this dream, but in going back and reading the emails I sent you, which I composed immediately after the dreams on your recommendation ... yes, I remember the dream. There was this golden cape ... and there were dividers surrounding it. I was a spectator. Then suddenly the cape was divided into sections like a pie. Then I woke up immediately after that. I have no idea what that was all about.*

Roger's dream contained powerful and fascinating imagery, but unfortunately he could not re-enter the dreamscape because he had no living memory of it; it no longer existed in his feeling body. It was briefly caught but never securely anchored. I attempted to amplify some elements of the dream, but the amplification did not reveal any new information since Roger could not go back into the dream and re-experience it. He was only able to reiterate what he has already said, which was read from a written record of the dream. Any work done on Roger's dream would now have to be done by a facilitator. No doubt many facilitators could come up with an interesting interpretation of *The Golden Cape* dream since it contains such powerful imagery, but it would be an interpretation, not a reexperiencing or a connection. This kind of situation happens quite often in the life of a dreamworker. I sometimes find it frustrating when it happens in my work with clients, but I try to put myself in the mindset of a catch-and-release fisherman, to honor our brief encounter with the dream and then let it slip back into the deep water.

Recording the dream

Ideally, a dreamwork client will keep an ongoing journal with dreams dated and named. In advance of the session, the client will pick one or two dreams that they would like to work on, e-mail a copy to the practitioner and arrive ready to delve in. A good dream record should include the:

- setting

- events that occurred

- feeling tones

When you record your dreams, try to cultivate the habit of including all these facets. Frustratingly (for we dreamworkers), many people record the narrative details of their dream very precisely but do not record or remember what the feeling tones were in the dream. Prompt yourself: "What was I feeling when ... ?" After a while, you will develop the habit of using a vocabulary of feeling-based words in your dream recounting. This will make it much easier to connect a dream to your life if you later decide to do some work on it.

Naming the dream

One good way to help anchor a dream is to give it a name. The act of naming confers a sense of value and relationship—if something is important enough to have a name, it cannot be easily dismissed and is less likely to be forgotten. A dream with a name can be much more easily accessed, recalled, and referred to. Also—it is good practice for the dreamer to consider what the most striking feature of the dream is and choose a name accordingly.

Consider Teresa's dream: it features the dream ego and four other figures, and it takes place in a public washroom setting. What would be a good name for this dream? When you're thinking of a name, keep in mind that it isn't too long or cumbersome; it should be catchy, otherwise it won't be of much help in remembering the dream. And it should hook onto something important, ideally what seems to be the most salient aspect of the dream, and bring it right into the forefront.

I'm in a public washroom. It's very large and sterile, with a stainless steel toilet. There's a jagged hole in the wall, and I'm not sure if the door works. There's a bird on the floor flapping around. It seems very flustered and agitated. A small white dog comes in and sees the bird. I'm worried that the dog might attack the bird. The dog doesn't seem aggressive, he's just nosing around curiously. But if he went after the bird, what would the bird do? Would it start to use its wings and fly out the jagged hole? Then I see a pair of legs lying on the floor of the toilet stall. They seem waxy and lifeless, like mannequin legs. The feet are crossed. I see a spider in between the feet. The legs seem to become aware of the spider suddenly, and they start to move—agitated, twitching, and jumpy. As they move I begin to sense that they are my legs and I wake up with my legs twitching and jumping, and afraid that there is a spider crawling on me. It feels so real that I search for the spider in my bed.

There is a whole host of naming possibilities here. If we try to include all the figures and call it *The Bird, the Dog, the Mannequin Legs and the Spider in the Washroom,* then we are getting pretty long and cumbersome. What if we were to limit it to the most important figure? Would this be the bird? If so we might name it *The Flustered Bird,* or *The Bird in the Washroom,* or *The Bird That Won't Fly.* This would help put the spotlight on something that is clearly problematic—a bird should not be flapping around on the floor of a washroom. Since Teresa used the word "agitated" in relation to both the behavior of the bird and the movement of the legs, we might consider calling it *Agitated in the Washroom.* This would put the focus on a very striking (and repeated) feature of the dream, the agitated quality of movement. This may well be the key that will help make the connection to Teresa's life. In the end she decided to name it *The Fluttering, Squished Bird and the Legs that Kicked the Spider.*

Summary: Cultivate these six habits to improve your dream recall

1. *Set your intention before bed.* When you go to bed at night, tell yourself that you intend to remember your dream in the morning. Having a dream journal and a pencil ready to go beside your bed is a good idea.

2. *Revisit an old dream.* If you are in a dry spell and can't seem to remember any dreams at all, go back to an old dream and run through it in your mind. Pick one that is still alive and mysterious.

3. *Allow yourself time to drift up to the surface in the morning.* As many mornings as you can, allow yourself the luxury of drifting slowly awake. In this state, you can practice "going back in" to the dream and retrieving more details.

4. *Capture a cue.* On mornings where you remember a dream but you have to get up right away, or you want to go back to sleep, jot down just one little thing from the dream. This may help you retrieve the whole dream later in the day.

5. *Make sure you anchor the dream before it drifts away.* Find out what *you* need to do to anchor your dreams and start doing it as a regular morning practice.

6. *Give the dream a name.* Naming a dream will not only help you remember it better over time, it will encourage you to take your dreams seriously and think about the messages contained in them.

CHAPTER 11

Clarifying the Dream

Clarifying is about getting a clear and complete account of the dream. More specifically, you want to be clear about the setting, events, feelings, and associations for each key dream figure (I suggest keeping the SEFA acronym in the back of your mind to remind yourself to cover all these key bases). All you need for successful dream clarification is attentive listening, open questioning, and good note-taking. If you are facilitating another person have her start telling the dream. Ask her to re-enter the dreamscape and describe it in the present tense if possible to experience it rather than read it off the page. If the dreamer is not able to relay the dream in this way, that's fine, just let her read it. The dreamscape may become reanimated as she reads, and she may be able to get back into it.

As you are listening, allow part of yourself to enter the dreamscape with her, keeping another part outside of it so you can keep notes and be attentive. Your eyes and ears are open for anything familiar that you might recognize. If you are confused or unclear about some aspect of the dream narrative, it's fine to interrupt and ask for clarification. Allow your dreamer to run once through the whole dream more or less uninterrupted, then go back and fill in the missing pieces. Ask for the dreamer's associations with the important figures and elements in the dream (i.e., if the dream features a friend named John you will need to know who John is, what the nature of the relationship is, what the dreamer thinks and feels about John, and what outstanding qualities John has).

Once you have all four pieces in place, you are ready to move on to the next step and start asking some orienting or connecting questions. If you feel you need more time, try asking your dreamer to say more about a part of the dream that you intuitively feel may be important. If you are using the method on your own dream, try doing it in exactly the same way. Divide yourself into two people, dreamer and facilitator, and interview yourself. If you use the method on yourself, you will probably be surprised at the results you can achieve.

Phrases and questions to use for clarification

Here are some of the basic phrases and questions I use in the clarification phase. They are generally neutral and nonleading. They are not designed to do anything except get more information and clarity about a dream.

- Go back into the dream if you can and describe it as if you are in it again.

- Tell me the dream in the present tense if you can, as if it is happening now.

- Take me into the dream.

- What is the setting of the dream?

- Where does the dream take place?

- Can you describe the part where ... happened a bit more?

- What do you mean when you say ... ?

- What happens now?

- What is the feeling when ... ?

- What do you associate with ... ?

- What qualities does ... have?

- What are the first three things that come into your head when you think of ... ?

Here is an example of a dreamwork session in which a considerable amount of clarification work was needed to unfold a complex set of connections and feelings, gradually leading to an important resonant connection. At age 33, Mary was diagnosed with a brain tumor. She went through one round of radiation therapy and several months later had a follow-up MRI to see if the tumor had progressed. This dream, *The Dead Floating Baby*, came the night after her MRI. Note that Mary is not accustomed to recognizing and reporting her feelings (either in waking life or in dream recall). This means that a lot of the clarification work has to do with drawing out the feeling tones:

It was like I was a male, but I was myself, and I had a crush on a girl. I looked up to her. I wanted to get closer to her. She was nobody that I could recognize. She worked in her family business with her dad, and I knew I wanted to get closer to her. So I applied for a job there and became a supervisor. One night the back doors were left open at the business, and it was my responsibility; but nothing happened, nobody broke in or anything. The girl that I had a crush on, told me that "you left the doors unlocked." Then I think I told the girl that I was interested in her, or somehow she found out that I like her. And she asked me to leave. I just remember it raining, flooding, and I was leaving in a car full of people. A car full of my friends picked me up, and my husband was there. I saw a baby floating in the water; it was dead. My husband supported me in terms of picking it up, and I was just about to pick the baby up, and I woke up.

Dreamworker: What was the feeling when you were picking the baby up at the end?

Just weird ... I didn't want to ... I didn't want to pick the baby up.

DW: Why?

Well, I knew it was dead.

DW: What were you feeling?

Just sadness. I didn't know or understand why this baby was dead, or floating around. It was by the road and it sort of floated. I knew it was dead. It was white, and I couldn't see its face, it was face down ... so, just anxiety, fear, sadness, not sure what to do.

DW: You say you didn't want to pick up the baby up ... but you did?

I was almost there, like, I was leaning down.

DW: So what made you decide to pick up the baby?

My husband was there, being very supportive, and I knew that was the thing to do.

DW: So ... if he hadn't been there?

I think I eventually would have picked the baby up. I felt like something needed to be done, and I was the one that was faced with this baby. I felt it was up to me.

DW: Tell me about the girl.

Tall, slim, long thin hair, I think blonde, very natural ... a sort of physi-calness. I don't even remember much contact with her in the dream. I just remember wanting to get closer to her.

DW: So ... let's zero in more on the feeling of why you want to get close to her.

The thought that just came into my head is that I want to get closer to myself. [Here she makes a spontaneous connection] ... *because that's more or less what I've been working toward. Feeling like I'm in my own skin more.*

DW: Why doesn't she want to get together with you?

I don't know. Maybe she's not quite ready yet. I think maybe I feel like there's a lot of work that needs to be done before I get there. So this dream could be about opening that up and accepting it and I know that it's going to be a slow process and that I have work to do. [This seems true and resonant to both the dreamer and the facilitator.]

DW: What's her attitude toward you when she finds out that you like her?

There's no hostility. It was just "I'm not interested," so I left. I didn't want to rock the boat any further. I chose to just go.

DW: And when she tells you that she's not interested, what do you feel?

It's fine. I'm not hurt. I'm not anything. I just chose to go.

DW: There is no feeling?

No.

DW: There's no disappointment?

No.

DW: That's a striking thing about the dream isn't it? You have a crush on her and you arrange your whole life to be near her, and then when she says no, then you immediately give up, and there's no feeling around that. There's no emotion. That's odd isn't it? [Up until this point I have done only clarification; now I am trying to help her make a connection using the highlight and ask technique— highlighting a certain aspect of the dream then asking her if she can see any connection to that.]

I mean I guess there's a little bit of disappointment, maybe.

DW: But things get pretty intense right after you leave, right? There's a flood and a dead baby. So let's try to connect those two parts.

Okay.

DW: She says no. You accept that. You leave. Then we're into this other part of the dream ...

[Thinks for a while.] *Maybe that ... that's maybe my feelings. Maybe the flood ... maybe I really am upset.* [This feels very emotionally charged and resonant.] *I think that's the way I've dealt with most of my life, I've repressed feelings automatically.*

DW: What happens when you repress something like that?

Oh, it builds up and [laughs] *then I lose sense of myself.*

DW: So the dream seems to be saying something about the problem of being disconnected from experiencing the full intensity of your feelings. In the dream you suffer an emotional blow but you don't let yourself feel it fully. You give up easily, and the giving up leads to a very dire situation. So what's the dream asking you to do?

To keep trying to get close to that girl? To not give up so easily? Yes, that's exactly it. And that girl is me.

DW: Yes. There needs to be some persistence there even though she's resisting.

Yeah. That's exactly what it is. [The dream is now connected—she has a resonant feeling of how it connects to her life. Step 4 is accomplished.]

DW: So stick at it. Find a way to get close to her. [Now we can move to step 5—responding to the message of the dream.]

We proceeded to talk about some ways she might work on getting closer to these two important parts of herself—the infant and the young girl. I advised Mary that both should be worked on concurrently, because the reconnection with the young girl probably cannot happen until the reconnection with the abandoned infant has been achieved. As is often the case, the creative use of the imagination is the most helpful tool. By simply imagining all three selves together—Mary and the young girl taking turns holding the baby and bonding with it—a healing process will be initiated.

How did the orientation happen in this session? It came from recognition of a universal motif. This is a characteristic example of a personal spirit motif. It shows Mary two parts of herself that have been traumatized and lost, and asks her to make the effort to reunite with them. The girl and the baby are personifications of two key traumatic foci in Mary's life, one very early and one in young adulthood. This dream now presents her with an opportunity to start addressing these old traumas.

Tip: While you clarify, stay on the alert for orientation

For a dream of average length and complexity, five to ten minutes of clarification may be needed to fill in all the details of setting, events, feelings, and associations. But keep in mind that you cannot go on indefinitely—that is, not if you plan to aim for the goal of connecting the dream to the dreamer's life. You will need to shift gears before long and get oriented so you can move toward helping facilitate a connection. Memorize the seven key orientation strategies (along with any others that work for you) and keep part of your brain on alert for any familiar guidepost. The use of an orientation technique is the watershed that separates simply listening to a dream (which can of course be very valuable in itself) from actual dreamworking.

What if you cannot make any personal associations?

Some dreams contain motifs that are utterly mysterious. You may have a sense that the dream is carrying a very important message, but the language and symbolism of the dream seems foreign and unfamiliar. The normal process of clarification does not yield much because you can't make many associations. As Marie Louise Von Franz said: "In archetypal dreams the dreamer often has no personal associations. In these cases you have to tap into the collective level—what are mankind's associations with that motif?" [6] In these cases, the dreamworker might be able to contribute to the process suggesting possible archetypal or cultural associations to the dreamer that may fit the dream. As always, these suggested associations must pass the Double Resonance test.

Here's an example. Adam, a 26-year-old man, was having difficulty both choosing a career direction and also settling into one committed relationship. Although he wanted both of these things in theory, he found that there was always something that didn't seem right about his current career path and current partner. He brought a dream called *The Young Man and the Old Man* to one of our sessions:

> *I'm traveling alone in the countryside. Near the end of the day I see a house. Thinking I might be able to spend the night there, I go knock*

---

6   Marie Louise Von Franz, *The Way of the Dream* (video).

on the door. An old man answers and invites me in. He is very friendly but there is something sad and painfully lonely about him. He seems to live here by himself. He shows me around. He has hundreds of beautiful artifacts and art pieces that he has collected from all over the world. Clearly he has had a fascinating life and done many things. As bedtime approaches he says to me with some awkwardness that since there is only one bed in the house we will have to sleep in it together. I tell him I'm fine with that. We get into the bed. It feels strange, but not like anything weird or really bad is going to happen—just awkward. I try to relax, but he is restless. He tosses and turns and eventually gets up and leaves the room. Soon I fall asleep.

We set about to clarify the dream but didn't get very far because Adam wasn't able to make many associations. It seemed to him that it was a very important dream, but a very mysterious one, quite unlike his usual dreams. As his dreamworker, I was struck by the archetypal feeling of the dream so I suggested to Adam that we might look at the dream as a meeting of the Senex (old man) archetype and the Puer Aeternus (eternal boy) archetype. This was new territory for Adam so I suggested that he read something about these archetypes before our next session. I lent him my copy of Marie Louise Von Franz's fascinating book, *Puer Aeternus.*[7] If he really got it, this would confirm that we were dealing with an important archetypal development in his psyche that had produced this archetypal dream. If the book left him cold, it would be back to the drawing board.

Adam did get it. He found the book very helpful because it helped him identify many of the Puer characteristics in himself, most especially the difficulty in narrowing down youth's sense of infinite possibility into one committed path. As is typical of the Puer type, this young man was afraid of becoming old and lonely, and thus he tended to balk when faced with any significant step toward maturity, including commitment in ca-

---

7   Marie Louise Von Franz, *Puer Aeternus.* (Boston: Sigo Press, 1981).

reer path and relationship. He needed to reframe his negative feelings about age, maturity, and experience; and the dream used the archetypal Old Man to bring this point home. The dream seemed to be asking Adam to spend some time in close company of the old man, even if it was a bit awkward at first. All this was presented in an archetypal story, using the old motif of the traveler and the stranger's house as a metaphor for an important encounter on one's life journey.

Summary

You will often feel like an explorer in a strange new landscape when you re-enter your dream, or another person's dream. What if you venture in only to feel utterly lost? If that happens don't worry, its normal. Make sure you have a clear and complete account of the dream. Now it's time to get un-lost. Pull out your compass and start to orient yourself.

CHAPTER 12

Getting Oriented

Orientation comes in different ways and there is no fixed way to go about it. Sometimes it happens spontaneously, sometimes not. Sometimes we know instantly what the dream is saying, sometimes not. Sometimes a sense of orientation is elusive and the dream remains a mystery for years. If a sense of orientation is eluding you, don't panic! Use one of the following seven orientation techniques. Some dreams naturally lend themselves to one technique or another, so you should be familiar with all of them and use them flexibly and intuitively. If one doesn't work, drop it and try a different one.

What have you made of it so far?

If you are facilitating another person, your first formal act of orientation can be simply to ask the dreamer what he has already been thinking about the dream. He may have already considered the possible meaning of the dream, and in some cases may have fully understood how it connects to his life. I will typically ask one or more of these questions:

- What have you made of the dream so far?

- Do you have a sense of what the dream is saying?

- Have you made any connections yet?

- What does it mean to you?

- Why would your dreammaker need to send you this message now?

- What do you think the dream is asking for?

If this leads to a promising connection, move immediately to step five, responding to the dream message. Remember, the connection should be doubly resonant, resonating as true for both you and the dreamer (the Double Resonance test is discussed fully in chapter 5). Often though, dreamers will have no idea what the dream is trying to say, or their insights will feel partial or unsatisfying. In these cases, you must now help catalyze the process of understanding. In order to do this effectively and reasonably quickly, you must have some sense of orientation about what the dream is communicating. If your instincts are leading you somewhere, by all means follow them. If not, try one or more of the techniques listed above and discussed in detail below.

Orienting by asking: What does the dream want?

Over the past few years, I have found that as I listen to my client's dreams and go about getting my bearings, my starting point has gradually shifted from "what does this dream mean?" toward "what does this dream want?" The result is a style of dreamworking I would describe as more direct and focused on personal growth. It has also enabled me to do rewarding dreamwork within a shorter timeframe, something that has been of great benefit for me and for the people I work with.

Here's an example—Harvey had the classic dream of a frightening figure trying to break into his house. He couldn't say much about the figure, just that it was male, big, and seemed to have vaguely nasty intentions. Instead of starting with what the dream could mean, we jumped right to "What does the dream want?" Harvey said immediately: "Well, usually in these dreams I am too frightened to go to the door and confront the figure, but I think that my dream is telling me that I should go to the door."

We now know that the dream is referring to a potential meeting that Harvey's unconscious *wants* to take place. It is setting the stage for an encounter that could be critical for him. Using Jungian terminology, we might say the dream is setting the stage for Harvey to have an encounter with a part of his own shadow. As Marie-Louise von Franz said: "In our dreams we are often assaulted by parts of our own personality"; although I would say rather—the dream ego fears that it will be assaulted, although typically no such assault actually occurs in this type of dream. [8] By using this shortcut, we have also arrived at the meaning of Harvey's dream within a few minutes. Some new part of him is emerging and trying to get into his sense of who he is, but up until this point Harvey has not let it in because of fear.

Dreamwork in the helping and healing professions

The "what does the dream want?" perspective is particularly well-suited for those of us who work in the helping and healing professions, for two reasons: first, it is faster and more direct than most other methods and can be used within the limited time frames often available to us. Second, because dreams constantly ask us to make changes—in behavior, lifestyle, mental attitudes, priorities, even how we handle our habits and addictions. In every one of us there is a constant stream of feedback and advice

---

8   Marie Louise Von Franz, *The Way of the Dream* (video).

coming from the inner healer, much of which comes through the dream life. So if health care practitioners hold onto the question "What are this person's dreams asking for?" they are in a good position to help the client tune into this inner guidance.

For me, holding this question has led to another question, related and perhaps deeper: what does our unconscious want for us? I suppose we all have our own answers for this question but for me the answer must contain the following elements: self-awareness, growth, wholeness, and healing. In other words, I believe that there is something in us that *wants* us to be conscious and self-aware; it wants us to grow and evolve; it wants us to be whole and not split apart by trauma; and it wants us to heal in whatever ways we can. This is why I think it is so valuable for those of us who work with dreams to practice putting the focus on what the dream wants. If you need further convincing regarding the healing potential of listening to your dreams, take a look at Marc Ian Barasch's book *Healing Dreams*; it makes a good case for the notion that our dreams may be asking us for something. [9]

Orienting through recognizing a universal dream motif

Imagine that you are channel surfing on your TV—you would probably be able to recognize what type of show you were watching within seconds—that's a sportscast, that's a commercial, that's news, that's a soap, that's a sitcom, another commercial, and so on. If you could not recognize anything about the type of program you were watching, it would be strange and unsettling, even if it were utterly fascinating. Most of us are so familiar with the stereotypes and conventions of TV programming that this kind of recognition is second nature to us. What if you had the same ability with dreams? What if you could recognize within seconds the type

9   Marc Ian Barasch, *Healing Dreams: Exploring the Dreams That Can Transform Your Life* (New York: Riverhead Books, 2000), chapter 2.

of dream you just had, or the dream another person was telling you? This is motif recognition, and it makes dreamwork a whole lot easier!

Motif recognition is the subject of part 3 of this book and will be discussed there at length. So we will not go too far into it here other than to give an example of how it can work in practice. Reese, 29 years old, had this dream when she was a teenager and still remembers it vividly; she feels it is one of the important dreams of her life. Reese was raised in a family with strong Christian values and throughout her childhood was fearful that she might go to hell. She called the dream *The Moon and the Mist*:

> *I'm sitting at the kitchen table at my parents' house. It's dinner time. My whole family is there at the dinner table except my dad. His place is empty. Outside I can see a very large, round, orange-yellow, very vibrant moon. My mom is trying to calm us, saying: "It's okay, he'll be here soon" (I assume she is meaning Dad will be here soon). I'm fearful. It's eerie and creepy. There's a feeling of suspense, like something is about to happen. Then there's this mist that starts coming through the door. I feel like the mist wants to get me. I think—it can't get me! Then suddenly I'm downstairs in my bedroom, up on the top bunk. I look out into the hall, and it's lit. I know that the mist is going to come around the corner and into my room. I look around in the closet. I'm frantically looking for something to protect me from the mist. I find a Bible or a cross. I find it just in time, just as the mist is about to get me, and I hold it up as if to say: "Go away! You can't get me! I have protection!"*

As I listened to this dream, my primary orientation came from recognizing a familiar set of motifs—something threatening trying to come into the house and get the dreamer; she responds with fear, trying desperately but ineffectually to prevent it from getting in; and and she has a feeling that she would be harmed, but in fact no harm is done to her. This is one of the most commonly encountered motif clusters in dreamwork. It is characteristic of a shadow dream—it means that some potentially positive new development is coming into Reese's life but she is afraid of it and is avoiding the encounter (see chapter 16: Shadow Motifs).

As soon as we recognize the presence of a shadow dynamic, we have some very useful orientation. Not only do we have a sense of what is happening in Reese's psyche, we also have an idea of what the dream is asking her for. In this case, it is asking her to stop running away from the moon and the mist, and to stop blocking the emergence of new life energies by hiding behind old religious constructs. It is asking her to do the very opposite of this—to willingly enter into an encounter with the moon and the mist. When I asked Reese to imagine walking out of the house into the misty moonlight, she immediately began to feel a mysterious and powerful energy, still a bit eerie, but at the same time very appealing.

At the time she had this dream (in her late teens) Reese probably would not have been able to successfully meet and integrate these parts of herself. They were starting to emerge (otherwise she would not have had such a dream) but she was far too fearful to work with them. So the dream remained vividly alive in her memory for over a decade until the time came when she was ready to walk outside her parents' house and start exploring this new part of herself.

Tip: An old dream may still be relevant and can be revisited

What does it mean when we still think about an old dream years after having it? It may mean that the dream was asking for something that has still not happened. Such dreams will tend to remain alive in our memory, or will repeat themselves in different versions, until the right circumstances are in place for us to address the problem. This is particularly true of shadow dreams—our dreams of threatening pursuers or intruders will happen again and again, often with increasing urgency, until we finally summon the courage to go to the door and open it.

Orienting through inner and outer

I have often heard it said that everything that appears in a dream is an aspect of the dreamer. If this were true, it would mean that we could not dream about anything or anyone in the outer world that is affecting us, which is clearly not the case. It is true that many of the figures and motifs that appear in our dreams are subjective, they are pointing toward something within us—but not all. It is very important that we are able to discern the difference. To take a very simple and common example—if a mother of a young child dreams of a sick crying baby, is the dream telling her something about her actual (outer) baby, or is it telling her something about the status of her inner child? It could be either or both, and the dreamworker must always be attuned to these dual possibilities. Thus, one of the most common and important orienting questions you can ask is the Inner/Outer question: "Does that figure in my dream represent a part of me? Or does it represent something or someone external that is affecting me?"

Tip: Ask the inner/outer question for each key dream figure

When working with a dream, the Inner/Outer orientation is something you will typically need earlier rather than later. Choose the most prominent figure or entity in the dream and ask the Inner/Outer question right away in relation to that figure. This will immediately give you some degree of orientation after which you can proceed into the dreamscape knowing that you have at least your basic bearings.

Here is an example of a dream where the most important orienting question is the Inner/Outer question. Is the man in Judy's *The Man With Two Guns* dream an inner figure or an outer figure? The dreamwork will go in very different directions depending on the orientation we choose right at the outset:

> *I was told there was a little guy hiding somewhere that I should watch out for. I suspected he was hiding in a closet full of stuff. I gave the clothes a*

good biff with my hand to get a sense of whether he was in there, noth-
ing happened. Then there he was—about my height with a slim body,
casually dressed in a white T-shirt and black pants. He had two guns, one
a bit bigger than the other. He was about three feet away from me. I took
the guns away from him (he wasn't very dexterous or very strong) and shot
him in the foot, I think his left foot. He was wearing a white shoe that
had no seams in it, no laces. I saw a drop of red blood appear where I had
shot him. We both looked at it. I felt that perhaps I did not need to shoot
him, I had already disarmed him so why did I have to shoot him?

Let's try the inner orientation first—taking the man with the two guns as an aspect of Judy, we might expect him to be a shadow figure (i.e., a not-yet-integrated aspect of Judy that is emerging and demanding integration). He has a characteristic commonly seen with shadow figures—they appear to be threatening at first, but as the dream ego musters the courage to encounter them and find out about them, they become less and less threatening. Psychologically, a shadow figure would represent the emergence of a dormant or repressed quality in the dreamer; he would be bringing important new potentials with him—in this case something to do with confrontation perhaps, since this figure confronts her with two guns. Does Judy need to be more confrontational and assertive in two particular ways, one more important than the other (since there are two guns, one bigger than the other)?

I asked Judy to be the man with the two guns. If she could easily identify with him and start to be aware of his potential positive qualities, it would suggest that we are dealing with a shadow dynamic. However, in this case she did not feel much identification with the figure; there was no real charge as she imagined herself in his role. When you hit a dead end like this in dream facilitation, it is usually a good idea to change your approach and try another way of looking at things.

So let's switch and try outer—if we take the man as an outer figure he would be a personification of someone or something external. We can help Judy make a connection by reiterating the pattern that occurs in the dream: "You find yourself threatened by someone, but you easily disarm him and turn the tables on him. You feel he could harm you so you harm him first. Then you look at what you have done and feel badly that you may have overreacted. Does this pattern exist anywhere in your life?" Or, in a similar way, we can facilitate a connection by focusing on the feeling tones: "You feel as if someone is attacking you so you must quickly attack back, but later feel like you have unnecessarily wounded him. Do you ever have this combination of feelings in your life?"

Now, with the help of this setup, Judy was able to recognize this pattern and these feeling tones and connect them to her life—she realized that in certain social situations she often feels that someone is being disrespectful or rude to her. She reacts automatically and unthinkingly with a scathing remark designed to hurt them, because she feels they could hurt her. Later, she usually feels that she overreacted and has probably done some damage to the person and the relationship, and she regrets her behavior. When Judy and I looked at the dream in this way—taking the man with the guns as an external figure (a personification of perceived threat that Judy overreacts to) rather than as an inner aspect of Judy herself—it had much more energy in it. It passed the Double Resonance test, whereby both the dreamer and the facilitator have a resonant feeling of trueness about the connection.

Now we recognized that we were dealing with an ego check motif, not a shadow motif. The dream is giving Judy feedback about how she is behaving. It is telling her that she is being oversensitive, too quick to react, unnecessarily defensive and hurtful, and that this is doing damage to her relationships. As is so often the case with ego check dreams, this dream uses exaggeration to get its point across—it depicts the situation of feeling disrespected as a scenario of having someone point two guns at you. It depicts the act of making an aggressively defensive remark as disarming and shooting someone. The dream scenario may be unrealistic and exaggerated but the feeling is the same feeling she has in her waking life when these kinds of interactions occur.

Here's another dream that illustrates how important it is to be able to discern between inner and outer. The dreamer is Erica, a 10-year-old girl with moderate learning challenges who is experiencing difficulties with her schoolwork. She had a frightening dream of her father that she called *My Dad Breaking Himself.*

> *One day I went to camp with my best friend. When camp was over she came to my house for dinner. When we opened the door to my house … my dad was smashing vases, and breaking bowls! Most of all, he was breaking HIMSELF! He had bruises on his legs, he was losing his teeth, and scars were on his forehead! I was so upset I started to cry and wonder what he was doing. After a few minutes passed, I couldn't take it anymore and I screamed, "Stop!" When my dad stopped, he was standing on the table with a baseball bat in his hand trying to break the TV, which was also on the table. He stared at me. I was too scared to talk; I thought that he might hurt me, but I spoke up. I said, "Dad, what are you doing?" He said, "I got so frustrated with my work that I started hurting myself to think of the right answer." Then I bandaged him up and we hugged. Then I woke up.*

If we took this dream to be pointing outward we would be very concerned that Erica is afraid of some potential violence or self-damaging behavior in her father (or some other external figure in her life such as a teacher, who is like her father). The outer orientation should always be considered, but if it doesn't fit as seems to be the case here, we should switch to inner.

If we look at the father figure as an inner aspect of Erica, this dream suggests that she has a tendency to get very frustrated with herself when she can't get the right answer, so much so at times that she starts to feel self-damaging urges. This was the perspective that made sense to Erica. Fortunately the dream is pointing out to Erica that she has the ability to stop this self-damaging part of herself once it becomes activated, and she can even treat it with love and compassion by bandaging it and giving it a hug.

Working on this dream was helpful for Erica in two ways. First, we connected the pattern seen in her dream to her waking life so that she could recognize it in the future. I said to her, "The dream seems to be describing the times in your life when you're having difficulty with school work and you can't get the right answer and you start to feel really frustrated with yourself. When you feel really frustrated and angry with yourself, you can't think really clearly and the whole thing probably gets even worse, right?"

Secondly, we highlighted and reinforced the positive and self-loving development that is depicted at the end of the dream: "So you can do just what you do in the dream—tell yourself to stop. Then try being nice to yourself, just like you are in the dream when you give your dad a hug, but it's like you give yourself a hug. Once you do that, your brain will probably work better and you'll feel better too."

Both these pieces of work are predicated on the assumption that we are dealing with Erica's *inner* Dad. The work would have gone in a completely different direction if we felt we were dealing with an outer Dad. We need not be too afraid of making a mistake by choosing the wrong orientation and arriving at a harmful misinterpretation of the dream. If we choose one path and follow it for a while only to find that it is not really leading anywhere, we can regroup and choose the other path. The acid test is the test of resonance (the Double Resonance test). This is your protection against forcing an inaccurate interpretation on your client—if it doesn't feel resonant to both of you it isn't right, so just try again.

Tip: Some people resist the inner, some resist the outer

The ability to recognize a dream figure as a part of oneself is a learned skill. It does not come naturally, and some people are very resistant to it. If an inner-resistant person dreams of a bully, he will not spontaneously consider the possibility that he may have a bullying part in his own nature; he may strongly resist this perspective even when his dreamworker asks him to consider it. If you encounter strong resistance and defensiveness when you suggest an inner orientation to your client, it does not mean you are on the wrong track. Quite the contrary, strong resistance is a kind of resonance, confirming that you are on to something. At the other end of the spectrum, some people too readily take the inner orientation on their dream figures and have difficulty imagining that they may be pointing outward. Be prepared to encounter both these variants.

Internalized figures—where inner meets outer

Often inner and outer merge and it is hard to make a clear distinction between them. This is in large part due to the phenomenon of psychological internalization—any important figure from a person's external world can become internalized. Our internal father image, for example, will almost always be strongly shaped and influenced by our actual father. Once this internalization has occurred, our father dreams can have several possible layers of meaning. If he appears in our dream, is he appearing as himself, as part of an internalized father complex, or both? This often blurs the Inner/Outer distinction in working with a dream.

Internalized figures, particularly if they have a negative aspect, can remain alive in the psyche indefinitely and become focal points for stuckness. They are often quite static, as if frozen in time, perpetuating a problem long after the original figure has changed or even died in the outer world. Psychodynamically, if an internalized figure has become a focal point for a complex of negative feelings, it should be handled as an introject—a construct forced into the psyche from the outside, never fully accepted and integrated as a true part of self, but yet occupying a deep-seated place in the individual's sense of self (see chapter 22: Introject Motifs).

As an example here is Allison's dream. Allison, 32 years old, grew up with an extremely critical and undermining father. After years of absorbing his criticism as a child, she developed an internalized version of him, an inner critic that she then carried forward into her adult life (what in Jungian psychology might be called a negative animus figure, or a negative inner masculine). This part of her operated in much the same way as her father did when she was a child, constantly undermining her confidence and her self-esteem. This in turn created a tendency in her to find herself attracted to critical and undermining men and repeatedly "allow" them to hurt her in a the same way that her father did and that her inner critic does. Allison tends to accept criticisms from her boyfriends as true because they fit with her inner reality, even though a part of her knows they are completely untrue and that she should not tolerate them.

Here's the question: if Allison has a dream of her boyfriend hurting her in an exaggerated way, what is the dream telling her? Is it telling her that her actual external boyfriend is very harmful to her and she must stop tolerating his behavior (an outer way of looking at it)? Or is it telling her that her internalized critical male figure is very harmful to her and she must do something about that (an inner way)? In such situations, it is usually both, and this is where inner and outer are inseparable. To phrase it another way: she will not be able to substantially change the outer situation until she changes the inner situation and vice versa. She must work on them concurrently. Here is Allison's dream of the *Sliding Snake Wound*:

I was with my sister M and a Snake Lady—a woman who knew all about dangerous snakes. The Snake Lady had all these things made from the different snakeskins, rattles, clubs, paint brushes. She was describing the different types of snakes, showing them to us. My sister was sitting on the couch and there was one snake that was crawling all around her. She asked me for help with it—she showed me all of her wounds, along her left torso, from the snake. They weren't healing. And the freshest one was on the upper side of her chest, right by her heart. She said the snake would get into her there, then slide back out and back in. I knew that's why her wounds wouldn't heal. So I asked the Snake Lady if she could help us get rid of it.

The first thing to get clear about is whether Allison's sister M was appearing in the dream as herself, playing a part of the dreamer, or both. Allison was clear that M was primarily playing the role of a part of herself.

Next we need to get clear on what the snake is representing—the snake that wounds and re-wounds repeatedly near the heart. Snakes and snakebites in dreams *can* refer to positive developments, but this one did not feel positive in any way to Allison; she was clear that it represented something harmful and thoroughly negative. She connected the persisting wounds to her current boyfriend, past boyfriends, and her father:

The way my boyfriend treats me at times triggers two parts in me—the one part that feels awful and wounded and sad because maybe I deserve it; and the other part that feels furious and angry because I know I don't deserve it and yet I am still wounded. It's the same way I've reacted to other boyfriends too (my high school one especially), and the way I react to my father now.

Thus the dream snake clearly had an outer aspect, representing current hurtful behaviors inflicted on her by her boyfriend and her father. But then we switched our orientation and considered the snake as an inner figure. This also made sense to the dreamer; there must be something inside her that is helping to perpetuate this pattern. The dream helped Allison understand that the healing of her self-esteem cannot proceed very far until she deals with the inner snake, since it makes her open and vulnerable to the hurtful behavior of key outer figures. She must tackle this problem on both fronts, working both the inner and the outer.

This way of understanding the issue certainly does not mean that Allison is somehow *creating* her boyfriend's (or her father's) critical behavior.

Nor does it mean that she is responsible for them or their actions. But it is giving her important information about why she tolerates their hurtfulness and allows it to continue. Her inner critical part organizes a field effect that allows critical and undermining behavior from key male figures; it does this in part by generating the feeling that she may somehow "deserve" it. Long ago, Allison's outer world organized her inner world, and now her inner world is in turn organizing the outer world.

But what can Allison do about this inner snake? Can we rid ourselves of these deep-seated negative introjects that have been in us for as long as we can remember? Can we kill them? Banish them? Weaken them? Learn to live with them? What are the options? Fortunately, there is a very positive element presented in Allison's dream—the Snake Lady. This figure appears to have a great deal of knowledge about snakes and their behavior. This would mean that the dreamer now has an opportunity to learn from this lady (who probably has both an inner and outer aspect) about how this whole snake situation works in her psyche and what can be done about it.

It is not easy to rid oneself of an introject. Although it is foreign in some sense, never having been fully accepted and integrated as a true part of self, still it may have been sitting in such a deep place for so long that it has been significantly incorporated into the architecture of the psyche. But when a dream like this appears, it is clearly asking for some kind of action to be taken against the harmful power of the snake-introject. Something must be done, or the snake will simply continue to re-inflict the same wounds and indefinitely delay the possibility of healing. In this case, the presence of a knowledgeable teacher figure in the dream suggests that the most important thing right now is for Allison to learn about the psychodynamics of how the snake-introject operates.

Orienting through Be the Part

This technique is one of our most valuable tools in dreamwork. When it works, it is very fast and very direct, allowing you to have a new and immediate experience of identification with a key element or figure in your dream. Someone or something that seemed completely external in the dream may now be experienced as a part of self. Often an immediate connection can be made to the message of the dream. The effect of the Be the Part technique is particularly striking with figures that have been cast in negative, nasty, frightening, and unsavory roles. When you suspect the presence of an ego check motif or a shadow motif, this technique is usually the most direct and fruitful way to proceed. If you or the dreamer you're helping are able to get into it (have an embodied and emotionally charged experience of being that figure), a stream of insights and identifications will typically start to flow.

Invite yourself, or the dreamer if you are facilitating another person, to play the role of another figure that appears in the dream by asking:

- "Can we look at this figure as a part of you?"

- "What part of you would the _____ be?"

- "Can you identify with that figure?"

- "Can you re-tell the dream from the perspective of the ___?"

- "Can you play the part of_____?"

- "Let yourself be the _____."

- "Be the _____."

If the dreamer has difficulty, it can be helpful to reiterate the qualities of the dream figure, and ask the dreamer if she sees any of those qualities in herself. Ask:

- "So, the man in the dream is loud, bossy, self-centered, and wants to be the center of attention … is there a part of you which is like that?"

Tip: You can be any aspect of your dream

When using the Be the Part technique, anything and everything in the dream is fair game. It does not need to be a person, or even a figure; you can choose *any* element in the dream to try on—a coldness, a darkness, a sense of being lost, a feeling, a frustration, a place, a mood, a removal from the action, a gap in the story—literally *anything*. Use your intuition about which element or figure to pick, and if the first one you pick doesn't lead anywhere, pick another one. If this way of approaching a dream interests you, I suggest finding out more about the Gestalt approach to dreamwork. As Gestalt therapist Kenneth Meyer says: "Gestalt dreamwork—enacting, miming, dancing, or singing in our dreams—enables the metaphors they present to become more alive and present for us. We show, rather than talk about, facets of ourselves." [10]

A 50-year-old man named Clayton came to see me primarily to address his social anxiety. He told this dream, which he called *The Baby With No Skin*:

> My wife D and I are sitting in front of an old-fashioned school desk. The desk has an area carved out of it, and inside this area is a baby. Somehow I feel that the baby is Somali. The baby has no skin. You could see all its organs, but it was alive. D was saying something about the baby, she was more engaged with it than I was, but not touching it or picking it up. I felt shocked. I didn't know what to do ...

Clayton started making associations with the skinless baby—a sense of trauma that he connected to his father leaving the family when he was a boy, his sense of being an orphan, a memory of being in great pain following a car accident, a memory of having psoriasis as a baby, and family

---

10   Kenneth Meyer, "Gestalt Dreamwork," in *Working With Dreams and PTSD Nightmares: 14 Approaches for Psychotherapists and Couselors*, eds. Jacquie Lewis and Stanley Krippner (Santa Barbara, CA: Praeger, 2016), 66.

lore that he may have received too much attention from his older sisters as a baby. But although these associations were all true in some sense, they were not resonant; they did not unlock the real potential of the dream. It was not until I asked Clayton to *be the baby* that a deep and resonant connection was made:

Dreamworker: Can you be the baby?

Clayton: *Okay.* (Closing his eyes)

DW: (After a 5- to 10-second pause) How do you feel?

Clayton: *Cold… vulnerable… supersensitive… so exposed…*

DW: And where do you feel these feelings in your life?

Clayton: *Everywhere. With people. In all kinds of situations.*
    I'm so sensitive that I have to dissociate. Like being in shock.

This was a very emotionally charged and resonant insight that connected to Clayton's chief concern of social anxiety—he felt so exposed and vulnerable around people that he could not relax and enjoy their company. Clayton's dreamwork session shows how being a dream figure can bring orientation simply and directly. It is also a good example of the technique of setting up a connection through feeling tones, a technique we will explore more fully in chapter 13. While Clayton was having the embodied experience of being the skinless baby, it was very easy to help him connect this experience to his waking life. It is also a good example of a personal spirit dream motif—a dream that depicts a traumatized part of the self that needs healing through reconnection (chapter 19). In this case, the dream tells us that the healing process will be gradual and difficult; it will be hard to bond with this baby because he has no skin, which suggests he cannot yet be picked up and held. An encouraging sign is the presence of his wife, who is more engaged with the baby than Clayton is. This suggests his wife could be very helpful in the reconnecting process that needs to happen.

A possible response here would be to have Clayton use his creative imagination to visualize the baby growing a layer of skin, and then another layer, and another. Eventually the inner baby will be ready to be picked up and held, and Clayton can now visualize this possibility. This is not a one-off visualization—it will require Clayton to commit to a series of imaginal exercises assigned as homework, leading incrementally toward a desired outcome.

Here's another example: 49-year-old Bonnie had a dream of seeing herself as a large turtle flipped over and lying on its back: "All my internal organs are exposed. And I can't flip myself back to the upright position. I can't move. I feel totally helpless and exposed. That's all it is, just that image." I asked her to be the turtle. As she did so, it became clear to her that the overturned turtle was a perfect representation of her feelings of vulnerability and fear. These feelings had been part of her for so long that they were taken for granted and assumed to be normal; they were her default emotional setting. Bonnie and I thought about a good response to the dream of *The Overturned Turtle:* she would draw a picture of the turtle and place it on her altar space. She drew this picture and revisited it every day for a week. Through this experience, she realized that she did not need to live with this default setting indefinitely. She began to feel that it could change.

What if you are not able to identify with the part?

If, after trying the techniques described above, you still find it hard to identify with the dream figure, it could mean one or more of the following:

- There is a deeper problem that needs to be understood; a specific block or resistance that prevents you from identifying with the figure.

- The figure is *not* depicting a part of you. Consider the possibility that it may be a depiction of an *external* person or situation that is affecting you or it may be a depiction of an *introject* (foreign psychological content that was forced into you*)*.

- The figure is indeed an aspect of you but it is just too big a stretch to identify with a figure so far removed from your current understanding of who you are. In this case, be persistent; keep trying the role-playing method. Accentuate the positive qualities of the figure to make it more palatable.

How do we know which part to be?

You must follow your intuition here, but a good rule is to select the part/figure/element of the dream that you *least* identify with for the Be the Part technique. This will help you shift into a perspective that you do not usually take and it will almost always yield more dynamic results.

Orienting through good thing/bad thing

It is often surprisingly difficult to discern whether the major happening that occurs in a dream is referring to something good or something bad. Usually it can be looked at both ways and considering each perspective in turn leads the way into an understanding of the dream. Again, the answer to this question is something that must pass the Double Resonance test; it must feel right to both the dreamer and the facilitator.

Consider Rachel's dream of *The Unwanted Pregnancy.* When she had this dream, Rachel was 52 and having a very difficult time finding a satisfying relationship (Warning: graphic content):

> *I was five months pregnant, by rape or by someone I didn't want to be with. It was an unwanted pregnancy. I was told that I should have an abortion. The dream was a pursuit of this abortion. I asked if my colleague C could perform the abortion. I was told he could not because he was an intern. A woman who was either a doctor or a nurse was going to do it. I had already cut myself open in the belly to try to do it myself, but*

to no avail. I told the woman that I had done this, and that I might have
left the incision open too long and wouldn't be able to sew it up again.
I was taken to a cabin for the abortion. I opened the door. There was a
room with an operating table and three nurses waiting to do the proce-
dure. It had a warm feeling to it… I woke up.

The intensely ambiguous situation of the pregnancy presented at the beginning of the dream seemed to call for the Good Thing/Bad Thing orientation, so I asked Rachel, "Do you think the pregnancy is referring to a good thing or a bad thing?" We first considered the possibility that the pregnancy was good—this led her to make a connection to her long-standing pattern of initiating a relationship, then suddenly getting cold feet about it and wanting to terminate. Looked at in this way, the dream might be asking Rachel to challenge this old pattern, ignore the cold feet, and stay engaged in one of these relationships longer than she typically would, thus giving it a chance to evolve and grow.

Then we switched it around and considered that the pregnancy might be referring to a bad thing. This led us in an entirely different direction— the fact that she had been impregnated by rape suggested that the dream might be pointing at an introject, the forceful intrusion of something foreign and unwanted from the outside. In this scenario, the dream could be asking Rachel to act immediately and decisively, aborting the pregnancy before the foreign intrusion grew too large to be expelled.

In most cases, one way of looking at it will be clearly more resonant and true than the other, unambiguously pointing out the direction for working further with the dream and responding to its message. In this case, however, both ways of looking at the dream seemed true and reso-nant to Rachel. We had to make a decision at this point—should we com-mit to one path or the other, or would it be best to keep both open until something new emerges? The fact that both paths seemed right to Rachel in spite of their oppositeness may mean that there is something deeper that unites the two somehow, and that this underlying truth has not been perceived yet. In these cases, it might be best to ask the dreamer to work on both paths concurrently. We cannot move to the level of responding to the dream yet since we are not yet sure what we should be responding to. So our response would have to be a pre-connection response helping create the conditions for further clarity and understanding, perhaps asking for another dream that would carry the story forward.

Let's consider another example—Clara was a 55-year-old woman who was raised in an evangelical Christian faith. Clara had a recurring dream, varying slightly in details but always similar in its emotional impact; she told me her most recent version of the dream, which she called *The Family Rapture*:

(This is a dream that has recurred throughout my adult life and caused me great anguish each time I experienced it. The dream always begins in the same way; the same people figure in the dream each time, and the ending is always the same.)

I am alone inside a house looking through a window. The window across from me is dark and I know the house is empty. There is an incredibly anxious feeling because I know that a nuclear war has taken place. An atomic bomb has been detonated and the aftermath is spreading across the world. The sky is a deep gray. Only a few people are around, trying to survive. I leave the house and hurry along the streets, trying to find a safer place where I can survive. Then the scene switches to another room where there is an elevator . . . my mother is waiting there for me. It seems that part of the world is coming to an end and it is also the Christian second coming of Christ or what is known as the Rapture. My other family members have gone ahead and she is waiting for me to join them. But I am not to go through. My mother is weeping and doesn't understand why I haven't been chosen to ascend. I assure her that God must have a purpose for leaving me behind. She steps inside and the door closes. The last image I have is of her weeping copiously and feeling her anguish wash over me. I usually wake at this point feeling overwhelmed with fear and with a desire to pray that my eternal soul be saved.

The dream poses a very clear question—should she get into the elevator or not? Throughout the long period of her life that she has been troubled by this dream, Clara has not been sure of the answer. The feelings of anguish and fear as the doors close suggest that she should try to get in and join her family. On the other hand, she has long had a deep knowing that the rapture is not for her—"I have a very strong belief in the higher power of God, but I live it and express it differently from my family. When I reached young adulthood I knew I could not follow the rigid, judgmental, and fear-based teachings that others in the church subscribed to. In my forties, I found a way to express my faith through joy and peace." The fact that the dream continues to happen also points to a lack of resolution. Clara doesn't fully know what the right choice is, and the dream is urgently asking her to resolve this terrible uncertainty. Obviously we cannot formulate a response to this dream until we know the answer to the central question.

In a dream like this that poses a critically important question and leaves it unanswered, the best orientation will often come from considering good thing versus bad thing. As we started to work with the dream, I asked Clara, "Do you think it is a good thing or a bad thing that you stayed behind on earth?" When the question was put to her in this way, she was clear about the answer: "I am meant to stay behind. My work is on earth. I work with people who have a desire to find their way back to the core of their soul. I need to help in the healing of the earth."

This was resonantly true for both of us. Now we know with certainty that she should *not* try to get onto the elevator, even though it means experiencing the grief of separation from her family; and it also means that she is left behind to follow a difficult path in a gray and troubled world. Now we can consider a response. The response would need to be something that strengthens Clara's resolve to say goodbye to her family and embrace her life on earth, something that will support her through the difficult transition that is trying to happen. She has long known in her head that she needs to make this transition, but it has not happened in her feeling body, so the dream keeps repeating and she is tormented by doubt and fear that she may be making the wrong choice.

As a response, I asked Clara to imagine simply saying goodbye and walking away from the elevator with an embodied knowing that she is doing the right thing. After doing this as a repeated imaginal exercise for a period of time she began to feel a shift: "I no longer have the dream and am very much at peace with the meaning of the metaphors. I can see the message now and it has brought resolution."

Tip: You do not need to know the answer to get the orientation

Pick out the central event that is happening, has happened, or is about to happen in the dream. You probably don't know yet whether this would be a good thing or a bad thing. Don't let the fact that you don't know the answer be a negative or confusing thing—take it as an opportunity to get oriented. The dreamer will usually find her way to an answer sooner or later. Your job is just to set up the question clearly and openly.

When you frame the Good Thing/Bad Thing question, keep your tone neutral and unbiased; ask it in a way that sounds completely open, even naïve, as if you really have no idea what the answer is. The dream ego will usually be strongly siding with one answer or the other, but you should not. I have tried many ways of framing this question, and I have found that the best is the simplest: "Do you think it's a good thing or a bad thing that...?" When switching from one perspective to the other I usually say: "Okay, good. Now let's try looking at it the other way."

Orienting through dynamic/stuck

Another reliable way to find orientation within a dreamscape is to ask yourself: what is dynamic and what is stuck? What is moving and what isn't? What is the evolution that is trying to happen and what is the problem that's holding it back? The human psyche is not static; it is always trying to change. But, like a shackled elephant, its desire to move toward change is often held back by insurmountably strong forces. When the human psyche is held back from changing in the way it wants to change, it is not happy. It protests, and the first line of protest often occurs at night, in our dream life. Our dreaming brain is very concerned with letting us know what changes are trying to unfold and also what impediments are getting in the way.

Many (I would go so far as to say most) dreams contain both dynamic elements and stuck elements. They tell a story in which something is starting to happen but then it seems that it cannot happen for some reason. These dreams show us that dynamic efforts of the psyche are engaged and working but have run into some kind of roadblock. They are pushing against it, trying to unfold something. Ideally, you should be able to recognize and then separate these two strands. Generally speaking, dynamic parts of a dream do not need any major intervention applied to them. They are already happening; they only need to be recognized, supported, and encouraged. Stuck parts, however, do call out for intervention. They will tend to remain stuck until something specific is done.

Here's an example of a dream that highlights both dynamic and stuck elements very clearly. Angela is a 38-year-old woman who has sustained significant neurological damage resulting from a brain tumor in the motor cortex and its subsequent surgical treatment. Angela called this dream *The Roller-Coaster Ride:*

> *I help design a roller-coaster and go on it. We shoot up really fast and then... the track ends! That's the way the ride is designed. The plan is that we were going to land in a big box filled with trees and other things for a soft landing but when we are off the track and in the air I keep asking: "How are we going to land in the box? How is this whole thing controlled? How is the landing supposed to happen?" I wake up before we landed.*

As we worked with this dream, neither of us were sure exactly what the roller coaster referred to but one thing was clear—Angela did not like the feeling of being suddenly launched midair with no landing in sight (or in mind). This was very dynamic, maybe even a bit too dynamic! And now that she was airborne, she suddenly found herself face to face with the stuckness—she had no sense of how the landing was supposed to happen! Because her dreaming brain could not generate any solution at this stuck point, she could only wake up.

We agreed that we needed to generate some new possibility and bring it into the scenario. So I suggested to Angela that we re-enter and explore some good landing options. She went back into the dream, re-experienced the feeling of the track suddenly ending and being vaulted up into midair. Now instead of panicking and waking up, she caught herself and created some new imaginal track under her. The track was coming down toward the ground...down...down...and into a safe and successful landing! Angela agreed to practice this sequence several more times as her home-work. At the end of this session, Angela and I both felt we had done some good and important work. But we still didn't know what the roller coaster referred to in her waking life. All we knew was that she wanted to have a landing plan. A few days later I received the following email from Angela:

> *I figured out my roller-coaster dream! When I went for my nap today, I was thinking about the feeling of coming to the end of the track and being confused and not understanding what happens at the end of the track. That is the exact feeling I get in my brain when I try to run. I take a few strides and then my brain just shuts down. It's so hard to describe but my brain just can't tell my leg what it's supposed to do next. I think because I need to make new neural pathways since I had the surgery, it's like they are not connected and I don't understand how to run. I started visual- izing extending the track, no drop, just straight and long. I have been able to jog on the spot for about 25 seconds, so today I started jogging on the spot, but then I told myself to GO—and I did! I moved very slowly*

but I was definitely going in the right direction! I feel like I have laid a piece of the roller-coaster track down and hopefully it will get longer and longer! I'm so happy!

In this case, it appears that Angela's dream set the stage for a visualization and the visualization in turn set the stage for a very focused and critically important neuroplastic event in her motor cortex. She is now literally laying down the neural circuitry for being able to run, circuitry she had lost after the surgical treatment of her tumor five years before.

Interestingly, around this same time period Angela had two other dreams in which she was able to run. Was her dreaming brain trying to remind her what it is like to run? Was it showing her that the body's memory of running still existed within her, only needing some connecting circuits to be laid down in critical motor areas of the brain? Was this also part of an inspirational nighttime pep talk to underscore the value of the effortful work that would be required for her to fully reclaim her running?

I am amazed (as I so often am in this practice) by the precision and creative power of the motif that her dreammaker crafted. It posed the question: what do you do when you are going along a track and the track suddenly runs out, but you want it to continue in a good direction toward a desired end point? The answer for Angela at least was: you have to lay down some new track that takes you where you want to go. This is neuroplasticity at work!

There's another valuable lesson in this story, a reminder that we do not need to know what the central image of the dream refers to in order to start working with it on an imaginal level. Angela and I did not know at first that this image of the roller coaster ending in midair referred to her interrupted neural network for running. All we knew was that the dream was asking her to extend the action toward a landing, and this is what she visualized.

The last thing I would like to say about this remarkable dream is that it highlights the conjunction of two great imaginal realms, the visual and the kinesthetic (the realm of awareness of the body, its positions, and movements). Angela began by visualizing extending the track. This work appears to have directly connected to the kinesthetic realm, whereby she was able to imagine moving her legs as if she was running. This in turn helped her actually start to manifest these same running motions in her physical body. All this is contained within the genius of the original dream motif: a roller coaster leaving her in midair. This motif is both visual and kinesthetic; I suspect some of us would feel it more powerfully in our mind's body than we would see it in our mind's eye, and vice-versa for others. In either case, the dream asked for some important work to be done in the area where these two realms meet and interface.

Here's an example of a dream where the stuck element is present at the beginning but it gives way to something very dynamic near the end. Carlo, a 40-year-old man, brought in a dream called *The Chameleon Concierge and the Wonderful Room of Gifts*:

I'm walking around a hotel trying to find my room. I have a card key in my hand, but I can't find it. Unsuccessful in my search, I go back down to the lobby. A concierge sees me in distress and approaches me. "Need any help, sir?" I reply, "Yes, thank you. I can't seem to find my room." I give him the room key. He says, "One moment" and walks away. He gives the impression that he knows everything that goes on in the hotel; he's part elf, part chameleon, part concierge. A few minutes later, he reappears and escorts me to the elevator saying, "Follow me." When we get off the elevator, I see a colorful, fancifully decorated upholstered door, partly ajar. I walk in. Inside the room there are two islands of gifts, stacked tall on top of each other. The concierge says, "Sorry for the inconvenience . . . these are for you." I feel privileged to be in this vast and luxurious suite, wall-to-wall windows, high ceilings, and gorgeous furniture. I nod to the concierge in acknowledgment and accept the gifts.

Carlo and I both noted that the stuckness (the unsuccessful search for his room) occurs at the beginning, whereas the ending is very dynamic and wonderfully positive. This is the reverse of the more common dynamic-then-stuck pattern. This often means that the dreamer has recently made some progress in relation to a long-standing stuckness and that the dreammaker is heralding this progress.

The concierge in Carlo's dream appears to be a guide of some kind, but is it an inner guide (what in Jungian terminology might be called a psychopomp, or soul guide), or an outer guide (an important teacher or mentor) that is being referred to? I asked Carlo, and he felt it was an inner guide. He also realized that he had recently been out of touch with his inner guide; he had been immersed in a very busy and externally focused period and his inner work had been relatively dormant. His inner guide had been available the whole time but he had not searched him out and asked for his help.

The dream points out that Carlo does hold the key to the wonderful room of gifts but must ask for inner help in order to find the room. This was a resonant connection for both of us. We now formulated a response that involved making a life change that would enable him to invest more time and energy in creativity, meditation, and inner work. With such a dream, it is important for the dreamer to be aware of what the gifts are referring to so he can fully receive them, appreciate them, and make use of them. In this case, Carlo connected the gifts to the skills he was developing in his healing practice.

Tip: Notice which comes first, the dynamic part or the stuck part

As a general rule, if a dream shows a dynamic motif at first that is later slowed or stopped by something stuck, it would mean that a dynamic change is trying to happen in your psyche but cannot because it is held back by something. If the reverse is true—a stuck motif followed by a dynamic movement later in the dream—it would mean that recently you have experienced some movement in relation to a chronically stuck situation. Your dreammaker is calling attention to this movement to recognize and encourage it; this is the characteristic pattern of the Positive Feedback motifs we will be looking at in chapter 26.

Repetitiveness in dreams

One of the surest signs that a dream is pointing at something stuck is repetitiveness. But how do we know if the dream is repeating in hopes that you will finally get the message (functional repetitiveness) or if the dream is repeating just because it is being generated by an old and now redundant neural field (dysfunctional repetitiveness)? This is often a tricky but very important distinction to make because it will determine the kind of dreamwork that is done and the type of response that is chosen.

For example, if you have a repetitive feeling of being unprepared for a test, it could mean that there is a situation in your current life which is testing you (or about to test you), and you are reverting to an old pattern of not preparing sufficiently. This is essentially an ego check motif (giving feedback to the ego about actions and behaviors that could be changed for the better), and it should be worked with and responded to as such. More commonly, however, this kind of repetitive dream of being unprepared for a test (one of the most common dreams in our culture) would mean that there is an old dysfunctional feeling of anxious unpreparedness left over from your childhood school experience (a brain fossil); it is not serving you in any way and the response would be aimed at reducing the power of this old field effect.

Tip: Ask yourself: Is there any value in this dream repeating itself?

When I'm working with a repetitive dream, either my own or another person's, I will pose the question: "Is there any conceivable good reason for this dream scenario to be happening again and again?" Try this with your own repeating dream scenario. If you can't think of any good reason, you are probably dealing with a dream motif arising from an old and redundant neural field (Simone's dream, *Can't Find My Boy!*, in chapter 14 is a good example). But if the answer is yes, you may be dealing with an urgent communication that your dreammaker is sending and re-sending because it is not being received and understood (this kind of repetitiveness is commonly seen with shadow motifs, personal spirit motifs, and ego check motifs).

I use the metaphor of a maze in trying to communicate the nature of stuckness. You may know exactly where you want to go, but the maze determines the contours of your movement. This is the predicament that we humans find ourselves in so often—we know exactly the changes we want to make, but somehow we cannot make them. Instead we find ourselves going round and round in the same repetitive loop, like an old turntable needle stuck in a groove. That's why it's not easy to change old behaviors, habits, and addictions. We all have habituated pathways of behavior and perception that, once developed, tend to be used again and again, thus becoming more and more entrenched. These pathways are to some extent fixed in our brains as neural fields (or neural networks). A strongly established neural field will not change easily. These field effects are symbolically depicted in our dreams every night; we just have to be on the lookout for them. This common and important dream type will be explored in brain field motifs in chapter 18.

Next time someone tells you an interesting dream, step back a bit. Ask yourself first, "What is trying to happen in this dream?" Then ask "Why is it not able to happen?" This will often give you enough orientation to proceed with some helpful facilitation.

Orienting through the body

There are some dreams that seem to draw attention toward the dreamer's body, or a part of it. For such dreams, the best way to get oriented is often through the body—through movement, through gesture, through postures, through dance, through use of the voice, through something physical. Most dreamwork tends to be sedentary and cerebral, but some dreams urge us to get up out of the chair, stop talking, and let the body lead the way.

Some of these dreams may be early health warnings—they may be putting the spotlight on a particular area of the body that is experiencing some difficulty, holding too much tension, or harboring an early manifestation of disease. Often you are completely unaware of anything going on in that part of the body and the dream is trying to alert you. Holly's two dreams that will be discussed in chapter 29, dreams that she connected to her body's early-stage difficulty with an IUD, are examples of this type. Obviously, developing the ability to recognize such dreams would be of great value to any health care practitioner.

Very often a certain part of the body/object is singled out and noticed for some reason: it is the wrong size, old or broken, unusually colored, injured, conspicuously missing, moving in a particular way, extremely hot or cold, charged up with energy, in pain, decaying, sagging, odd, exaggerated, etc. Somehow a part is calling attention to itself.

How might a problem with your body appear in a dream?

Be on the lookout for all these elements, which are commonly borrowed and used by the dreammaker and may be appearing as a metaphor for your body or a part of it: a house or other structure, a vehicle, a vessel or container of some kind, a tool or instrument, another person's body, an animal's body, a bodylike object, a plant, or tree.

Physical, functional, or figurative?

If you suspect that your dream might be calling attention to something going on in your body, you need to discern whether the reference is physical, functional, or purely figurative. For example, if you dream of a problem with your foot (either your actual foot or something standing for your foot) it could be pointing at any of the following:

- **Physical** *(there is some problem going on in your actual physical foot)*—an old unresolved injury, a body memory, the beginning of a disease process; poor circulation, fungal infection, loss of bone density, etc.

- **Functional** *(referring to some issue that has to do with the function/role/purpose of feet)*—a problem with balance, with lack of support, with grounding, with lack of exercise, not walking enough, wanting to kick someone, etc.

- **Figurative** *(the foot is appearing as a figure of speech rather than a physical or functional foot; here we must be attuned to wordplay, puns, and double meanings)*—you need to take a stand, you're getting cold feet about something, you have a soul (sole) problem, you don't have your feet on the ground, you need healing (heeling), you have really put your foot in it, etc.

With all of these, especially the first two, the best way to get oriented could be through working directly with your physical body.

Some suggestions for working with dreams through the body

- As soon as you suspect a body focus, tune into that part of your body. What do you feel there? Is there any sensation? Does that part of you want to do something?

- What associations do you have with that part of your body? Have you ever had a problem there? An injury?

- Use the Be the Part technique ("Be your foot" … "Be the rusty old car" … "Be the leaking roof").

- Use exaggeration: If a gesture, movement, or posture appeared in the dream, do it in an exaggerated way. Repeat it. If you are facilitating another person, you may want to do the movement along with him. If the dream contained a subtle sensation or feeling, imagine that the sensation is very strong—make it more intense than it was in the dream.

- Are you holding a particular feeling or emotion in a certain body part? If so, try to bring it out into words or movement. What would your sore thumb want to say if it could speak? If you cannot express it verbally, try movement, gesture, or posture.

- If you cannot make a direct literal connection, perhaps the connection is functional, based on the role of that body part. What is that part of your body supposed to do; what is its job?

- What are some figures of speech involving that part of the body? If a figure of speech or wordplay comes to mind while facilitating, go ahead and suggest it to the dreamer, "Do you think it might be a reference to shouldering a burden?" Be prepared to drop it if it doesn't quite fit the dream or resonate.

The goal is to make a connection to something relevant going on in that part of your (or the dreamer's) body. Once you've got that, you're done. You can sit back down and move on to the next step.

Here's an example of a dream that seemed well-suited for a physical approach. Naomi, a 43-year-old woman, was experiencing a very frustrating dynamic with her body. She felt the urge to be active and physical, but when engaging in any vigorous activity, she had the tendency to injure herself, reactivating old injury sites that had not completely healed. The injuries were not only painful but also extremely discouraging, preventing her from living the physical life she craved. Naomi had the following dream, which she titled *Scooped Up By a Gorilla*:

> *I'm in a swimming pool with a bunch of people. There's a gorilla upstairs behind a plexiglass barrier and he's trying to get to me. He's banging on the glass and he's really pissed off. He breaks through or gets out somehow and he's coming downstairs to get me. I assume the fetal position while on my feet in the pool; I think everyone else does too. I know he's looking for me. I'm terrified… I'm not sure if he gets to me but I have a visual of him behind me scooping me up, hands on breasts in a sitting spoon position.*

The physical quality of this dream seemed to suggest that it would be a good candidate for some kind of body-based dreamwork; it features a dream figure full of energy and potential movement (the gorilla) and also two noteworthy postures (fetal position in a pool of water and being spooned by a gorilla). So Naomi decided to work on this dream in a group session led by a practitioner who combines dreamwork with movement and dance therapy. When the session began, Naomi immediately began to identify with the gorilla; she felt his anger and frustration at being held back behind the plexiglass and his desperate eagerness to find her in the pool. Identifying with the gorilla, she experienced a powerful throwing motion in her body, as if she was picking the hiding woman up and heaving her out of the water. Naomi wrote in her post-session notes:

> *I am the gorilla, isolated, blocked, trapped, my gift of physical strength restrained. I'm not able to join the rest of the world on its physical journey. I have to inflict pain, it seems, to be me. Breaking through means injury. I want her—she can show me or give me what I need. I will have her as mine. I will meld with her. She needs to let me take her and carry her. There has to be fusion between us.*

This strong and spontaneous identification with the gorilla made Naomi aware that he was a part of her, a shadow part that was holding her frustrated physical energies. The gorilla displayed the quintessential quality of the shadow—wanting to be let in.

Summary

For me, orientation is at the very heart of dreamwork. When you work with a dream, you will know when you're oriented and when you're not. If you're not, *don't panic.* Reach for a compass. This chapter gives you seven different compasses, any one of which might suddenly give you your bearings. If you've tried a few of these orientation techniques and you still don't feel connected, don't worry—you can now try one of the connection setups described in the next chapter.

CHAPTER 13

Connecting the Dream to Your Life

The primary goal of this dreamworking method is to help you understand how your dream connects to your life. Connection is an Aha! phenomenon. It is rather hard to describe in words, but quite unmistakable when it happens in practice. It is the moment when you really *get* the message, and you know what the dream is trying to say about your current life situation. Often a resonant connection will spontaneously happen during the clarification or orientation phases (about 60 to 70 percent of the time in my experience). But what if it does not spontaneously happen? Or what if you're facilitating another person and you can sense a connection but the dreamer cannot? At this point, it is often very helpful to use some kind of setup to try to spark the insight. These setups are connection catalysts that still allow dreamers to experience Aha! moments themselves. This is important because the experience of arriving at an insight yourself is more useful than having someone explain the same insight to you.

The difference between orienting and connecting

Orienting and connecting often overlap and blend into each other; what is the essential difference between these two? During the orientation phase, neither the dreamer nor the facilitator yet has a sense of how the dream might connect; both parties are still trying to get oriented. The facilitator is guiding the process by asking certain questions that are designed to focus the orientation quickly. At some point in this process, the facilitator may feel that he has a good hunch about where the dream connects. Now it's time to shift gears and put the focus on connection. Let's consider an example and use it to highlight the difference between clarifying, orienting, and connecting. Douglas, a 56-year-old man, has adult ADHD tendencies, mainly distractibility and difficulty staying focused on a task. He had this fascinating dream we called *Stuffing an Octopus Into a Sack*:

> *I'm in an indoor pool. There's about three or four feet of water, and there's this octopus there. I'm trying to do some research with it, but I don't quite know what it is that I'm trying to do. And I don't know very much about how to handle the octopus. There is a feeling that I have been given some instructions, but not enough to be comfortable that I know what I'm doing. It could be a bit dangerous—will it grab on to me with its suctions? At one point I am trying to get it into a gunnysack. That is scary. I am trying to force it into some bag where I could hang onto it, and I don't know what it would do. I feel uncomfortable and like I don't have enough instructions. I wake up.*

Now, if we ask Douglas whether he was actually in the water with the octopus, we are clarifying. If we ask him what his associations with octopus are, again we are clarifying. If we ask him how he felt as he was trying to stuff the octopus into the sack, we are still clarifying.

If we ask Douglas whether he thinks this is an inner octopus (something in him that he struggles to understand and deal with) or an outer octopus (someone or something in his external world that he is struggling with), we are orienting (through Inner/Outer). If we ask Douglas whether it is a good or bad thing that he is stuffing this octopus into a sack (should he be trying to do this or should he stop trying to do this?), we are still orienting (through Good Thing/Bad Thing). If we ask him to be the octopus to find out more about what it might be representing, we are still orienting (through Be the Part).

But if, after having done one or more of the above, we strongly suspect that the dream octopus is a representation of Douglas's ADHD problem, which he is working very hard to understand, control, and contain, then we are starting to make a connection. If you, as Douglas's facilitator, feel the time is right to try out this connection, you can say something like: "In the dream you are struggling with something you can't control. You feel uncomfortable and like you need more instructions. Where in your life do you feel these feelings?" Now you are attempting a connection. You are using a carefully chosen construct in the hopes that Douglas will be able to forge the connection in his own mind. If he can, it will be of more use to him than suggesting: "Do you think the octopus might be a depiction of your ADHD?"

If Douglas cannot make a connection right away, it might be helpful to reiterate just the key feeling-based words: "struggling, not able to control, uncomfortable, needing more instruction..." Often when someone has his own words reflected back like this he will be able to grasp the connection.

How do we know if the connection is true or accurate?

Remember the Double Resonance test we talked about in chapter 5? When you are facilitating another person, your proposed connections must pass this test, resonating as true for both you and the dreamer. If the dreamer has made the same connection you already suspected, chances are you have reached your goal. To make sure, you can ask a double-checking question like "Does that seem to fit?" or "Is that where it connects?" or "Does that seem right?" If the dreamer makes a connection that you were not expecting, then you must again subject it to the Double Resonance test. If you both feel it is a resonant connection, then you have arrived. Now you must decide if you want to suggest *your* original suspected connection as well and see if that one is also doubly resonant (since there can be more than one connection point between a dream and the dreamer's life). If you do not resonate with the dreamer's proposed connection and feel yours is more likely, then you should put yours forward for the dreamer to consider. Typically, you would use a phrase like: "All right, so that's a possible connection. And is it also possible that XYZ?" In cases where multiple possible connections have been brought forward, all of which seem to have some degree of resonance, try to pick the one that has the most energy and work with that one.

Tip: When working on your own dream, emotional charge is the most reliable sign you have made a good connection

If you are working alone on your own dream, you won't have access to this Double Resonance test, which makes it more difficult to be sure if you've made an accurate connection. Feedback from the other is one of the great advantages of working on a dream with another person, but we don't always have this advantage. It is all too easy to delude ourselves and sell ourselves a story about what our own dream may be telling us. If I have a dream insight that seems to be entirely mental, I typically do not trust it. If it did not happen with any spontaneous emotional charge, I am suspicious that my mind is telling me something comfortable and nonthreatening, something I probably already know about myself. But if I have an emotionally charged reaction I know from prior experience, it is much more likely to be accurate. This emotion will often be a negative one—if my insight makes me wince with shame, embarrassment, self-disgust, self-directed anger, or frustration,

I know I am probably on the right track! (This is especially true of ego check motifs, shadow motifs, and limiting field motifs.) Feelings of grief, pain, loss, and great suffering are characteristic of personal spirit motifs, and are strongly correlated to unresolved trauma.

What about more positive emotions? Feelings of amazement, awe, and wonderment often come with inspiring contact motifs, rebirth motifs, self-discovery motifs, and positive feedback motifs, and these typically require no waking insight or connection to catalyze them. These powerfully positive emotions are generated within the dream itself and continue to suffuse the waking memory of the dream whether or not the dreamer has any sense of what they are connected to.

This emotional/feeling level of the dream experience is critical for the dreamwork process, not only because it can lead us toward a good connection, but also because it can be used to gauge the accuracy of any potential connections we are making.

There are many possible ways to set up a connection for the dreamer. The common element is that they all involve shining a spotlight on some element of the dream, then asking the dreamer where that element may exist in his or her life. Let's look at three versions of this technique with dream examples.

Connecting through highlight and ask

This technique has three essential steps:

1. Extract one key feature of the dream that has caught your attention

2. Spotlight it by saying it to the dreamer, preferably in one short sentence of no more than three phrases

3. Ask the dreamer where that may exist in her life

I suspect that some version of this technique is used by dreamworkers around the globe, regardless of what name they give it or whether they are even doing it consciously. It is very simple and direct in its essence. Some variation of this method lies at the heart of many dreamworking styles that are client-centered rather than interpretive or analytical.

Rob was in the midst of a relationship crisis. He was 44 years old at the time he had this dream of *The Hobbit Door*. For many years, both he and his former partner had declared that they were not interested in having children. More recently his partner had begun to change and found that perhaps she did want to be a mother after all. Rob still felt that having a child would be too disruptive to the life he wanted, but now he found himself considering the possibility with a new sense of urgency:

> I'm in a bungalow-style house. I'm with the owner of the house. He asked me about the possibility of adding a small door to the house. He said it would be a separate special door for Hobbits, but it could be used for kids and animals too. We were having a problem because we couldn't find anywhere to install the door where it wouldn't cause a structural problem, like cutting through major support beams. In other places we saw the cement foundation that would be too hard to get through with a jack-hammer. We kept searching for a spot. After a while the owner got tired of searching and said, "Let's forget about it. Maybe it's not that important," but I wanted to keep looking. I finally found an option that would work. He was losing interest, but I encouraged him to go through with it. I can't remember if we actually built the door or not. But if we did, I imagine it was workable but not perfect, partly below grade, partly above... it got the job done. Now there would be a way for the little people to get in.

As his facilitator, I suspected that the making of hobbit door referred to some way in which Rob had recently become open to something that he had formerly not been open to. So I asked, "The dream suggests that recently you have made an opening for little people to come in. Has that happened in some way in your life?" With this setup, Rob immediately made a strongly resonant connection to his openness to having children. It was in fact starting to change, from a resolute no to a definite possibility.

This is an example of a self-discovery motif, a motif that informs the dreamer about important changes that are happening just under the surface of consciousness; these dreams often involve discoveries of new and previously unknown parts of a house. This dream also provides a clear example of the Dynamic/Stuck pattern discussed in chapter 12. In *The Hobbit Door*, the dream ego (Rob in the dream) carries the dynamic energy that wants change; this part wants to make sure the Hobbit door does get built. The stuck part is played by the house owner who gets tired and will easily give up on the whole project. This is very important information for Rob—he can anticipate that a part of him will indeed be very eager to open up to the idea of parenthood, but it may be waylaid by another part that will quickly lose momentum if the new initiative runs into difficulty.

Here's another example of a connection setup being used. Kristy was 29 years old; she had this dream of *The Babies in the Freezer* a decade earlier, and it was so intense that she still vividly remembered it years later. Not only did she still remember it, she also felt that it still had an important message for her that she had not yet understood:

I'm in an old house. It's very run down, it's all gray and white, I can see an overturned sofa in one room. A toddler comes up to me and takes my hand. It leads me downstairs to the cellar. I see a freezer, and I go over and open it. A frosty mist and a blue light come up out of it when I open it. I gasp—there are frozen babies in the freezer! Suddenly I'm upstairs again. (The dream continued but the facilitator decided to work with this one key piece.)

As her dreamworker, I sensed that the frozen babies were the most critical element of the dream, so I wanted to keep the focus on them as I tried to set her up to make a connection. Kristy had some resistance to this and wanted to pull the focus away to other parts of the dream, but I resisted. I brought the spotlight back to the babies: "The dream seems to say that something very young and very important has been frozen for a long time. How would this apply to you?" With this setup she was immediately able to make a resonant and very emotionally charged connection: "It's my singing. My music. It's so important to me, but I haven't been doing it. It's in a deep freeze."

The motif of the lost, abandoned or traumatized baby/child is universal in dreams, and always critically important, I call these personal spirit motifs. Its importance will almost always trump every other element in a dream since it is pointing to a wound in the innermost part of the psyche that urgently requires attention and healing. This dream is emphatically saying that Kristy's soul and spirit *must* sing; she cannot let this part of herself remain as a frozen potential that is not allowed to live.

Tip: Keep it short and stay close to the dreamer's own words

When you set up the dreamer using the highlight and ask technique, your choice of words is critical. Try to stay very close to the words the dreamer actually used. Also try to make sure that the sentence you use does not have more than three distinct phrases; if it is too long, the dreamer may lose track of the beginning before you get to the end.

Connecting through feeling tones

Feeling tones are simply the feelings that the dream ego experiences in the dream. In the dream example from the beginning of this chapter—*Stuffing an Octopus Into a Sack*—the dream ego felt, in the dreamer's words, "struggling, not able to control, uncomfortable, and needing more instruction" as he tried to force the octopus into the sack. These are the feeling tones of this part of the dream. Feeling tones may change during the dream of course; as a facilitator you will often be focusing on one particular part of a dream that has the strongest and clearest feeling tones.

A problem often encountered in dreamwork is that the feeling tones have not been caught and anchored properly, so that by the time clients are describing the dream in session, they no longer have a clearly remembered sense of what the feeling tones were. This is why it is so critical to train yourself to focus on the feelings in your dreams and develop the habit of recalling them and recording them.

If you are helping someone with a dream and you sense that a connection point is close at hand, you can follow these basic steps:

1. Identify a part of the dream with strong clear feeling tones

2. Extract just the feeling words and phrases (use between one and four feeling words or phrases; not more than four)

3. Reiterate these words or phrases to the dreamer using the following construct: "In the dream you feel: A, B, and C. (pause)...where do you have these feelings in your life?

If you're working on your own dream, do it in exactly the same way, playing both parts in turn—as facilitator you set up the question and as the dreamer you try to answer it.

Here's an example—42-year-old Hannah was trying to make a big life decision following a breakup, debating whether or not she should relocate her life to the West Coast. At the height of feeling stuck and unable to make up her mind, Hannah had a dream that she called *Into the Tunnel*:

> *I need to get to the parking garage to get my car. I see this big area of water... sort of like fountains but it's just mucky water. So I go through this mucky water, and I get to the edge where there are these cement tunnels going up a hill. To go through these tunnels, you had to put your nose down into a black rubber thing and squirm your way all the way up through this small tube. Other people were there and everybody seemed to be doing it okay. But I was too afraid to do it... that if I went through the tunnel I'd get stuck in it... how could you breathe? And where would you fit your arms? It just seemed too small to fit through. And then there was another lady that was doing it... she had her arms out and around, which I thought would be maybe easier to do. So I thought maybe I could*

do that ... but she had her arms going up and around this tube ... and I thought if I did that I might get my arms stuck ... and then I'd get stuck in the tube, and that would be worse, because my arms are stuck. So I ask if I do it that way, which looks a little bit more freeing—can you guys get me out if I stop breathing? They say no they couldn't. So then I sat there thinking "Well, I can't do this."

Dreamworker: So in the dream you feel afraid to do something that other people can do, and you're afraid that you would get stuck. What can you connect that to in your life?

Being stuck everywhere in my life. Right now, the suffering I put myself into about the breakup. I'm stuck ... I'm really stuck in that ... that's heavy on me. I'm stuck ... I don't know what I want to do in life, where I want to go in life, where I should live, whether I should move, who I am.

This was a resonant connection point—the dream was a depiction of Hannah's fear of moving ahead into the unknown. Her dreammaker seemed to be pointing out that she need not be so fearful; everyone else is easily able to move through the tunnel without getting stuck. Why couldn't she? As her dreamworker, I wondered why Hannah's fear was so strong. It had a life-or-death urgency to it. Also the dream contained some specific imagery that made me suspect it was a reiteration of her birth pattern, the fear of suffocation, fear of getting stuck in a particular posture, the need for outside help to rescue her—all these were strongly suggestive of a paralyzing fear of transitioning into the birth canal. To explore this further I asked her:

DW: If you imagine moving into the tunnel ... what do you feel?

Very dark ... very confining ... and I think I would panic thinking that I wouldn't be able to breathe and make it all the way through ... and then the panicking would cause me to not breathe even more ... cause my breathing to stop.

It appeared that in her feeling body (not in her rational mind), Hannah equated change and transition with suffocation and possible death. This would make it very difficult for her to commit to any major life change such as the move to the West Coast that she was currently facing. Whether or not this is a replaying of her actual birth pattern would be hard to know for sure, and impossible to prove. In her case, I suggested the possibility that it might be connected. Hannah was intrigued and undertook to research her hospital birth records, which showed that she had required an application of forceps to turn her into the position needed to move into the birth canal.

This way of looking at it made some strange kind of sense to Hannah—there must be a deep unconscious reason she had a lifelong pattern of becoming paralyzed on the brink of making any big change. Together we developed a response to the dream; she would use her creative imagination to imagine the following scenario—she would approach the tunnel, summon her courage, enter the tunnel in the position that felt best, visualize moving through it without getting stuck, and finally emerge safely on the other side. This helped create for her a new template for facing major life transitions that proved very valuable.

In my experience, dreams often shine a light on deeply unconscious patterns that contribute to our inexplicable blockages, habits, compulsions, and intractable stuckness. I suspect that birth (including prenatal and perinatal) patterns resulting from our intense and very early experiences form a very significant part of our unconscious psycho-physical patterning. Many dreams seem to emanate from and expose this level of human experience; the imagery that appears in certain dreams is hard to account for in any other way. We will consider this in more detail in "Rebirth motifs" in chapter 24.

Tip: Good note-taking or a good memory is needed

When you set up a connection through feeling tones, you will get the best results if you pick out two to four of the feeling-based words your dreamer just used in describing her dream. Use *her words,* not your own paraphrased approximation of her words. For this reason, you will probably want to have the words written down, unless you trust yourself to remember them accurately. In my practice, I write down most of the dream verbatim. Even when I have a written copy in advance, I record the key words and phrases that the dreamer uses as they re-enter the dreamscape and describe the dream. For purposes of setting up a connection, it is better to choose words they have used recently if they are different from the words in the written transcript. If they left out a key feeling word that was included in the written version when they retell the dream in session, I remind them of the word, making sure it still fits and bringing it back into the mix. The words you choose for the setup should still be reverberating and hanging in the air.

Connecting through spotting a figure of speech

Dreams will often employ a very specific figure of speech, an idiomatic expression, a pun, or play on words. One of the most direct ways to connect quickly to the meaning of a dream is to spot the figure of speech that the dream is using. We have already looked at some of the ways these language-based elements are used in dreams in chapter 3.

Some people have trouble accepting that the unconscious mind would stoop to playing with words, even at times making outrageous puns; but the evidence is indisputable. Over the years I have learned that the dream-maker will employ whatever device it can to get its message across. In fact, these wordplays come up so often in dreamwork that it brings up the old chicken-and-egg question: do we dream in figures of speech because they exist in our language, or do they exist in our language because the dreaming brain works that way? I suspect it may be a bit of both. Here's an example, the dream of a 61-year-old woman named Gayle; she called the dream *Spoons Push Their Way Out*:

> *In this dream I see myself but I'm also the person I'm seeing. I have a spoon stuck in my chest. Then I sense that it's trying to push its way out. I could see the outline of the spoon pulling the skin taut on the back of my neck. It's trying to come out, pushing on the flesh and skin. Then it came out. There are two silver spoons that emerge; one has a handle longer than the other.*

Prior to the session, Gayle had already been struck by the possibility that the dream was using the idiom "to be born with a silver spoon in the mouth," meaning to be born into wealth and privilege. Indeed, she had been born into a wealthy family, and she often wondered if this had somehow hindered her from finding her own path to independence and self-sufficiency. As we discussed the dream, it seemed resonantly true that the silver spoons were referring to Gayle's privileged upbringing, and it also seemed to be a very positive thing that the spoons were now leaving her body. This expulsion of the spoons is characteristic of an introject motif, a motif that depicts the psyche ridding itself of a set of ideas and beliefs that were instilled in childhood. Gayle agreed that her parents—probably unwittingly and unconsciously—had led her to believe that she would not have to suffer deprivation and hardship like most people because they would always be there to provide for her. This belief system had lived within her for many years but now she was trying to push it out—a very positive psychological development.

The instant Gayle recognized the central metaphor of the dream, given in the form of an idiomatic expression, the message of the dream began to unfold itself. If you are helping someone with a dream and you have spotted wordplay the dreamer has not yet spotted, you should call attention to it. These are some of the phrases I use to set up a possible connection, using the *Spoons Push Their Way Out* dream as our example:

- Have you spotted any figures of speech or wordplays in this dream?

- The dream features two silver spoons … is there a possible wordplay there?

- What would you connect to "silver spoon"?

You must (as always) use some version of the Double Resonance test to assess whether or not the figure of speech you have spotted is really a key to the meaning of the dream. Our language uses so many idiomatic expressions that we can spot them all over the place when we are attuned to them. If you point out a figure of speech and it is not resonant for the dreamer or leads ultimately to a dead end, just drop it and move on to another connection strategy. For example, the most obvious idiomatic expression in the dream of *The Man With Two Guns,* would be "to shoot oneself in the foot." But this turned out to be a herring of the red variety; the operative metaphor of the dream had to do with being easily triggered, not shooting oneself in the foot.

Summary

Of course, there are innumerable ways to help yourself or another dreamer arrive at a resonant connection to a dream. Often the Aha! connection point will arise spontaneously in the course of the dreamwork, but often it will not. For those cases where a formal strategy is called for, keep these methods at your fingertips. If you remain mystified after attempting both orientation and connection, don't worry; some dreams take longer than others to give up their treasure. Let it go for now; you can always come back to it later. You can still respond to the dream, but it will be a *pre-connection response*, designed to keep the dream image alive in your mind in anticipation of some future insight and connection. In many cases, your efforts will reward you with a satisfying insight about how the dream connects to your life. When this happens, you are ready to move to the fifth and final step of the method: responding to your dream.

CHAPTER 14

Responding to the Dream

If your dream is a message, then what is the purpose of the message? Why did something or someone bother to send it to you? What do they want from you? These questions take us beyond the realm of understanding the dream and into the realm of responding to it. A response can be anything—anything you actually decide to do because of an insight obtained from your dream. The most common kind of response would be to resolve to change your behavior or attitude as a result of understanding a dream message, but there are many other possibilities.

Dialogue between ego and dreammaker

Responding to a dream is a powerful stimulus for the channel of communication that can exist between the conscious and unconscious mind. The dreammaker is very responsive to being responded to. If the dreamer cultivates the habit of responding to dreams, the dreammaker will reciprocate and a powerful axis of communication will soon be in operation:

- dreammaker makes a dream ("I am sending you a message")

- ego catches and anchors the dream ("I got your message")

- ego connects the dream to his or her life ("I think I understand your message")

- ego responds to the dream ("I get the message and I'm going to try to do something about it")

- ego awaits the next development in the unconscious, the response to the response ("Now what?")

- dreammaker makes another dream, arising from an inner landscape that has been somewhat altered by the previous dialogue ("I got your response, and I'm sending you the next message")

If this axis of communication is not opened and developed, the dream life will tend to have a repetitive quality ("I haven't heard back from you. I'm sending you the message again").

Dream-based homework

My twenty-five years of dreamwork practice have taught me many things; one of them is that a lot of people don't do their homework! A dreamer may leave a session very excited about a response we have come up with together, but at our next meeting it often turns out that he or she has forgotten all about it. I find that many people simply will not make *any* response to their dream unless I push the agenda in some way. But how pushy should I be? If I insist homework be done, this sets up a potential problem for the next session if the homework has not been done. If I merely suggest the homework, there is an implicit agreement that my client may decide to do the homework or they may not. For some clients, this will be the best way to handle the response phase—if the homework assignment really resonates with them they will do it, if it doesn't they probably won't. So be it. And then there are some clients who only want to tell the dream, have the experience of working with it, and perhaps gain some insight from it; they do not want to feel any pressure to act on it. For these people, requesting homework would be too pushy and would likely prove counterproductive.

In recent years I have made a point to ask, "How hard do you want me to push the response homework?" If the client wants the process to be dynamic and results-based, there should be some response homework agreed upon at the end of every session; this will drive the process forward quickly by fully activating the dialogue between ego and dreammaker.

Pre-connection responses

You've had a powerful dream. You've done some work with it and it's still puzzling. You've even taken it to your dreamworker but understanding has remained elusive. That Aha! moment has not come. You're still not sure where it connects to your life. You know it is asking for something but you can't figure out what. What can you do? Try one of these pre-connection responses, all of which can serve to keep the dream alive in your mind and create the conditions for further insight and (hopefully) eventual connection:

- Ask for another dream that will shed further light on the mystery

- Go back into the dream in your imagination and explore further

- Do some kind of ritual amplification of the central dream image

- Do some research on the central dream image

Remember Ellen who had the dream of *The Big Grasshopper* back in chapter 6? Ellen's dream intrigued her but it also mystified her; she did not understand why she would dream of a grasshopper. She had no particular association with the grasshopper and could not connect to any sense of its personal meaning for her. So I gave Ellen some pre-connection response homework—I suggested she could ask her dreammaker to send her another dream of the grasshopper. It obliged with the following dream a few months later, which she called *The Traveling Minstrel Grasshopper Show*:

> *The dream was about a traveling minstrel who was making a show about caring for a grasshopper. It was a magic show—he made the grasshopper go through transitions, it sometimes changed into something else. There was also a mouse. I was very interested in the show. My daughter was with me and we were both trying to figure out how he could turn the grasshopper into different things. It was very magical and intriguing. And I was involved in some way—my job was to hold back the dogs, so they didn't get involved and spoil everything. That was it.*

Dreamworker: What would happen if you didn't hold back the dogs?

> *They'd probably jump in and kill the grasshopper... and the mouse.*

DW: So what would the dogs represent? Something you have to hold back that could jump in and spoil something magical and intriguing ...

> (After some thought): *My lack of belief that I can have any future. My depression. My dark thoughts.*

Here Ellen had arrived at a very resonant connection point that showed how important it was for her to try to keep her depressive thinking in check. It became clear now, after this second dream, that the grasshopper was a symbol of her new possibilities. It was very small, very fragile, and very vulnerable; but it was also magical and held potential for a future transformation. I would treat the grasshopper as an inspiring contact motif for this dreamer—something absolutely unique and special to her (see chapter 25). If she can be convinced of its importance and can hold back the black dogs of depression from destroying it, it will gradually become an important inner reference point for her.

Adam's dream of *The Young Man and the Old Man* discussed in chapter 11 gives us another example of a pre-connection response. His dream, like Ellen's, remained mysterious and was not well connected by the end of our session. His response homework was to do some research into the archetypes of the Puer Aeternus (eternal boy) and the Senex (old man), and it was this work that helped him arrive at a satisfying understanding of the dream.

Post-connection responses

Now let's move on to post-connection responses. You have worked on your dream and the Aha! moment has come—yes! That's what it's about! Now you're connected. If this is as far as you want to go with it that's fine, you've already done some important work that will likely pay off for you. *But* you are only one small step away from getting an even bigger benefit. Now that you understand what the dream is about, ask yourself, "What does the dream want from me?" You will be taking this next critical step. This will bring you right to the potential change point. You now have the chance to make a real life change based on your insight from the dream.

Remember the IRA (Imaginal-Ritual-Actual)

Here's an insider trade secret for you; something I have learned from many years of helping people formulate dream responses—start with the imaginal, then do something ritual, and finally (if you still want to and need to), do something in the actual realm. This is the order that brings the best results. To quickly clarify exactly what I mean when I use these three terms: the imaginal response takes place entirely in your imagination. The ritual response involves doing or creating something that does exist in the external world, but only in your private world, like placing something on your personal shrine. An actual response involves committing to a fully actualized life change.

Why not go to the action phase straight away? It's not always a good idea to plunge straight into action when contemplating a life change. If you give yourself a chance to rehearse the change you are thinking about, to experiment with it, modulate and refine it, you will often find that your end result turns out better. All this work can be done through imagination and ritual, without involving anyone else in your drama or creating any new mess or stress in your outer life. Once you have done the imaginal and ritual groundwork you will probably feel clearer about what, if anything, needs to be taken out into the actualized realm.

Fifty-year-old Morgan recently told me the following dream, which he called *The Colorful Toad:*

> *I'm in my upstairs office in my house. The room is fairly dark. On the floor I see a glowing orange toad. I approach him and tell him that he doesn't belong here; he should be outside. I gently pick him up and I carry him outside onto the front porch. I carefully place him down at the edge of the landscaped border that opens onto a garden. The garden slopes down to a street. The toad hops down the slope but then starts tumbling. I feel bad for him, I'm concerned if he'll be okay. I run down the slope and I see him crash against a rock. He now loses his orange glow and turns into a regular-colored toad. He appears to be stunned by the crash, but after a few seconds he recovers and collects himself. He now turns bright blue and hops away across the garden and up the slope toward the trees. As he's doing that, I get distracted by a couple walking down the street. I lose track of the toad. I wake up.*

As we worked with this dream, we were gifted a natural connection point that Morgan spontaneously experienced as he told the dream—when he said the words "I tell him that he doesn't belong here; he should be outside" there was a very resonant moment, a brief but unmistakable few seconds of poignant insight. We could both feel that this dream was about a part of him that doesn't belong inside, that should be outside. Morgan was easily able to connect this to his career. He works in a 9 to 5 desk job in an office setting (the dream begins in an office). This job pays the bills nicely but he has no great love for it. For many years Morgan has longed for more meaningful work, for a vocation, or at least for some kind of work that is more aligned with his soul values. And when he ponders what that work might be, his imagination most often takes him outside; he has fantasized about owning a wilderness retreat, an outdoor activity center, or a small hotel in the countryside. The toad seems to have appeared to underscore this quality of "being not-in-the-right-place," and even perhaps to lure Morgan outdoors, off into the forest.

Now that we have achieved the first goal of the dreamwork (a resonant connection between the dream and the dreamer's life), we can move on to the second goal—generating some kind of response to this insight. For the imaginal response, I always begin by working within the setting and parameters of the dreamscape. Making the translation to waking life can come later, but in the beginning we just go back into the dreamscape and pose the question, "What is trying to happen?" or "What is the dream asking for?" Morgan and I agreed that the desired direction of change that we want to support is a movement from inside to outside. He has already taken the toad outside; this transition has proved to be a bit bumpy, and it involves some very dramatic changes (depicted in the dream as the toad changing color), but it seems to be working in that both Morgan and the toad are now out of doors. However, Morgan then gets distracted and loses touch with the toad. This is problematic; it may mean that in waking life he has good initiatives toward important changes that would feed his soul but he also has a tendency to get distracted and not follow through with the changes. There are at least three indicators in the dream that the toad is something soulful: its mysterious and sudden appearance in his office, its numinous glowing colors, and the tender care with which Morgan intuitively knows to handle it.

So, I asked Morgan, what about a visualization in which he finds the toad again and follows it as it moves into the trees? He agreed that this felt right and he tried it with me in the session. We are now supporting and extending a desired energy and movement that is trying to happen in the dream. The implicit underlying message of this exercise is: "the encounter with this toad is very important, it's good that you have taken the toad outside, now don't get distracted, don't lose touch with this important thing, follow it farther into the outdoors, see where it might lead you." Everything in this message is in alignment with what Morgan and I have already agreed is trying to happen. Typically, I will ask the dreamer to repeat a visualization like this between three and ten times over the next week or so after we do it in the initial exercise together in my office.

Now, let's go further to a ritual response. The toad seems to have something to do with Morgan's soul and what it wants; such dream motifs often lead us very naturally to the ritual level, a level that intersects the imaginal and the actual. How about finding a toad pendant and wearing it for a time? Or buying a toad figurine for the office? Or finding a picture of a toad and putting it on an altar, or the fridge, or the computer desktop? All these would serve to do two important things that we human beings use ritual for—ritual elevates the relevance and importance of a thing, and ritual can help keep something alive and forefront in our awareness, it renews and reminds. I suggested in this case that Morgan might get two toad pictures, of an orange toad and a bright blue toad, since this color change was so striking (and to this day so mysterious).

On to the third level; an actual response is much more serious and more involved. The stakes are higher because now other people are brought into the mix, and there could be real and lasting life changes made. This is why it is often not a good idea to rush in to the actualized realm, and why I advise doing the imaginal and ritual responses first. These two (or even just the imaginal by itself) will often open a very natural pathway toward making an actual life change; and indeed sometimes doing these first two will even render the making of an external change unnecessary.

Morgan has made some forays into the actual realm. He has traveled to a number of places to feel out their suitability for a potential future career endeavor. He is still working in the office at time of writing. But who knows? Toads can pop up at any time.

Different types of dreams call for different types of responses

A response could be almost anything that is change-oriented and arises from a dream insight. Let's take a look at some possible responses, organized roughly into IRA categories, just so you can start to collect them for your own list of potential responses:

Imaginal

- Imagining a new reality, a new outcome, a new action
- Having an imaginal conversation with someone

Ritual

- Putting something on your altar, fridge, shrine, or computer (and so on) that symbolizes some key part of your dream (a photo, an object, a drawing)
- Doing a formal ritual of completion or closure (burying, burning, releasing into water or air)
- Working with a symbol that appeared in the dream (e.g., wearing a ring, stone, key, coin, symbol, etc., like the one that appeared in your dream)
- Writing an unsent letter to someone

- Creating something (a picture, a photo collage, a poem, a tattoo)

Actual

- Resolving to make a life or behavior change

- Resolving to attend to some unfinished business

- Resolving to speak to someone about a key issue

Your imagination is your most powerful tool

What is the most frequently used and most effective tool in a dreamworker's toolkit?—I would say it is the creative use of the imagination. Your dreams will so often depict your struggle to move and evolve in a certain direction. You want to move but you cannot because of some stuckness or block. At times like this you can recruit your creative imagination to move your dream scenario along toward a desired outcome. You are literally initiating the process of change at its headwaters. From there, it can flow forward toward the changes that you have been wanting to happen in your waking life. In the Jungian world, this technique might be called "active imagination." Many excellent chapters and books have been written within the Jungian genre on this subject; indeed, some of the best examples of active imagination in action can be found in Jung's own autobiography. [11] I like to think of it this way: you can re-enter your dream and look around for a possible new outcome. Try it, see if it feels right. If it doesn't feel right you can try something else. When you have found something that feels good, you can rehearse this new possibility until it starts to become a real part of your life. Don't let anyone tell you that you can't do this, especially your own pessimistic side. You can do it. Here's how.

---

11   Carl Jung, *Memories, Dreams, Reflections* (New York: Vintage Books, 1965).

The essential steps of an imaginal response

- Go back into your dreamscape.

- Identify the stuck or problematic point in the dream and go to that point. Feel what it's like to be there.

- Catch yourself. Become aware that you can change the scenario.

- Ask yourself (or the dreamer you are facilitating): What do I want to do? How do I want to change this scene?

- Start doing this new thing. If it has energy and momentum, follow it as it unfolds.

- If you're facilitating and your dreamer cannot generate any new possibilities, you may have to make specific suggestions.

- Remember, you're not committing or locking in by trying something. If your new direction doesn't feel right, you can always go back and try something else. Remember the famous quote from Yogi Berra: "When you come to a fork in the road, take it."

- Don't be thinking about what this new thing might mean in your waking life. You can translate it into waking life later; for now just stay within the dreamscape.

This technique is in essence very similar to Imagery Rehearsal Therapy (IRT), a well-established and well-validated therapy for the treatment of nightmares, including post-traumatic nightmares. In IRT, the nightmare sufferer chooses a dream to work with, writes it down, decides how they would like to change the outcome to something more positive, and then rehearses this new outcome in their imagination. [12]

---

12   Barry Krakow and Joseph Neidhardt, *Conquering Bad Dreams and Nightmares* (New York: Berkley Books, 1992).

Here is an example of a dream that called for an imaginal response. It is the dream of a 36-year-old woman named Yolanda, called *The Mechanical Scorpion*:

The dream takes place in my grandmother's place, in the room that used to be my bedroom. There are chairs set up in the room. Three authoritarian men sit in the chairs and there is a chair there for me as well. It feels like a grand decision is about to be made. I try to avoid the whole scenario, walking around the house with this automated scorpion in hand. It is small but with a very fierce energy … it moves, constantly moves and has its own intention. Its intention is to go inside me and carve my insides; carve in a destructive way. And I know that at some point it has been in my right shoulder —right in the heart of my right shoulder, and was carving my insides. Somehow it is outside my body now … so I'm looking down at my hands; looking down at this object that is moving continuously and very quickly. It has its own objective and intentions—to go inside me. It is horrible! I don't want that! But I don't know how to manage it … I wake up.

Yolanda's dream is another example of an introject motif; it depicts her struggle to rid herself of a foreign and harmful psychological content that was forced into her in childhood. The opening scene gives us some clues as to the time of her life (when she slept in that particular bedroom) and the circumstances (the authoritarian men who make a grand decision concerning her) surrounding the origin of this introject.

Now the dream is showing that Yolanda is on the verge of being able to expel this scorpion-introject. It is currently outside her, but there is a danger that it will get back inside her if she cannot manage it somehow. What can she do? Because of the emotional intensity of the dream, Yolanda had trouble generating new possibilities—the scorpion felt too powerful to fight against. She needed some active help and facilitation, so here's what I coached Yolanda to do:

- *Identify the stuck point*—the scorpion is still a very active threat, Yolanda has no plan for managing it. It's terrorizing her.

- *Re-enter the dream and go to the stuck point*—Yolanda allowed herself to feel the horrible carving energy of the scorpion.

- *Ask the dreamer what she wants to do from this point*—Yolanda replied that she might want to kill it but she didn't think it was killable (indicating that this scorpion-introject still has significant power and energy). I suggested that perhaps it could be trapped and held in a container. She agrees that this might work.

- *Invite the dreamer to imagine this happening*—Yolanda imagines capturing the scorpion in a jar and sealing it tight. She feels a sense of relief and hopefulness. She says that perhaps it can be killed or disposed of at some future time.

Once Yolanda generated the possibility of being rid of the scorpion in her imagination, it began to seem possible that she could rid of what it represented in her waking life. Now, translating from the imaginal realm into the actual realm, we put our heads together and thought about what that might be. Yolanda knew it was something to do with her early school experience, and specifically the strict and punitive measures that were inflicted on her to force a change from left-handedness to right-handedness. This early traumatic experience had forced something into her body that remained there more than thirty years later, something foreign, destructive, and painful. Now Yolanda's dreammaker had depicted this foreign content as a mechanical scorpion and had brought forth the exciting possibility that she could be rid of it.

Responding by resolving to make a change

Diana, 32 years old, had identified that one of her key goals in therapy was to be less impulsive and rash in the way she makes decisions and life changes. She had a dream called *Going Feet First*:

> *The dream begins when I'm at a family gathering. It's in a big school-type yard. There are lots of trees and I'm with my in-laws, including my mother-in-law who I'm very close to, and have a very strong feeling for. She's a mentor to me, and I care for her opinion. At one point she asks me to go into the big old type of farmhouse, and go into the cellar part, and help her bring some food out and some things for the dinner. We get there and she goes down the steps, it's a very tight opening, it looks like, very, very steep small steps. It's almost like someone has dug this hole out of the ground, like ... it's a little ominous to look down there. But she just trots right down the stairs and she's waiting for me to follow her. And I look at this opening and I'm claustrophobic looking at it because I'm pretty sure that not even my head will fit. I don't want to put my feet down first and then get my body stuck in it then I'll be stuck, and I won't be able to go any farther. So I think I'm going to put my head down in and just dive in and maybe I'll just be able to fit through, but I can't even do that because it's so claustrophobic feeling. So I just put one foot down in and test it out ... and then I feel all this room after the foot goes in! There's a sense that there's lots of room down there. As soon as I get past my knees and my feet in, all this room opens up. It's so much easier, it's still tight at the top but the bottom is just completely open and I'm in and it's fine! [laughs] Imagine what would have happened if I'd gone head first and fallen down the stairs and broke my neck and ... big mess!*

Dreamworker: So the dream seems to be highlighting the contrast between going head first and going feet first. What can you connect to that?

Well, since working on this dream, I went through the feelings of what it felt like to go head first... there's this panic. I have to hurry up, and get it over with. I just have to do it. It doesn't matter what the consequences are, this is the fastest quickest way. It's going to be painful, but it will get the job done fast. Let's just get down there fast.

DW: And that used to be your style?

Yes—that used to be my style of working at making decisions, life decisions, working at things, if I'd come up with a problem that seemed impossible... well, too bad! I was going to make it work! I was going to do it no matter what, and I realize that often these were inappropriate ways of behaving, and of making decisions that never served me well in the long run. I would feel so claustrophobic after acting like that, that I'd have to then get out of the situation again. It never would work. So in this dream the feeling of going feet first is a careful, mature, thought-out, planned, cautious way of doing things, of making decisions. Now this dream has become a tool in my head. So that now when I'm facing decisions and doing things in my life, I'm thinking about doing them feet first. It's the security of knowing that if I do it feet first I will get there.

The presence of a respected mentor figure in Diana's dream is a clue that some teaching is trying to be imparted or modeled via the dream. The dream then proceeds to show her something about the way she acts (the classic function of an ego check motif); it tells her: "When you are presented with a difficult situation, your first impulse is to jump in head first without considering your options." Many ego check dreams stop at this point; they do not suggest a solution, they merely depict the current problem in an exaggerated form. But Diana's goes on to point out a possible solution: "Might it not work out better if you catch yourself, consider your options, and try a more cautious approach?"

In this case, we can see that Diana received and understood the message of the dream, then responded by resolving to make a deliberate change in her thought process and her behavior. She realized that her dreammaker had devised a very clear and helpful metaphor and presented it to her for her to adopt and make use of. Diana uses this feet first/head first metaphor as a tool in her head, and it has helped her in many critical life situations.

Responding by doing a ritual

When a dream suggests that some closure, completion, letting go, or saying goodbye are being called for on a certain issue, then the most fitting response may be a ritual of some kind.

At age 61, Tina had a dream of preparing a grave for her mother. In waking life her mother had been dead for more than ten years, but Tina still felt that her mother's influence was a strong and not always positive force in her life. She dreamed often of her mother; this dream she called *The Long, Shallow Grave*:

> *I'm trying to bury my mother. I'm digging a grave that seems very long,*
> *but too shallow to accommodate a proper burial. It's strange. In the*
> *dream it seems like the right thing to do but as soon as I wake up*
> *I know it won't work.*

Tina recognized that this dream image connected to her healing process of putting to rest her mother's negative influence on her life—it was, like the grave, very long but too shallow. Tina decided to do a ritual response. What kind of ritual would support and perhaps complete the task that her psyche was trying to accomplish? Since the dreammaker had already suggested burial (a common element in rituals), it seemed appropriate to continue along these lines. But this time Tina resolved to go deeper; she decided to dig a very deep hole in her garden and bury in it some significant objects that symbolized her mother's stultifying influence on her life.

In designing a ritual, it is important that the symbolism resonates with what the dreamer wants to accomplish. Humans have hard wiring for responding to ritual, so it will often be psychologically effective even for people who do not especially "believe" in it. A ritual designed to help with resolution of an unresolved issue would typically consist of an element of acknowledging followed by an element of release.

Responding by creating something

Occasionally, an object or figure appears in a person's dream that seems to have some special significance. When describing this object or figure the dreamer will use words and phrases that have a connotation of amazement and specialness ("incredible," "awesome," "beautiful," "mysterious," "weird feeling," "there was something about it," "important," "wow," etc.). In Jung's writing, the word "numinous" is often applied to such dreams, meaning "having a sense of the divine." Kate had such a dream, she called it the *Crystal Prayer Wheel*:

> *I'm on a beautiful beach in a place like Goa. There's glowing light everywhere. There's no one there except this one woman who has a stall where she's selling all sorts of different things—statues and pieces of jewelry. There's this one piece that I'm really drawn to and it looks like, a Tibetan prayer wheel. A long cylinder with carvings in it, and at the end there are two pyramids made of metal, perhaps brass. It looks almost like a puzzle. I have the feeling if I could figure out how to take it apart carefully that there would be something inside that would be very powerful, very helpful for me. Helpful for me in my personal healing, but also helpful for me in helping other people heal. I feel this object is somehow really important. I really want it, I just know I really need to have it. The woman shopkeeper looks diminutive and hippie-like, but she is pretty fierce when she sees I was looking at it. She says: "I don't think you're ready for that yet." At first I kind of feel defeated, like she must be right, I'm not ready for it. But then I feel that—no! I really need to have that and I am ready for it. That's where the dream ends—it's a bit of a standoff. I don't get the prayer wheel and we never really resolve it.*

The prayer wheel was exquisite. It had that quality of numinous importance that comes in some special dreams. She wanted it badly; it was something very important for her but she wasn't quite ready for it. Kate sensed that it referred to something in her waking life that she wanted badly but that she wasn't quite ready for. She made a connection quickly—she knew it had something to do with her confidence as a healing practitioner and as a person. She wasn't quite ready to step into her power and fully believe in what she was doing; and this is why the woman on the beach didn't want her to have the prayer wheel.

Creative responses are very well suited for this kind of dream motif. The investment of time and energy into an act of creating something matches the high value of the dream image. Kate made a lithograph print of the Tibetan prayer wheel (one copy of which hangs in my office). In creating this piece, she was declaring to the prayer wheel, to the vendor woman, and to herself: "I recognize how important you are. I'm honoring you with a new creation in my waking world to show you that I am now ready."

Responding by finding a way out of a negative situation

Do you have a version of the old school anxiety dream? You're back at school or college and something is wrong—you're not prepared, haven't been going to class, won't graduate, whatever your version is. Do you worry that this repeating dream might be delivering a dire and important message? (Why am I still having this dream?!) But ask yourself—is there a message? Or is it just an old brain fossil that won't go away? You must make this distinction with every repetitive dream. Consider the possibility that your brain is caught in a repeating loop. If this loop is playing itself over and over again, long after the circumstances that generated it have changed, chances are it is not serving any useful purpose. Unfortunately, these old brain loops ("brain worms" as some people call them) have real staying power; they tend to remain active in our brains (asleep and awake) long after they have outlived their usefulness.

Simone has been tormented by a repeating and horribly anxious dream for over five years. She is now 64 and the dream is about her son (now in his early forties). It is called *Can't Find My Boy!*

> *It's always the same dream, but in different settings. The most recent one—I am in a forest with big trees. We are on some kind of outing. My son gets lost. I run around frantically looking for him, calling out his name over and over! I wake up in a state of panic…*

This a very common (I would say universal) anxiety dream that young parents have about losing their children or having some harm come to them. But why is Simone dreaming it now, forty years after her son was a toddler?

The first thing we need to do is make sure that the dream is not repeating itself in its attempt to deliver an important message that the dreamer is blocking or ignoring. I asked Simone: "Is there any conceivable good reason for this dream scenario to be happening again and again?" She replied with no hesitation that she did not think so—"No. I've thought about it so many times and wondered if it was telling me that I had missed something as a parent or done something wrong. But then why wouldn't it give me more of an answer? It's just always the same; it's just redundant!"

Now we are sure that the repetitiveness of the dream is dysfunctional and not functional (message-delivering), we can proceed to treat it as a brain field motif (see chapter 18). Our goal is to help Simone find a way out of this deeply ingrained and tormenting neural field. Using the actual problematic situation in the dream as our starting point, I asked Simone to re-enter the dreamscape (in the woods, anxious about her lost boy). But now we bring in a new element—I ask her to catch herself, to be conscious that this is just a repeating loop she's caught in. What new outcome would she like to imagine? She decided to visualize herself moving out of the forest into a clearing. As she enters the clearing she sees her son as the adult he is now.

Simone practiced doing this in our session, then I asked her to repeat the imaginal exercise two or three times a day over the next two weeks.

Why is this repetition needed? The repetition of the newly generated solution, similar to the rehearsal phase in IRT (Imagery Rehearsal Therapy), is required to counteract the ingrained repetitiveness of the original problem. If your brain keeps taking you back to the same problematic place, you need to help it find a way out of that place, and then you need to practice *using* that way out. This principle of finding a solution and then practicing it applies to the waking brain (working on bad habits, addictions, negative thoughts, and negative beliefs), and it is equally true for the sleeping brain when it generates repeating bad dreams. Simone felt immediate relief from doing the imaginal exercise, and within a month the frequency of the nightmares started to decrease. She may soon be completely free from that old dream that has brought her nothing but panic and worry for decades.

Responding by working with a symbol that appeared in the dream

There are some dreams that shine a spotlight on a particular object or figure that seems to have an important symbolic meaning for the dreamer. Usually the meaning of the symbol is not fully understood but nevertheless its importance is clearly sensed. If you've had such a dream, try this for your response—find something to stand for the special object or figure that appeared in your dream and keep it close to you for a period of time.

Here is an example. This is the dream of 58-year-old Candace, who was anticipating a visit in which she would try to reconnect to her parents from whom she had been significantly estranged for many years. She called this dream *The Key and the Hook:*

> *I have lost my key. I'm searching for it in my old high school. My partner T is there with me, helping me look. We go out the back door. There are some bad men there, four of them. They spot me and start to follow us. They are going to rape me. Three of them go toward T and one of them comes toward me. He has a small hook as a weapon. I take the hook from him and sink it*

into his neck. Then I try to call the police, but nobody takes me seriously. A young woman saw the whole incident and I want her to give evidence that I was about to be raped and was trying to defend myself…

Candace immediately connected the dream to the anticipated visit with her parents. She had a fear of being psychologically and emotionally raped by them, as had happened on many previous visits. She had a fear of being hooked by her father into feeling like a disempowered child, and she connected this to the hook in the dream. She recognized that her tendency was to defend herself against her father's hook attack by lashing out and hurting him back; this she felt was depicted in the dream as her wounding the rapist with his own hook. And Candace also understood that this kind of defensive counter-attack always left her feeling guilty about hurting him; this dynamic was represented in the dream as the fear of being in trouble with the police and the need to justify her attack as necessary self-defense.

Candace understood the psychodynamics of the situation quite well but was still very concerned that when she actually entered the force field of the family home she would not be strong enough to prevent the anticipated rape and hook attack from happening again. This is an example of a family field motif which we will look at in chapter 20. The dream seemed to be warning her about the danger, but it also contained a new symbol—the key. What was the key referring to? As we considered the possible meanings of the key, Candace made an interesting connection. Perhaps the key was the awareness that both her parents were very immature and very damaged people who needed her compassion and love. If she could hold this awareness in her mind on the visit, perhaps it would protect her from the negative pull of the old family patterns. But at the same time Candace understood that the compassion she felt for them also had a hook-like aspect; it made her feel responsible for helping them find a way out of their own tormented webs of dysfunction. It also made her feel guilty when she had to hurt and disappoint them in order to look after herself; after all, they were only acting like the wounded children that they were. Candace realized that her compassion for them was both the hook and the key. It could work both ways.

As a response, I suggested a symbolic amplification—perhaps it would be helpful to bring the hook and the key together and wear them on a pendant as a kind of protective amulet that would help her stay clear and conscious when she went to visit them. Candace liked the idea and decided to try it. If and when she started to feel triggered and disempowered, she could think of the hook-key of her compassion and try to let it focus on the energy of the key rather than the hook.

Summary

If you're having trouble thinking of a good response for your dream, try approaching it from the perspective of what the dream is asking for. If you can answer that question, you should be right on the doorstep of formulating a good response. Practically speaking, most of us won't have the time and energy to respond to *all* our dreams, it would be a full-time job! Use your intuition to choose which of your dreams you will run with for the full distance, from the imaginal into the ritual, and in some cases all the way to manifesting an actual change in your life.

That brings us to the end of part 2—now you know the method. Start practicing it and developing your skills if you haven't already. Let's turn our attention now to the common dream motifs—how to recognize them and how to work with them.

PART 3

Common Dream Motifs

CHAPTER 15

Overview of Dream Motifs

Dreams are wild and therefore difficult to categorize. They seem to defy attempts to organize them into groupings of any kind. They can be so multifaceted and layered that it can be very difficult to say "this is an X type of dream and that is a Y type of dream." So why try? Why do we need to impose a typology on the dream world? Can we not just let them be what they are without trying to fit them into categories?

Yes we can, if we have a lot of time to mull over our dreams and feel no urgency to get anywhere quickly. And indeed this kind of mulling over approach can bring very rich rewards. However, if we are attempting to help someone else understand a dream within a limited time frame, mulling over will usually not suffice—it takes too long and it often ends up nowhere in particular. In dream facilitation, we need to use some kind of method, and we need ways to become oriented within the dream sooner rather than later. We need some kind of map to help us find our bearings, and often what this dream map essentially amounts to is the recognition of familiar motifs we have come across in dreams before. So, like it or not, I think we *are* trying to categorize dream motifs (at least those of us who work with dreams regularly); so we might as well set about to do it in a way that is as helpful as possible.

For me, the most useful way to categorize your dreams is to consider what the dream is asking you for. What does your dreammaker want you to do in response to understanding the message of the dream? Almost all coherent dreams can be looked at in this way (it is not the only way to look at a dream, of course, but it is always possible). In my experience orienting toward a desired response helps us do the most dynamic kind of dreamwork; it helps us reach deeper and faster into the potential of the dream and it sets up and supports a strong gradient toward self-awareness, change, and personal growth.

Many dreams contain more than one motif

Our dreammakers do not limit themselves to one motif per dream. A dream may contain more than one central motif and may be asking for more than one response. I have found that dreams with good working potential often present two central motifs. For example Domenica's dream of *The Big Loon* in chapter 3 opens with an ego check motif (she attempts to drive an unsafe car) and moves on to an inspiring contact motif (she sees the big loon). Both motifs are critical to understanding the dream and each calls for its own response. In my own dreamwork practice, I have made it a rule not to engage more than two motifs in one dream even in complex dreams where there are more than two. It just gets too confusing and I don't want to get overloaded, so we select the two most important motifs and work with those.

I have organized the dream motifs into fourteen groups, each of which has a chapter devoted to it. I present them in order of how frequently they are encountered, although all of them are very common and very important.

Each of the fourteen is essentially different from the others as it delivers a different message and asks for a different response.

The fourteen motif groups

1. Shadow motifs

Essential message: "An emerging part of you is being kept outside. It is now knocking at the door trying to get in."

Asking for: disowned, repressed, and potential parts of yourself.

2. Ego check motifs

Essential message: "Hey! Look what you're doing! Do you want to keep doing that?"

Asking for: a change in your ego position, attitude, and behavior.

3. Brain field motifs

Essential message: "At certain times you are stuck in a repetitive brain loop; when this happens, your mindset is such that you cannot choose and perceive freely."

Asking for: you to recognize the problematic neural field and find a way out of it.

4. Personal spirit motifs

Essential message: "Your spirit has suffered a trauma; since then you have not been whole. A chance for healing is now presenting itself."

Asking for: you to support the reunion of the orphaned part of your spirit with your whole self.

5. Family field motifs

Essential message: "Here is a depiction of a way you are still influenced by old conditioning from your upbringing and family of origin."

Asking for: you to recognize how the limiting family field operates and change it.

6. Relationship field motifs

Essential message: "You and your partner are stuck in a rut in the way you are relating. This is preventing you from perceiving and experiencing new possibilities in the relationship."

Asking for: you to recognize how the limiting relationship field operates and change it.

7. Introject motifs

Essential message: "You are trying to rid yourself of something that was forced into your psyche in the past."

Asking for: you to identify the foreign psychic content that was inculcated and support your psyche's attempts to weaken or purge it.

8. Self-discovery motifs

Essential message: "You are discovering more of yourself. Keep it up!"

Asking for: you to invest more energy and intention into self-discovery; to venture into new areas.

9. Rebirth motifs

Essential message: "You are in a period of profound change and creativity. You are reinventing yourself, reconceiving yourself, rebirthing yourself, or giving birth to something."

Asking for: you to identify where you currently are in the creative rebirth process and support that phase.

10. Inspiring contact motifs

Essential message: "Be amazed! Be inspired! You have something unique and remarkable within you!"

Asking for: you to support a full realization of the encounter that is happening.

11. Positive feedback motifs

Essential message: "You have just accomplished something very positive. Be aware of it, support it, encourage it, keep doing it!"

Asking for: you to invest more awareness and energy into the positive trend that is already happening.

12. Rogue part motifs

Essential message: "A part of your psyche has broken away from the whole; it is now acting autonomously and harming you."

Asking for: you to be aware of how the rogue part functions, so there can be a reduction in the harm it causes.

13. Dreambody motifs

Essential message: "Your dreambody has its own abilities, its own desires and needs."

Asking for: you to be attentive and supportive of what your dreaming body does and wants to do.

14. Somatic motifs

Essential message: "This is your material body here. You're close to being awake and I'm coming into your dream."

Asking for: these motifs do not typically ask for anything other than awareness of the material body and what it is experiencing.

Why motif recognition is so helpful in dreamwork

There is no doubt that we get great benefit from talking about our dreams, even when we do not recognize the type of dream we are talking about. But in order to do dream facilitation and be consistently helpful, I believe that motif recognition is critical. If you do not have some idea of the kind of message your unconscious is sending you, and what it might be asking you for, you cannot go much further. You simply do not know which of many possible paths to take.

Here is an example of a dream that illustrates how important it is to be able to recognize a dream motif. Fran was a 38-year-old woman who had a strict religious upbringing. For most of her adult life she has been subject to sudden and dramatic changes of her emotional state. She will be feeling fine, and then all of a sudden she will be feeling horrible, for no apparent reason. Fran had a very vivid dream that she named *Bag of Bugs on a Timer:*

> *I am in the bedroom of my current house, but I know that I'm in my parents' old house, where we lived when I was 7 to 16 years old. (This house shows up in many of my dreams.) I'm facing the closet and notice on the top of the shelf a small kitchen timer and a small drawstring bag. When the timer goes off, large cockroaches and spiders crawl out and cover every part of the room (walls, ceiling, furniture, windows, floor, etc.) leaving nothing resembling my bedroom. I don't recall if I ever turn away from the closet to look at them in my dream (I don't think I do), and at some point they fade. The timer goes off again and the whole thing repeats itself over and over until I wake up. I wasn't terrified in the dream (although when I woke up I was disturbed) but I definitely was asking "what the f—?"*

We worked with this dream in a group setting. Our first direction was to consider the bugs as a shadow aspect—an emerging part of Fran that was trying to be let out of the bag and gain entry into her sense of self. If the insects were a true shadow part they would, once allowed in and encountered, soon morph into something very positive. We asked Fran to try to make a positive identification with the cockroaches and spiders. She gave it a good try—but it didn't work:

> *I tried to turn around and speak to the bugs, trying to negotiate with them one at a time, but my dream self couldn't actually say anything to the bugs, or try to even reach out to engage them. I was frozen when trying to interact with the bugs. I tried to consider the positive aspects of the bugs, along the lines of tough, resilient, creative, sassy. But no matter how I tried to create a positive encounter with the insects, it just wouldn't stick.*

As the main facilitator, I felt that we were not on the right path; it just wasn't working. It was time to shift gears and try a different approach. I suggested looking at the bugs not as a shadow motif, but as an introject motif (a depiction of some foreign content that was forced into Fran's psyche in the past). If this were the case, then the goal would not be integration, but expulsion—a 180-degree turn in a different direction.

As soon as we started to look at the bugs in this way, the dream's meaning suddenly came into focus—Fran needed to kill and purge the bugs, not encounter them and integrate them. Even before she fully understood what the bugs referred to she now wanted to use the enormous energy of revulsion and hatred she felt toward them: "I burned a small corner of bugs as a way to start ridding them from my life...I felt a thousand times lighter when I did that."

Eventually, Fran connected the bugs to the early indoctrination of religious ideas and constructs from her childhood—"I immediately resonated with the understanding that the cockroaches and spiders represented the many lies, stories, influences that I have taken to be truth, when they in fact are not." The dream was a very graphic depiction of the struggle going on in her psyche to keep these ideas contained, a struggle that was only partially successful. Sometimes the bugs were safely sequestered in the bag, but at any moment they could all burst out again in full force. Before having the dream, Fran had never considered that she could aim for something more than containment, that she could actually try to expel these old constructs from her psyche. Understanding the message of the dream gave her permission to imagine this possibility for the first time.

Tip: When a dreamwork session bogs down and loses energy, it is usually because the central motif has not been recognized

When you think you're barking up the wrong tree, the essential message of the dream cannot come through clearly, which in turn means that it is hard to know what the dream is asking for; therefore, it is premature to try to think of a fitting response. When you find yourself bogged down in working with a dream, don't keep slogging through the same bog, try something different. The best thing to do is to revert to the method—go back to one of the orienting methods until a better sense of orientation comes into focus.

As you head into the next fourteen chapters, you will be presented with a lot of information. If you feel overloaded, I would suggest coming back to this touchstone—the whole point of being able to recognize dream motifs is that it can give you an immediate sense of what the dream is asking for. That's what you're looking out for. Every motif will be presented and discussed in the following format:

- the essential message of that motif

- what that motif may be asking for

- one or two dream examples of that motif

- the psychodynamics that give rise to that motif

- distinctive features of that motif

- dreamworking suggestions for that motif

A quick reference chart of the distinctive features of each motif can be found in Appendix 2. This will be helpful when you are working with a dream and trying to differentiate between two or more possible central motifs.

CHAPTER 16

Shadow Motifs

Essential message: *"An emerging part of you is being kept outside. It is now knocking at the door trying to get in."*

Asking for: *you to meet this disowned, repressed, or potential part of yourself, and let it in.*

Terri was 12¾ when she had her *Teenagers* dream; she was just beginning to enter puberty. She had many fears, especially about something bad happening to her or her family members. She named this dream *Teenagers Want to Come In*:

> *I'm with my family, doing something at home. Then some high school students come over our back fence into out yard. They're coming toward the house! I quickly lock all the doors. Then I realize I left the basement door open. I quickly run down and lock it just in time. The high school students are on their knees, pleading and begging to get in.*

Terri does exactly what most people do in their dreams when threatening figures approach—she runs to secure the door. Her first instinct is to keep the teenagers out. But (this is a hallmark of shadow dreams) her dreammaker points out that the "threatening" figures are not actually doing anything threatening. The teenagers are pleading and begging with her, they are not breaking down the door, hurting anyone, or doing any mischief. So … what does the dream want Terri to do? It seems to want her to change her attitude toward the teenagers, to challenge her reflexive fear reaction and consider opening the door to let them in.

From prior experience with this kind of dream, we suspect that if Terri does let them in (in her imagination) she will immediately experience a positive shift; she will start to appreciate the good qualities and energies that they bring. So I asked Terri to visualize opening the door and inviting one of the teenagers to come inside (just one for now to be cautious). How does it feel? "It's okay" she said, "it's fine. She's actually really nice."

The teenagers in this dream display the quintessential characteristic of shadow figures—they want to be let in. Psychologically speaking, this means they represent something that wants to come into Terri's personality, to be accepted by her as a part of her. The simple act of visualizing opening the door and letting one of the teenagers come inside will send a powerful signal to Terri's inner self that she is now ready to let this transformation happen. Terri is on the cusp of puberty, she is about to become a teenager herself, and this dream is a depiction of her fear of growing up. The transformation it refers to is inevitable, but things will go much more smoothly if she lets the teenagers inside proactively and willingly. If she refuses to let them in, they will gather energy, they will get rowdier. When they appear in the next dream, they will probably seem more insistent and more threatening.

This sense of inevitability arises from the psychological fact that you cannot keep the shadow out because it is a true part of you, only it's a part of you that you don't know much about yet. It's emerging, and we humans often find new and emerging things very threatening. This quality of being impossible to keep out is often represented as the dream ego fumbling with flimsy insecure locks and frantically trying to secure multiple entry points. As Terri said: "I quickly lock all the doors. Then I realize I left the basement door open!" It is as if the dreammaker is saying: there's no point running around trying to keep everything locked, the shadow will eventually find a way in.

Here's a different kind of shadow dream. This is the dream of a 47-year-old man named Brandon, he called it *The Outrageous Man:*

> *I see David Suzuki through a door, just a brief glimpse. Then I am up*
> *in a big room like an auditorium looking down at a stage. A young man*
> *walks into the room. He is super dynamic and full of energy. He grabs the*
> *edge of the stage with his teeth and somehow vaults himself up onto the*
> *stage. I'm surprised… amazed!*

Brandon's dream presents us with a very different take on the shadow figure. This outrageous man is not a frightening or negative figure, but he is someone very far removed from the person Brandon believes himself to be. In the dream this "far removed" state of affairs is depicted as an exaggerated distance between the outrageous man on stage and the dream ego, watching from a distant vantage point far back in the auditorium seats. Was the dream asking Brandon to approach the stage, to get closer to this outrageous man, perhaps even to meet him? I sensed that it was, so I asked Brandon to be the part of the outrageous man. Through this imaginal exercise, he began to feel that he might indeed possess some of these outrageous attributes himself. Brandon was aware of a strong resistance to going up on stage ("I'm not the kind of person who takes center stage") but perhaps he needed to challenge this resistance.

The cameo appearance by David Suzuki at the beginning raised the voltage and urgency of the dream. For Brandon, Suzuki represents a very inspiring and admirable figure, someone who is actually living out his full potential and purpose. Putting the two parts together the message seemed to be: "You have great potential, but to unfold it you must now overcome your resistance to taking the stage, sink your teeth into something that challenges you, and allow your outrageous side to come out."

Here's a dream where the shadow appears in a more frightening guise. 48-year-old Evan told me this dream, he called it *The Big Bear:*

> *In this dream people are trying to stay safe from a bear. He's brown at first, and then he turns into a sort of polar bear. I'm inside a warehouse with a girl, we're trying to explore sexuality, but we're aware of the bear being around outside. The fear of the bear coming is great. At one point we're outside on the corner in front of the warehouse, and the bear comes, scaring everyone. We just make it back into the warehouse door and I barely have time to lock it. Then he's there at the door. His massive head is butting the lock. The lock is too small, no sense of security. I wake up …*

This was a familiar cluster of motifs for me—a fearsome figure outside, the dreamer hurrying to lock the door, the inadequate lock—all are characteristic of a shadow dynamic. So I suspected that this bear might be a part of Evan that he was afraid of, a big strong part. I asked Evan to go back into the dream scene and be the bear on the other side of the warehouse door. He closed his eyes and started to imagine. He could not get into a strong identification with the bear, but a stream of associations started to come. Notice that his associations are a mixture of good and bad:

> *I like being the bear. But I don't really want to break in and scare people either. It reminds me of my father when he was sick—just lumbering around, not aware of other people's needs. Bears can just do what they want. Bears are hairy. I've been thinking of growing a moustache and a beard, and they would be white now … like this bear (laughs). Just let the beard come out the way it wants to come out. Whatever comes out is me. I've heard horror stories about bears—people caught in the woods, a bear comes along and no matter what they do the bear just mauls them and eats them. The bear nightmare. But this bear didn't do that. I feel he's*

more about my own power than anything else. He's the threat of my own masculine power. Being big. Being adult. Being initiated.

As Evan spoke, I witnessed the positive shift happening right in front of me. His bear monologue wove in and out of a tangle of negative associations (scaring people, selfishness, being insensitive to other's needs, lumbering, mauling, horror stories) but as it went on the good part emerged more and more clearly, and it ended up with Evan experiencing a strongly positive set of associations: masculine power, big, adult, initiated.

Evan's dream is a good illustration of how an essentially positive quality (masculine power) can become contaminated with negative associations from childhood (the selfish insensitivity of his sick father). Once this contamination has happened, it is hard to remove it from the psyche, and it will often result in a dream life that is populated with very ambiguous figures— mafia thugs and gangsters are extremely common shadow role players.

If you are not sure what kind of figure you are dealing with, use the re-enter and explore technique to meet the figure and find out more about it. If it shifts positive, this confirms that you are dealing with a shadow figure. If it doesn't, and particularly if it does some harm to the dream ego, you are probably not dealing with a shadow figure. We will be focusing on how to differentiate the many types of frightening dream figures in chapter 31.

Psychodynamics of the shadow motif

"Shadow" is a term coined by Jung referring to the parts of the personality that are despised, rejected, and ignored. For our purposes in this book I use the term "shadow" to include the meaning given above, and, more specifically, these three meanings:

- the parts of the potential personality that were repressed during the process of socialization

- the parts of the potential personality that are disowned and disliked because they are contaminated with bad associations and experiences from the past

- the parts of the potential personality that have not yet emerged and manifested

Thus, your shadow consists of all the true potential parts of you that have not yet been allowed in (into your personality and your sense of who you are). One of the most characteristic traits of a shadow figure is that he or she appears in dreams having a mixture of negative and positive traits, with the negative traits being more pronounced or appearing first. One reason that the shadow often makes its appearance in a "bad" disguise has to do with contamination from negative childhood experiences. If a child grew up with a frighteningly angry father, he or she will tend to mistrust all anger, even healthy anger; and will tend to disown and repress all types of anger. This anger does not disappear—it cannot because it is a true part of self—so it has nowhere to go but into the shadow. Later in life it will come back and knock at the door; and when it does the person will almost certainly have the same fear and mistrust toward it that he or she did as a child. Robert Bly's *A Little Book on the Human Shadow* provides a good description of how the socialization process contributes, often unavoidably, to the repression of true parts of self—parts that are "pushed into the shadow."

For movie lovers, there are many great movies that depict shadow themes. Two excellent examples are *Dr. Jekyll and Mr. Hyde* and *Fight Club*. In both these stories (spoiler alert), what at first seems to be two people turns out to be only two aspects of the same person, the known self and the suppressed and fearsome shadow. This is the very same plot twist that unfolds when we work with a shadow dream—the scary figure lurking outside your door turns out to be a part of you.

Yet we must encounter and ultimately welcome these shadow figures in order to grow. Our dreams will repeatedly present us with the opportunity to work on this issue. If the dreamer can find the courage to encounter the shadow figure, a transformation immediately begins—a transformation from negative to positive (the positive shadow shift).

Whenever change is afoot in the psyche, the counter-change forces are also mobilized, the conservative elements in the personality that want to keep things more or less the way they are. These elements characteristically appear in dreams as police, security guards, border guards, or other figures that enforce the powers of establishment and authority. Thus it is extremely common in shadow dreams for the dream ego to think of calling the police. This depicts a fundamental human tendency—to respond to impending change with apprehension, to attempt to stop it from happening and return to the status quo.

When your shadow is just starting to stir but has not yet emerged, it makes you hypersensitive to other people who possess the same qualities that it does. If your shadow is flamboyant, you will be triggered and irritated by flamboyant people. If you allow this flamboyant part to emerge and accept it into your sense of who you are, that irritation tends to disappear. Now that you are more flamboyant you can accept and appreciate this quality in others. Thus, any time you find yourself inexplicably triggered by a certain person, you should ask yourself: "What is it about him that bothers me so much?" It is very likely that this person is offering you an important shadow clue.

Distinctive features of a shadow motif

- somebody or something scary at the door that wants to come in
- being chased or followed by a scary figure
- a sense of danger and anticipated harm, but no harm is actually done
- trying to lock doors, flimsy or ineffectual locks

- trying to secure multiple entry points

- trying to call the police

- being triggered by figures that are wild, uninhibited, outrageous, crude, hypersexual, sacrilegious

Dreamworking suggestions for a shadow motif

I will describe the following dreamworking techniques as if you are using them by yourself on your own dream, but they can all be used just as effectively for facilitating another person:

- *Positive re-frame*
  If you recognize a shadow figure in your dream, imagine that figure as an aspect of yourself. *What would it be like if I had a bit more of that_____energy or quality? What would the good side of that be?*

- *Use of the imagination to encounter the frightening figure*
  Re-enter the dream scenario in your imagination (e.g., you are hiding in the closet, a scary figure is at the door). Decide to go to the door and encounter the figure. Greet him: *Hello. Who are you?* If you now start to feel more positive feelings about the figure, invite him to come in. Ask him: *What do you want?* Very often his answer will be some version of: *I want you to be more assertive, stronger, bigger, bolder, more yourself.* If this imaginal exercise opens up some new positive feeling, repeat it several times over the next few days. With this work you will be giving yourself the very thing your shadow dream is asking for—an encounter with an emerging part of yourself.

- *Be the Part*
  Switch places with the frightening figure at the door. Try being him for a while. Feel what it's like to be feared and

locked outside. Interview the figure; ask a question then switch roles and answer the question. *What do you want from me? Why are you here? Are you a part of me? What part? What will you do if I let you in?*

Further examples of this motif

Can't Find a Private Bathroom to Use, chapter 3
The Big Gray Dog, chapter 8
Scooped Up by a Gorilla, chapter 12
The Moon and the Mist, chapter 12

CHAPTER 17

Ego Check Motifs

Essential message: *"Hey! Look what you're doing! Do you want to keep doing that?"*

Asking for: *a change in your ego position, attitude, and behavior.*

Have you ever had an anxious dream of being in a car? Is it you driving the car? If not, what might that mean? Are you having trouble slowing down? What could that be referring to? Not sure where you're going? Can't see the road ahead? Can't get the car started? Can't even find your car? All these (and many more) are common variants of the driving problem dream, one of the top ten most common dreams in our culture. Why would your dreammaker send you such a dream? Feedback. It is giving you feedback on what you're doing and how you're living your life.

Stephanie, a 58-year-old woman, was dealing with a number of serious health concerns. In our first session she told me her dream of *Sliding Over the Edge:*

I'm standing at the top of some high bluffs looking out over a cliff toward the lake. I start down a path. I fall on my bottom. Then I'm sliding down these rocks (they're a nice brown color). I zoom down around a corner and out over a precipice … and I land on a jut-out … one leg on either side of this jut-out. I'm just sitting there, comfortably, with this canyon beneath me … and I wake up. I don't feel scared or anything. Just … "oh, here we are."

The first clue that we may be dealing with an ego check dream is the high elevation at the opening of Stephanie's dream; this is a very commonly used metaphor in dreams when a person is in a precarious or dangerous position in her life. The first fall is minor (onto her bottom) but it is followed by an uncontrolled slide toward a dangerous edge and a much more serious potential fall. This escalation of seriousness is typical of ego check motifs that are trying to warn the dreamer about dangerous behaviors and looming health problems. There is also a curious lack of concern displayed by the dream ego; a comfortable, matter-of-fact demeanor that is strikingly at odds with the life-threatening danger of the situation. This very short dream delivered three important warnings to Stephanie: first, you are at risk of a fall (she connected this to the current deterioration of her health situation); second, you need to stop the sliding as soon as it starts (by making active interventions) and not let the slide gather momentum; and third, you need to take this whole matter much more seriously because it could take you right over the edge.

I will never forget my dream of *The Little Furry Creature,* though it happened more than twenty-five years ago. It consisted of one single horrific scene:

I am hitting a small creature over and over and over again. It is a gray-brown color, the size of a mole or a mouse. I'm trying to kill it but it just won't die. Then I suddenly make eye contact with the creature somehow; as soon as I do this a powerful feeling of remorse and compassion for the wounded creature floods into me. I pick it up and hold it tenderly, hoping that it won't die. What have I done?! I wake up crying.

I knew instantly that this little creature was an aspect of me, a part of myself that I unthinkingly and automatically try to kill. As soon as it appears I try to kill it. It was as if I had been trained to do that, that's just what you do when the furry creature appears. I knew this dream was trying to get me to become aware of some trained behavior of mine, something that was hurting a small and vulnerable part of myself. As I thought about it, the connection dawned on me—the creature was the part of me that felt vulnerable and easily hurt. My stoic persona had been trained to kill (repress) this part as soon as it appeared in my feeling body.

My imaginal response to this insight was to visualize picking up the tiny wounded creature and talking to it, nursing it back to health, and re-assuring it that I would try to change this deeply conditioned pattern. My ritual response was to find a picture of an injured mole and place it on my altar space. My actual response involved cultivating a better awareness of what happens in my emotional body whenever something hurts me.

Since the time of this dream, I have come across many other dream versions of this same universal story. Remember Wendy's dream of *The Bug-Bird* discussed in chapter 9? It had the same pattern as my dream—an unthinking act of violence against a small animal followed by sudden identification, compassion, and deep remorse. Over the years I have found that the harsh treatment or killing of small and defenseless figures (animal or human) in dreams usually depicts strong repression of one part of self by another. These dreams characteristically employ extreme actions and strong emotional charge to get your attention and reflect back to you something problematic that you are doing. This mirroring and feedback function is the essence of the ego check motif.

Psychodynamics of the ego check motif

The key psychodynamic of the ego check dream is *feedback*—from the unconscious to the conscious ego. These dreams try to hold up a mirror, to compensate, to suggest, to correct. They point out where you are off track, dangerously out of balance, or just might be able to do a bit better. This kind of feedback may be hard to accept, and it is often vigorously resisted by the ego, but it can always be framed and understood as constructive in nature.

The inner intelligence of the unconscious mind can communicate with the ego in many ways, but the most common way is through the dream life. When we have a dream where this communication seems to be trying to hold up a mirror and get us to see something about ourselves that we haven't yet seen, then this can be called an ego check dream (or an ego check motif within a larger dream).

When a figure in your dream behaves badly, you may not be inclined to consider this as a depiction of some aspect of you. Try it on anyway. See if it fits. If you dream of a dictator always take a moment to ask yourself: is it possible that I'm being dictatorial? This is the basic Inner/Outer orientation that you should do for every seemingly external figure in your dream. If you feel an emotional charge as you try it on, this suggests that the dream figure is indeed pointing inward. In the case of an ego check motif, this emotional charge will usually be a negative one, anything from mild embarrassment to horror (like the horror I felt as I woke up from my dream of the small furry creature). You are being shown a glimpse of yourself that you could not see before; this is good news, not bad news! If you don't accept the feedback as true, you may miss a good opportunity for self-reflection, self-change, and personal growth.

Distinctive features of an ego check motif

- a dream figure or the dream ego acting in a problematic way

- driving difficulty

- a famous or infamous figure in a dream

- the dream ego or another figure killing or harming a small and defenseless figure

- the dream ego or another figure is up precariously high or in danger of falling

Dreamworking suggestions for an ego check motif

The following dreamworking techniques are described as if you are using them by yourself on your own dream, but they can all be used just as effectively for facilitating another person:

- *Moving from Outer to Inner*
  Unwelcome, shameful, and unfamiliar attributes of self are usually projected outward onto other people and institutions, both in waking life and when we look at our dreams. If you dream of a figure acting badly, always activate the Inner/Outer orientation and pose the question: "Can I look at this figure as a part of me? If so, what part would it be?" If it doesn't fit, that's fine, don't force it; but you should always try it on before you dismiss it.

- *Be the Part*
  If you're having trouble seeing a dream figure as a part of yourself, try playing the role, being that part. If you dreamed of a wasp try being the wasp; you may suddenly become aware of a waspish part of your own nature. If you can succeed in doing this, you will gain something: self-knowledge, integrity, humility, coherence, a new way of being, and often an increase of life energy.

Further examples of this motif

The Tiny Neglected Puppy, chapter 1

The Big Loon, chapter 3

Pit Bull Kills My Cat, chapter 3

Eddie Shooting Me Again and Again, chapter 3

Knocking Out the Two Monkeys, chapter 4

Big Man Sticking Me With Pins, chapter 6

The Bug-Bird, chapter 9

The Man With Two Guns, chapter 12

Going Feet First, chapter 14

The Weird Handshake, chapter 21

CHAPTER 18

Brain Field Motifs

Essential message: "At certain times you are stuck in a repetitive brain loop; when this happens, your mindset is such that you cannot choose and perceive freely."

Asking for: you to recognize the problematic neural field and find a way out of it.

Why do human beings find it so hard to change, even when they have a clear idea of the kind of changes they want to make? This is one of the most perplexing problems in psychology. Dreams give us one important answer; they point to the presence of a kind of matrix of stuckness that appears again and again in the dream life. The dreams that arise from and depict this stuckness are repetitive and have frustrating and negative feeling tones. These dreams seem to say: "This is why you cannot make the change you are trying to make. It is as if you are under the influence of an invisible magnetic field that is affecting you in a very significant way."

I refer to these phenomena as limiting fields. I define a limiting field as: a field effect that can limit and distort a person's perceptions, emotional reactions, and freedom of choice. In dreamworking I have found it helpful to delineate three kinds of limiting fields. The three are very similar and have broad overlap, but they are asking for slightly different responses: the brain field is asking you to do some brain training to address self-imposed limitations; the family field is asking you to do some strategizing and brain training to address limitations that arise in connection with your family of origin; and the relationship field—asking you and your partner to work together to change ingrained relational patterns. In this chapter we will be focusing on the brain field motifs.

Here's an example of a typical brain field dream. The dreamer is Grant, a 55-year-old man who is very accomplished and successful in his career, yet he still has a nagging repetitive dream of being held back in school. He called this dream *Missing One Course:*

> *I'm always taking some class in this dream. Often it has to do with math. But it's always an entrance requirement into university. Passing this course is the barrier between me and the next step in my academic progress. I'm struggling, I just don't get it. I don't pass. The sensation in the dream is of being caught in limbo; not able to move forward because I have this one piece missing.*

The first thing we need to distinguish with this type of dream is whether its repetitiveness is functional (delivering and redelivering a critical message that Grant has not yet understood and acted upon) or dysfunctional (the result of an old and outdated brain fossil). I will usually ask: "Can you think of any positive reason why you would need to get this dream message again and again? Or do you no longer need to have this dream and the feeling it creates?" In most cases the dreamer will intuitively know the answer. Grant considered the question carefully and decided he would like to move on from this whole scenario. He had already moved on in his life, in the dream he just seemed to be stuck in a time warp.

Having decided to work with the dream as a brain field motif, we now know what our goal is—to help Grant recognize when he is caught in the brain field (in either waking or dreaming life) and practice finding a way out of it. We used the re-enter and explore technique. Grant closed his eyes and went back into a recent version of his dream. He felt the old familiar anxiety and frustration for a few moments, then I asked him to catch himself and let himself become aware that he is caught in a time warp. It was time to make a little change. I asked Grant to consider a new option—he can walk away from the whole scene. He visualized walking right out of the school, down the front steps, and off toward a new horizon.

I have found through trial and error that when working with dreams like this one the best results come when you begin your visualization in the problematic place, then catch yourself, realize that the scene can be changed, and finally exit that place, leaving through a door, closing it behind you, and walking right away. The symbolism of escaping from a place translates into the possibility of being able to escape from an old and ingrained neural network. Usually some repetition is required to "convince" your brain that there really is a way out. I asked Grant to repeat his imaginal exercise of walking out of the school once a day for a week. Over the following months, Grant began to notice that his vague feeling that he was somehow held back from progressing further in his profession was beginning to shift. The repetitive school dreams did not come nearly as frequently, and when they did Grant went back to the imaginal exercise of walking away.

Lidia, a 27-year-old woman, consulted me for her health issues, but her most pressing concern was anxiety about death and dying, her own death and dying. It terrified her and she could not stop thinking about it, although there was no apparent medical reason why she should be so concerned with her death. She told me the following dream, we called it *Can't Find the Spider*:

I live in a house in a field near the top of a mountain. I live there with my husband. One day I sense that a spider got into the house. I look for it but can't find it. I have to find it or I can never rest! I cannot relax with the possibility of that spider being somewhere in the house. My husband looks for it but he can't find it either.

What does Lidia's spider represent? You can't just go to the dream dictionary and look up "spider" (well I suppose you can, but it probably won't help you much). The spider is clearly something very negative and frightening for her. In my experience, when you come across a frightening dream figure like this you need to consider a range of possibilities:

- It could be a shadow figure—an emerging part of Lidia that she should encounter and integrate. In this case, the desired response would be to summon the courage to find and face the spider.

- It could be an introject—a negative belief system forced into Lidia in childhood. In this case, the desired response would be to expel or kill the spider.

- It could be a brain field motif, a depiction of a negative thought pattern that Lidia cannot control, that her brain keeps doing to her. In this case, the desired response would be to train her brain not to think about the spider.

- It could be a depiction of a disease state, something lurking within Lidia's body. In this case, the response would involve a focused effort aimed at finding out where the spider is and how dangerous it is, and perhaps taking specific action against it.

- It could be a depiction of an external figure or problem in Lidia's life, perhaps someone who is spider-like is lurking and hiding in some corner of her life. In this case, the dream might be trying to warn her about the seriousness of this situation and asking her to address it more proactively.

You cannot be sure. Only Lidia can be sure. As we worked on the dream together, Lidia became more and more convinced that the spider was a depiction of her fear of death. Somehow this awful fear had got inside her, and now that it was inside her she could find no peace. She suffered from a terrible restless anguish that was probably at the root of most of her other health concerns. Lidia ran from one practitioner to the next desperately trying to find answers and reassurance; in the dream this was depicted as a frantic search to find the spider and get it out of the house. But, like in the dream, nobody can find the spider and the terrible uncertainty remained.

With this insight, Lidia identified the spider as a brain field motif. We were dealing with a deeply ingrained neural network that generated intense fear and uncertainty about death. This is what we need to treat, and it can only be treated by getting out of it. I asked Lidia to imagine walking out of the house, out of the field that the house is situated in, to close the gate behind her, and walk away down the mountainside. An immediate and palpable sense of relief came to Lidia as she did this. She had never considered walking away before, all her energies had been spent on searching for the lurking spider inside the house. This relief was not an instant cure, of course; Lidia needed to practice the visualization many more times. But even this first time gave her a precious sense of hope—perhaps it would be possible to get to a place where she wasn't anguishing about the spider!

Psychodynamics of the brain field motif

These dream images depict and arise from firmly ingrained neural networks that have become seemingly "hard-wired" in the brain. Some of these neural fields are very old; they are like brain fossils—remnants of something that existed a long time ago. They may have outlived their usefulness and can give rise to repetitive and dysfunctional thinking. They also give rise to repetitive dreams. Such dreams can show the dreamer in a clear and exaggerated way where his brain is caught in an old repeating loop.

Surprisingly often, you will find that field-like dream settings (fields, pastures, meadows, malls, courtyards, schools, and large public buildings are all common) are signaling the presence of a limiting field motif. One of the definitions of a "field" in physics is "a region in which a particular condition prevails." When your dreammaker locates your dream in a field-like setting it may be pointing out: you are now under the influence of a particular condition. In Lidia's case the prevailing dream condition was: in this place you cannot rest or find peace until you find the fearful hiding thing that cannot be found.

Can new and healthy neural fields be developed to "replace" old dysfunctional fields? This is a central question in psychology and psychotherapy. I believe that they can, but it usually requires a lot of hard work—a new and better neural field must be established through repeated effort and sustained focus of intent. This kind of retraining of the brain lies at the heart of the cognitive behavioral therapy (CBT) model; it is also a cornerstone of many mindfulness and meditation traditions.

Brain field motifs are most easily recognized by their negative and repetitive sense of familiarity, a feeling that the same dream or the same feeling or situation has happened many times and is always the same ("Oh no! I can't believe I'm still having that dream!"). Our childhood schools were, for better or worse, the places where we received much of our early brain training, so it is not surprising that traces of this training would still be present and active within us, even decades later. A dream that is set in your old school or college is probably arising from, and drawing your attention to, the presence of a brain field, especially if it has a repetitive and negative feeling tone. This is also true (to a somewhat lesser extent) of the very closely related family field motifs and relationship field motifs.

These dreams ask: do you want to stay stuck in this old pattern for the rest of your life?

Distinctive features of a brain field motif

- back at one's old school, tested, unprepared, unqualified, late, in trouble, held back from graduation

- being locked in, imprisoned, restrained, having a binding contract, having no choice

- moving but not able to choose the direction, on a train, a track, in a force field or a maze, running through corridors or stairwells

- trying to communicate or make a connection but can't

- feeling triggered, overwhelmed by extreme surges of inappropriate emotion

Dreamworking suggestions for a brain field motif

- *Re-enter and explore*
  Go back into the dreamscape, Let yourself feel the old familiar feeling of being there. Now catch yourself. Realize that you can change this scenario. Choose an action that feels right. You may want to use the literal imagery of exiting from a place—find a door or a gate, open it, go outside, close the door behind you, and walk away. Now check in with yourself—how does it feel to be out of that space? Any regret? Any unfinished feeling? Do you want to go back and do it differently? (If so, you absolutely can.) If it feels right you have found a way out! Well done!

- *Using your imagination to reinforce your new neural field*
  Once you've found a way out, rehearse it a few more times
  until this new exit strategy itself starts to become ingrained.
  The more deeply ingrained a neural pathway is the more
  easily it can be found and used. Practice makes perfect. Take
  full advantage of your brain's neuroplastic potential. Until
  this kind of work has been done, asking yourself to choose a
  new response over an old established response is like asking
  water to run downhill in a faintly etched groove and not find
  its way into a nearby deep channel.

Further examples of this motif

Can't Leave the Meadow, Introduction
Pit Bull Kills My Cat, chapter 3
The Roller-Coaster Ride, chapter 12
Can't Find My Boy!, chapter 14

CHAPTER 19

Personal Spirit Motifs

Essential message: "Your spirit has suffered a trauma; since then you have not been whole. A chance for healing is now presenting itself."

Asking for: you to support the reunion of the orphaned part of your spirit with your whole self.

At age 58, Virginia had been divorced for many years and was not currently in a relationship. She wanted to be, but she felt this desire was somehow blocked and sabotaged by a part of her nature that she could not understand or control. She told me her dream of *The Two Urchins:*

> *I'm driving and my ex-husband is sitting beside me. I turn down a major street, and as I make the turn an urchin girl pops up right in front of the car. I stop, she's in front of the car with her bicycle, and there's a show-down. She's staring me down, and she won't move. I'm getting a little impatient. So I move the car just a little bit and I just "bump" her bike. She erupts into a huge outburst of how I've hurt her; she's making a huge*

scene. So I stop the car, get out, and take her to the side of the road, on the sidewalk. I need to calm her down. I try to be patient with her. I start asking her where she lives. And at some point she morphs into two children—an 8 or 9 year old and a 4 or 5 year old, so there are two of them now. The older one is petulant and manipulating; the 4 or 5 year old is extremely frightened.

The opening scenario (a couple driving and running into some impediment) can be seen as a retrospective relationship field motif (you'll be reading more about relationship field motifs in chapter 21). It is giving Virginia some information about how her old relationship became stuck. The dream points out that this problem of the two girls blocked her relationship from moving ahead. And now, many years later, she still has the same problem—the urchin girls are still orphaned and living on the street. Is it now the right time to get out of her car and deal with them? I suspected it was. I soon discovered that Virginia's attitude toward the urchins was primarily one of impatience. When she re-entered the dreamscape to talk with the urchins she felt irritated, inconvenienced, and manipulated. She could not feel much sympathy for them and it was blocking any evolution of her relationship with the girls. This was our working point.

I asked Virginia to be one of the urchins, preferably the older one, since it was the older one with whom she was most impatient. Gradually, a sense of identification and empathy began to develop. Virginia's emotional body opened up and she started to feel what it was like for these two girls, orphaned, living on the street without any adult around to care for them. Virginia started to open up to the possibility of an ongoing relationship with the urchins. She wasn't sure she wanted to adopt them and take them home, but at least she could spend some imaginal time with them. She was also beginning to understand why there were two, an older and a younger; the younger one was holding most of the fear, pain, and trauma, and the older one was brought into existence as the best that could be done under the circumstances to look after the younger one.

The older urchin was a depiction of the self-care system Virginia had created to make life bearable after some rupturing trauma occurred in her childhood. The original trauma, she was sure, dated from attachment issues in early childhood. At this stage of her process, however, it is not so important to look back toward these old traumas, but to keep the focus on the re-uniting and healing that is trying to happen in her present-day psyche, and also address the feeling of irritation that is blocking it.

Here's another example, a more urgent and horrific depiction of a personal spirit problem. Anita had recently had a difficult experience at work, a bad experience with a client that sent her into a tailspin of severe self-criticism. She had the following dream; she called it *The Hungry Ghost:*

> *I'm in my house. Something terrible has happened in the basement. My friend Shelley has been attacked and killed by a hungry ghost. The ghost has a male energy, very dangerous. It has attacked Shelley and cut her up into pieces. I'm trying to ignore this situation, hoping that somebody else will take care of it, but nobody does. I'm cuddling with my grandmother, trying to pretend that nothing bad has happened. I feel that I can't hide it anymore, I've got to tell someone. I go to my grandfather, but he's old and in a wheelchair, there's nothing he can do. I know I have to go tell my father. I'm dreading this, but I have to do it. I tell my father: "Shelley has been murdered!" Then I break down and start sobbing. Oh my god! I'll never recover from this! I wake up terrified.*

I asked Anita what qualities her friend Shelley has (here I am working in step 2 of the method: Clarifying by asking for the dreamer's associations). Anita described Shelley as: "soft, innocent, virginal, the kind of woman that male sexual predators prey upon." Next I asked her what she would associate with the hungry ghost. She replied that this term came from her exposure to Eastern Buddhist mythology, referring to an insatiable evil spirit capable of great harm. I asked what she would associate with being "cut up into pieces." Anita connected this to the case of an infamous sexual predator who cut his victims up into pieces; she went on to make another spontaneous and very resonant connection: "I cut myself up severely for making mistakes of any kind, even small mistakes." I asked her to say more about this. "My father would yell terribly when I made a mistake, so I felt the mistake would be unfixable and I would lose all my sense of self-worth."

In an instant the dream was connected. It is about the harm done to a soft and vulnerable part of Anita by another part, a severe critical part that was originally introjected by her father but has its own autonomous life in the basement of her psyche. Anita had lived with this internal problem for her whole life, but recently for some reason it started to become intolerable. Anita agreed that although the dream may have been triggered by the recent life event (her bad interaction with a client and subsequent barrage of self-criticism), its real roots were much deeper and older.

Anita and I pondered—what can be done right now to help the wounded Shelley part? When it comes to personal spirit motifs, always work with the assumption that the dream figure is not literally dead, even if it is portrayed as dead in the dream. In almost all cases, the wounded figure will come back to life when the dreamer imagines approaching them like Snow White or Sleeping Beauty awaking from the kiss of the prince. Shelley did come back to life as Anita imagined approaching her, her body now re-formed and no longer in pieces. I asked Anita if she could express an intention to Shelley—that she would stay with her and care for her. This is the essence of what the personal spirit wants from the ego—reunion and loving care. Anita imagined saying this to Shelley. Now the healing of an old traumatic wound was underway.

As a ritual response, I suggested that Anita get a doll to represent her Shelley-like part, do an enactment of bringing the doll up from the basement, and keep it close by in her bedroom for a time. Ritual reminders like this can be very helpful in personal spirit work because they counteract the tendency for the dreamer to "re-forget" the painful memories and feelings the dream brought to the surface.

In the months following their original dreamwork sessions, both Anita and Virginia experienced the feeling of coming into a fuller sense of self that happens after re-gaining a lost part. They both became less troubled, happier, more energized, and more optimistic for the future. If you think you've had a personal spirit motif appear in your dream, put this at the top of your dreamwork priority list; these motifs have an urgency that trumps other inner work. Your goal is quite simple—reunification with a part that you have been separated from. Your work will be well rewarded.

Psychodynamics of the personal spirit motif

The personal spirit can be defined as the aspect of a person that needs to be whole; to have a firm sense of self and an unbroken continuum of personal history. If your wholeness is split apart by trauma you will want to reunite yourself, and this will give rise to dreams of lost and abandoned figures who appeal to you for relationship and connection.

Personal spirit dreams are extremely common, universal in fact. They are the dreams of the inner child, of abandoned babies and lost children. They have a characteristically poignant and painful feeling tone because they tell the story of an old hurt that caused a separation within the self. And they are perhaps the most hopeful and positive type of dream we can possibly have, because they indicate that the psyche is now trying to re-unite itself and become more whole. If a person is traumatized past the point where his or her coping mechanisms can hold everything together, the psyche suffers a rupturing wound and the personal spirit becomes, to some degree, uncoupled from the ego consciousness. The person is no longer whole and no longer has a continuous personal story. When this happens a whole cascade of defensive adaptations may occur, including splitting, dissociation, developing soothing inner worlds of fantasy, using food and substances to avoid feeling, and forgetting parts of one's life.

People who have suffered this kind of wound become to some degree dis-spirited; they have lost a part of their full self, and there is a corresponding loss of energy, vitality, and security. Now there is a tension created in the psyche, since the personal spirit does not like to be in the "unnatural" state of being separated from the ego. Philip Pullman's novel *The Golden Compass* (*Northern Lights* in the UK), part of a series together called *His Dark Materials*, captures the terrible poignancy of this state of separation. If a person is split apart from their *daemon* (a personal spirit in the form of an animal) in this fictional world, they suffer a terrible soul wound and become a ghostly, dis-spirited shell, still alive but only barely. The unbearably painful feeling might break through the protective wall of forgetting at any moment and produce the flashback phenomenon characteristic of post-traumatic stress disorder (PTSD). This tension gives rise to a whole category of dream motifs—the personal spirit motifs. These motifs depict the ongoing drama of the personal spirit trying to get back to a state of wholeness. For more excellent resources on trauma and the dreams of traumatized people, see the Recommended Resources section at the back of this book.

Distinctive features of a personal spirit motif

- a figure who is dead, murdered, abused, badly injured, suffering, sick, or starving (it could be a baby, child, adult, animal, or plant)

- a feeling tone of loss, suffering, separation, grief

- an abandoned baby, child, or animal

- orphans, parents separated from their children

- suddenly realizing that you were supposed to be looking after a baby, child, or animal

- two lost children, one younger and one older

- fragmentation of something that should be whole

Dreamworking suggestions for a personal spirit motif

- *Re-enter and explore*

  If you have a dream of a figure who is suffering, lost, wounded, or dead, the first question to ask yourself is "Is this figure a part of me? Did I just get a glimpse of my own wounded spirit?" If you get the sense that the figure is pointing inward, the urgency of the situation will start to dawn on you. This is serious! What can be done about it? Remember, you do not need to know what part of you this is or what traumatic event in your life is being referred to; that will come later. Right now your task is to help the suffering figure. Using your creative imagination, re-enter the dreamscape and move toward the suffering figure, consider picking it up, holding it, caring for it, assessing what it needs. If you are able to do this, the work of reconnection has begun. If not, there may be some block standing in the way. This block needs to be identified and addressed.

- *If there is a block, investigate it*

  Personal spirit dreams often exhibit the classic Dynamic/Stuck pattern—the dream ego will feel an urge to make a connection with the orphaned figure, but some problem presents itself and prevents the connection from happening. In the *Yuri/Ari* dream you will read in chapter 27, the problem is the obstinate foster father. In *The Two Urchins* discussed earlier in this chapter, the problem is the dream ego's impatient and irritated feeling. The dreammaker is usually very clear and insistent in such dreams in pointing out "X is trying to happen but cannot until Y happens."

Typically, this will set the table for a twofold response, one part to support the dynamic urge and the other to address the blockage.

Further examples of this motif

The Tiny Neglected Puppy, chapter 1
The Dead Floating Baby, chapter 11
The Baby With No Skin, chapter 12
The Babies in the Freezer, chapter 13
Come Find Me, chapter 24
Yuri/Ari, chapter 27

CHAPTER 20

Family Field Motifs

Essential message: "Here is a depiction of a way you are still influenced by old conditioning from your upbringing and family of origin."

Asking for: you to recognize how the limiting family field operates and change it.

Family field motifs have much in common with brain field motifs—both arise from and depict strongly ingrained neural fields that can be activated in your brain. But the family field does not just exist within you, the individual, it exists collectively around your whole family of origin. It is a shared field that includes not only your nuclear family, but your extended family, and to some extent your whole clan (cultural community with shared identity and values). It can be re-activated whenever you are in proximity to your family of origin.

Here's an example—this is the dream of a 31-year-old man named Ben. He called it *The Everything on Fire Bear:*

I am in a house. It is in the town where I grew up, but it is not a house I recognize. Two evil TV sportscasters are in the house. They are glaring at me. They unleash the "Everything On Fire Bear" on me. I feel confused. I see a bear made out of flames come around a corner into the living room, lumbering toward me at a slow, methodical pace. As it bumps into things, they catch on fire. I run outside, avoiding their attempts to trap me in the house. Then I find myself outside, in a backyard of a house I do not know. It is a house that many of my friends lived in when I was a child, and where we used to play. So I'm hiding in the backyard, and I can see the evil sportscasters with the Everything on Fire Bear out on the street, causing havoc. Three white unicorns come running into the backyard toward me. I can see in their eyes that they are scared, but I also sense that they are full of love for me. We hide together. I look up, and see the evil trio come into the backyard and walk toward us...

Next thing I remember, we are back in the original house. The three unicorns' heads are mounted on plaques on the wall. There are about two other plaques on the wall that I can't quite see, but I feel like they are other animals or people they killed. The evil sportscasters once again send the Everything on Fire Bear to get me. It starts lumbering toward me again, but this time I can't find a way out. I know that I can outrun it, it moves at such a slow pace, but this time all the doors and windows are locked and I can't get out. I run to the kitchen, where I see a friend of mine from my current school. She is washing dishes. She is encouraging me, cheering me on, hoping I can get out. Then I notice there is a patio door in the kitchen (as there was in my childhood home). The door is open just a crack, about 6 inches. I go to open it more but it's jammed. I try frantically to squeeze my way through the small opening. I can see a huge green field outside with lots of room to run. I'm so close to getting out, but just can't squeeze through. The evil trio are right behind me now. I am panicked. I wake up.

As Ben and I looked around for some orientation in this dream, I suspected the presence of a family field motif because of the setting—it takes place in Ben's childhood neighborhood. Next, our key watershed question is about the fiery bear—is this an inner or an outer figure? If we take it to be inner, it would most likely be a shadow figure, frightening at first but shifting toward the positive once encountered. This was Ben's first inclination, so we started out along this path. Working with the dream in a group setting, we asked Ben to "be" the bear. He immediately listed several positive potentials of the fiery bear but something did not feel right. There was a sense that he had researched the fire+bear qualities in advance and was plugging them into the dreamwork rather than spontaneously feeling a sense of identification with the fiery bear. The energy was not there (usually a sign that the central motif has not yet been recognized).

So we switched our bear bearings from inner to outer; I set up a connection attempt based on my suspicion that we were primarily dealing with a family field problem and not a shadow problem: "If the dream is pointing to some problem in your family of origin, who would the fiery bear be?" Ben immediately knew that the bear was a depiction of his mother, the most inflammatory figure in his childhood life. Suddenly the energy in the room went up. Now we were on the right track. The desired response also came into focus: the dream was asking Ben to find a way to get out of the house, exactly what he was trying to do, but was not quite able to do at the end of the dream. This response would be the 180-degree opposite of the desired response for a shadow motif, which would be to summon the courage to face and encounter the threatening figure.

There are several warnings in the dream that Ben should not try to work on this family field problem by making a heroic stand and challenging his mother in some way: the size of the bear, its lumbering and inflammatory nature, the presence of an "evil trio" (being outnumbered three to one), and the ominous sense that three unicorns have already been killed in this place. All these elements indicate that this house is still very dangerous to him. This would mean that his family of origin and the family home are still dangerous to Ben in some critical way. He needs to do his personal work elsewhere, then someday he may be strong enough to return and try to change the family field, but not now. So our response was aimed at getting out. What was blocking the door from opening enough to allow his escape? This was the immediate problem that Ben needed to solve.

Here's another example of a family field motif. Rita, who was 40 years old and of Italian-Canadian background, consulted me for help with depression. She connected her depression to three major issues: a stressful and unsatisfying job, the lack of a life partner, and a feeling of troubling incompletion around her father's recent death. Her father was an abusive alcoholic and they had a very difficult relationship. She told me her dream of *Mending the Black Apron*:

> *I am lying in bed and I am in the arms of a man, but there is no face to the man, it is just his chest. I feel very safe. Then there is a knock at the door—it is my father, who wants to come in. He is very frustrated so I let him in. I ask the man who is standing naked to hide behind the door as I open it because I don't want my father to know he is there. My father comes in and begins looking for something; he seems very annoyed and frustrated. He finds what he is looking for and walks out of the room, and I follow directly behind him. We go into another room and my father walks over to a cousin of mine, an older woman, and just stands there next to her. This cousin hands me an apron—my grandmother's black apron. I know it had to be mended so I think—I need a needle for this. So then I see the needle… it is a large needle. As I am taking the garment I think: "I can't use this needle"… it's too big of a needle… I am going to have to find a smaller needle to mend this." And that is the end of the dream.*

Dreamworker: What do you associate with your grandmother's black apron?

Repression. Having lots of children. She was a housewife and had lots of children. She was a slave to everybody and lost herself. Her identity was taken away from her. She wore the black apron when she was mourning for her husband.

DW: What would it mean if that apron was given to you?

If that role was given to me? I'd be dead. I'd be spiritually dead.

Rita's dream has a common structure—it shows something dynamic and positive trying to happen in her psyche, then shows something that is blocking this promising change. It suggests that Rita has recently been learning how to trust intimacy with men (relaxing and feeling safe in the arms of her lover at the beginning of the dream). This is a very positive development, but it is blocked from happening by two things—first, the intrusion of her father, and second, her acceptance of the black apron. The intrusion of her father she understood and connected quite readily—he is still (even after his death) so intrusively and abusively present in her psyche that this interferes with her developing good relationships with men. To put it another way—she has always found it hard to trust men because she anticipates that they will suddenly start to behave like her father.

The acceptance of the black apron was a bit more mysterious, but with a bit of facilitation Rita was able to make the connection through association—she associated her grandmother's black apron with the repressive identity she was expected to accept as a woman raised in a family with traditional Italian values. This is a very good example of a family field dream—it shows the lasting effect of old conditioning and belief systems from the dreamer's upbringing. Rita does not consciously accept these old beliefs anymore, but they are still exerting a powerful influence in her unconscious, which is limiting her perceptions and choices in the area of relationships. By the end of the session, Rita understood that she needed to address these two specific problems before her love life could become unblocked.

Psychodynamics of the family field motif

We must all grow up within a family of some kind. Most of us grow up within concentric family rings with the nuclear family at the center, moving out through extended family, community, clan, and culture. Each of these family rings exerts its field effect on the young child and helps form them, for better and worse. Later in life, as the individuality of a person asserts itself more urgently, he may need to liberate himself from the influence of these early field effects. What had in the past been accepted as a given may now seem limiting and even intolerable.

Thus a family field can be defined as a type of limiting field sustained not only by your own individual psyche but by the collective psyche of the larger family units you are a part of. As with the other types of limiting fields, these fields are developed in childhood and give rise to pervasive distortions of the way one perceives, feels, and reacts to the world. These distortions are often not readily explained by your current life situation and are not responsive to normal therapies. One of the reasons they are not typically responsive to normal therapies is that the fields are re-constellated whenever you find yourself in the presence of an original family member. Even if you have come a long way in your own personal process of growth and individuation, you might still be powerfully influenced when you re-enter the collective field of your family of origin. You will often feel childlike, disempowered, and easily triggered by events that might not affect you in any other context.

Many people have a fear of becoming parents because they may pass on some negative trait that will cause great suffering in their children, similar to the suffering that they themselves feel. Very often this concern is due to the presence of a strong and negative family field effect that will be clearly depicted in their dreams. Working with these dreams may, in some cases, allow them to diminish the negative influence of their family field, and even open up the possibility of parenthood.

Distinctive features of a family field motif

- dream setting is in your childhood home or neighborhood

- dream features your parents, siblings, and other figures from your family of origin

- two or more generations of one's family in the same dream

- feeling childlike, immature, over-sensitive, disempowered

- unquestioned assumptions and roles derived from the family of origin

Dreamworking suggestions for a family field motif

- *Recognize and highlight*

  The presence of a family field effect is often hard to recognize, both in dreams and in waking life. Like the famous fish that is unaware it is living in water, we are often unaware of effects that persist from our childhood experience. We cannot see the field because we've always lived in it, even when it is aggravating and stressing us. Here's my suggestion: whenever you have a dream that features your original family members or is set in your childhood home, always consider the possibility of a family field motif. What is the dream showing you about how your family field operates? How does it affect you? Would you like to change this effect? Would you like to get away from its influence? Reduce its influence?

- *The use of the imagination to find a way of leaving the family field*

  Ben's dream of *The Everything on Fire Bear* offered him a choice: should he try to change this whole family situation (which would involve not only changing himself, but also other key figures and the way the whole family culture operates)? Or should he try to move away from the powerful influence of the field and do personal work at a safe distance? After working with his remarkable dream, he chose the second option—to get away. Family field effects can be very strong, and they are further strengthened by close proximity. Many of us need to do our growing up outside the family field and then re-enter the field once we feel ready.

Ben and I agreed that his family field effect is too strong to allow him to thrive and grow, so his response was aimed at finding a way out of the field. His imaginal response was to visualize being able to squeeze successfully through the patio door, close it behind him, and walk away. In my experience most dreamers, if given a clear choice, will opt for getting out. Ben had an intuitive sense (made clear and evident by this dream) that the family force field was just too pervasive, too entrenched, and too damaging to his spirit. Leaving does not mean that he was abandoning his family or giving up on them. What it meant is that he would journey elsewhere to become his full self.

Further examples of this motif

CHAPTER 21

Relationship Field Motifs

Essential message: "You and your partner are stuck in a rut in the way you are relating. This is preventing you from perceiving and experiencing new possibilities in the relationship."

Asking for: you to recognize how the limiting relationship field operates and change it.

Some of us tend to put most of the blame for our relationship problems on our partners. Others of us tend to take too much of the blame ourselves and let our partners off the hook too readily. A good dream about your co-created relationship field can be a very helpful reality check; it can give feedback to both of you about how you are both contributing to a chronic problematic pattern. Any dream you have that includes your current relationship partner or an important partner from your past and has a negative and repetitive feeling tone is likely to be a relationship field dream. These dreams depict a matrix of stuckness co-generated by both members of the couple. They will often give a double dose of feedback to both parties in the relationship: *"Your partner is being like this... and you are being like this. Perhaps you should both try to change."* Thus, the responses to these dreams can often include a suggestion for the partner as well as for the dreamer. Is it legitimate to involve your partner in a strategy for change based on your dream? Definitely... if it's a relationship field dream.

Paula, a 30-year-old woman, brought the following dream to her session. She called it *Kidnapped!*:

> *I see a man kidnapping a woman. I'm desperately trying to save her. He has his back turned to me, taking her away. I get hysterical! I attack him but it doesn't help. I take his ring off his hand. Then he's gone. Later I tell my partner, Brian, about the whole incident. We're both scared that the man will come back because I've got his ring, and he could harm us. We have to be prepared... "*

I suspected a relationship field motif here, both because of the presence of Paula's partner, Brian, and the strongly negative feeling tone. There is also an implied feeling of repetitiveness in that Paula fears the problematic figure will return to threaten her and Brian, which suggests that he represents an ongoing unsolved problem that threatens their relationship. But is he an inner or outer figure? Paula felt he was likely to be inner. This was a natural point to attempt a connection through feeling tones, so I asked her: "Where in your life do you have this hysterical feeling?" She answered that it would only happen in her primary relationship, when she felt Brian was shutting her out. To use the metaphor of the dream—when Brian turns his back on her it feels as if her normal state is kidnapped and she is left feeling hysterical. The dream is asking for a response from both members of the couple. Brian needs to be more aware of how he turns his back on Paula and how intensely it affects her. Meanwhile, Paula needs to recognize when she has been kidnapped by this overwhelmingly strong emotional state and find a way to "get herself back" (or get back to herself).

Here is another example of a relationship field dream. Leonard is a 61-year-old man in a long-term relationship; he and his wife, Deborah, have been married for almost thirty years. Leonard had a dream he called *The Weird Handshake*:

> My wife, Deborah, and I are driving. Somehow we've got stuck in an awkward spot that we can't seem to get out of. I try driving forward, up a rocky, muddy hill. That doesn't work. Then I try going backwards. I'm going on an angle. Deborah suggests that I go on a different angle. She's uncomfortable and getting anxious about the situation we're in. She gets out of the car and slips in the mud. Then a man who owns the property we're on comes out of a barn and walks toward us. He seems rather menacing. And then he gives Deborah this strange kind of handshake in which he scratches her palm with his right index finger. This made her feel very uncomfortable and defenseless. I'm trying to figure out how to deal with him, so he and I are carrying on this joking, bantering conversation about the mud. But beyond the conversation is the problem of how do we get out of this trapped awkward situation.

The opening of the dream is a metaphorical depiction of the current relationship field that Leonard co-generates with Deborah. The dream points out that Leonard has a tendency to get himself stuck (he is at the wheel) and he responds to this by going ineffectually back and forth. Now Deborah and the relationship are also stuck. Deborah gets upset and gets out of the car. Leonard connected this to a feeling that Deborah often abandons him emotionally when he is floundering. The dream now introduces a new character, the menacing landowner. We can sense that this figure must be very important in generating and maintaining the relationship field since he is the one who "owns" the field that the dream couple are stuck in (a large number of limiting field dreams, including relationship field dreams, actually take place in fields or field-like settings).

We must now consider the Inner/Outer orientation—is the landowner playing a part of Leonard (inner) or is he a depiction of an external figure or force that contributes to the stuckness of his relationship (outer)? I strongly suspected it was an inner figure and asked Leonard to be the part to see if he could start to feel some sense of recognition and identification. There was some resistance at first, but gradually Leonard was able to sense that he might in fact be behaving like the menacing landowner at times. There was a part of him (not a fully conscious part) that tended to hold power over his wife and keep her in a vulnerable and uncomfortable state. The actions of this part of his ego were contributing to the overall stuckness of the relationship. This aspect of the dream could now be handled as an ego check motif—asking Leonard to recognize a problematic aspect of his ego stance and consider trying to change it.

But the more immediate response we agreed on was to visualize getting out of the menacing landowner's field. Leonard imagined getting back in the car with Deborah, finding some new more effective gear, and driving away. It's important to remember your goal with this kind of response work. With relationship field motifs, the goal is almost always for both members of the couple to get out of the problem field. Keep this in mind when designing your imaginal exercise.

Psychodynamics of the relationship field motif

A relationship field is one of the limiting fields that will regularly appear in your dream life. I define a limiting field as a field effect that can limit and distort your perceptions, emotional reactions, and freedom of choice. A relationship field includes key fields in your brain, your partner's corresponding brain fields, and the shared field created by the way these two mesh with each other. These field effects are always present in long-term relationships, for better or worse. To the extent that they are negative and limiting they will tend to give rise to a type of dream that highlights the problem and poses the question: "This is a stuck pattern that keeps happening in your relationship. Do you want to try to shift it?" As the old saying goes, it takes two to tango. Relationship field dream motifs show how the tango is unconsciously choreographed by both parties.

As with brain field motifs, notice when your dreammaker locates your dream in a field-like setting; it may be pointing out: you are now under the influence of a particular condition. In Leonard's dream of *The Weird Handshake*, the prevailing condition was: when you get stuck and start going ineffectually back and forth, Deborah gets aggravated and she leaves your side, and this in turn activates an unconscious part of you that wants her to feel uncomfortable and defenseless.

Often these dreams will also present important information about how an older family field is influencing the current relationship field. Rita's dream of *Mending the Black Apron* discussed in chapter 20 was an example of this—the opening of this dream showed Rita's father disrupting her ability to relax into the arms of a current lover. In the terminology of psychoanalysis, we might say Rita's father complex was interfering with her ability to find a healthy relationship.

And what about repetitive dreams about old relationship partners? Let's look at an example. Thirty-year-old Iris was about to get married to Miles. She was a bit concerned when she had a dream of an old boyfriend, and she wanted to explore its possible meaning. Here is her dream, *Three Weeks Before the Wedding:*

> *It's three weeks before I'm getting married to Miles, and Jake (an ex-boyfriend) appears back in my life. Feeling an attraction to Jake, I tell Miles that I need to see this through and spend some time with Jake. Miles agrees and seems not to be very upset by this ... at the time. Jake and I are hanging out, but as much as I'm excited by his presence I'm also a little bored and the relationship seems shallow. I start second-guessing my decision. Suddenly I feel like oh my god! What have I done? I walked away from the best person in my life for this guy! I'm hoping I haven't damaged things with Miles. I go back and find Miles, and now he is upset. I'm afraid I might have ruined everything.*

As we discussed the dream, Iris was aware of the disturbing repetitiveness of this dream theme; she had many dreams of old boyfriends, not just Jake. It connected to something she didn't like about herself in waking life, a tendency to compare relationships, daydream about old partners, to wonder if she was making a mistake and could perhaps do better. The response we agreed on reinforced something that was already starting to happen in the dream—Iris imagined moving out of the place of comparing and second guessing and going to a place where she felt a sense of resolution and contentment with her current choice, Miles.

And what about Miles's role in this relational field? Does he have some responsibility for co-generating the problem? There is an interesting detail that the dream calls attention to—he is not upset that his bride-to-be is going off to rekindle things with an old flame. Why not? Later we see that he *is* indeed upset, so why does he not express this emotion earlier? What is this saying about him? I asked Iris to consider what this might be pointing at, and suggested that she might even want to share the dream with him and ask for his thoughts. She was understandably hesitant because of the possible threatening implication of the dream.

Distinctive features of a relationship field motif

- dreams that feature you and your current partner in a problematic situation

- repetitive dreams of previous partners

- dreams that feature family of origin figures and your current partner

Dreamworking suggestions for a relationship field motif

- *Recognize and highlight*

  Your first task is to recognize the presence and influence of the relationship field. Be on the lookout for any dream that depicts you and your partner in a problematic situation. Ask yourself: Is this dream depicting a force field that we both get caught up in? How does it affect us? What can we do about it?

- *Re-enter and explore*
Typically, the dream will offer insight and feedback to both members of the couple, so ideally your response would be something both members participate in. On the imaginal level, when you visualize getting out of a problematic place try taking your partner with you. Arrive together at a new place. Think about ritual responses that include your partner as well as yourself.

- *Consider sharing your dream with your partner*
Would you ever share a dream of your partner with your partner? Does it depends on the dream? This is something that many people never consider, but with relationship field motifs it can be a wonderful thing to do. If you do this, you are inviting your partner into your inner life, and including them in your process of self-discovery. One suggestion: after you've told the dream, ask your partner what he or she thinks before you say much about your own insights; this generates the feeling that you are working together to understand a message about both of you.

Further examples of this motif

Face Down in the Pool, chapter 3
Flying Paper Ride, chapter 3
The Two Urchins, chapter 19
Mending the Black Apron, chapter 20

CHAPTER 22

Introject Motifs

Essential Message: "You are trying to rid yourself of something that was forced into your psyche in the past."

Asking for: you to identify the foreign psychic content that was inculcated, and support your psyche's attempts to weaken or purge it.

Have you ever had a dream of something inside your body that shouldn't be there? A parasite, a worm, an insect, insect eggs, an implant, a microchip, a pocket of pus, a bullet, a foreign object? These dream motifs, with their accompanying feeling of horror and revulsion, are surprisingly common. Such a motif may be a metaphor for something that was forced into your psyche long ago but never fully accepted and integrated as a true part of you, occupying a deep-seated place in your sense of self. Introjects can result from any forceful inclusion of ideas into a human psyche. They happen from child-rearing techniques that involve shaming or strong repression, abuse and the covering-up thereof, coercive teaching, conditioned behaviors, belief systems, moral codes, value systems, religious constructs, lies, propaganda, indoctrination, and brainwashing.

Here is an example of an introject dream, it is the dream of a 38-year-old woman named Heidi. She gave it the name *Snakes and Globes*:

The dream is set in my bathroom at home and the bathroom is mirrored on three sides, three walls. So there are lots of mirrors in the dream. The first part of the dream is that there are these large squirmy, snaky creatures coming out of my face ... and there are multiple snakes. First they seem like worms because they are a pink-white color but they're very large so I want to get a closer look at them to see exactly what they are and they're all falling into the sink in the bathroom. In order to get a closer look at them, I lean up close to the sink and look at the wormy creatures and notice that they have snakeheads on them. So they are actually like snakes and I think one or two of them have a little snake tongue coming out and they've got dark eyes. They're moving a bit in the sink but not much. And then the next part of the dream is that I am squeezing out of probably a silver dollar sized hole in my left cheek these large spherical globes of what is basically yellow pus. And the globes are made of this gelatinous form of pus so it's like semi opaque and it's quite bright yellow. But they're definitely spheres; they are perfectly formed globes and I am pushing them out of my face, this hole in the side of my face, my left cheek. And I can't remember exactly how many of them there are, probably at least two or three. And when they come out they just float in the air. Meanwhile the snake-worms are still in the sink.

Dreamworker: What's the feeling at the end when you're looking at the floating globes?

Well, throughout there's horror and revulsion, but there's also relief ... and with the globes there's a kind of fascination because it's not just free-form pus that's coming out, it's these spherical globes. I'm kind of fascinated by the fact that these are perfectly formed spheres coming out of my face. So there's a mixture of emotion—revulsion, relief, and a little bit of fascination.

The setting of the dream is Heidi's bathroom. Bathrooms have many functions; which function is being referred to here? The presence of many mirrors suggests that the "place where we look at ourselves" function is the critical one. The snake-worms coming out of Heidi's face are strongly suggestive of an introject motif. The combination of the mirror emphasis and the face emphasis suggests we may be dealing with something about her appearance, how she feels about her looks; and also possibly her face to the world, i.e., her self-presentation or persona. There are many snake-worms, not just one. This is noteworthy—does it mean that she has been living with multiple introjected beliefs about her face?

The fact that the snake-worms are definitively out of her and in the sink suggests Heidi has already accomplished an important piece of psychological work. But now there is an aftermath—something else is coming out, the globes. The pus, the sense of encapsulation, and Heidi's morbid fascination with her own pus, all these elements are common in introject dreams. But when I asked about the globes of pus she said something unexpected and interesting: "They are some kind of horrifying alchemy. There's a magical fascination to them, they're horrible and magical at the same time." I asked Heidi what she might be able to connect this to in her life, something both horrible and magical. She said she could connect to an old belief she had that pain and suffering are necessary for her creativity. "I romance my pain, I'm almost afraid to give it up" she said, "and this reminds me of the magical globes. I don't want them inside me but I'm somehow worried that I'll lose them too." This was a very resonant moment. It had that strange quality of being perfectly logical and true in dream terms ("dream logic"). We worked out an imaginal response that would allow her to get rid of the snakes but keep the globes around for a while. She visualized flushing the snakes away (she had no ambivalence about doing this), but gathering up the globes and keeping them safe in a glass container. Heidi was pretty sure she didn't want to imagine the globes back inside her face, but perhaps she might want to hold onto them for a while and experience her life with the globes outside of her.

Introjection is not always the result of abuse or cruelty, it can happen in the course of well-intentioned parenting and teaching. Here's an example—at 40 years old, Patti was recently pregnant and delighted to be. She told me the following dream, *There's a Shark Following Us!*:

> *I'm at my parents' lake. It's dusk, getting dark, and I'm with my boy-friend. We're swimming a bit and then walking on the rocks by the shore. We see a shark following us. We realize it is actually after us! It is very scary. At one point I grab another shark out of the water and rip it into shreds to scare off the first shark as if to say , "This is what will happen to you if you keep bothering us." But it doesn't affect him at all, he just keeps coming toward us. I run toward the house. I almost make it to safety, but I feel the shark right behind me, and I wake up ... "*

I was struck by the setting of Patti's dream, at her parents' lake; a lake where she had often played and swam as a child, and a body of water that certainly did not contain any sharks. As a very general rule, if a dream depicts a problem and situates it in a childhood setting, we can deduce we are dealing with something problematic that originated in that time and place of the dreamer's life and has persisted until the present. I asked Patti why the dream might have been situated there.

> *Usually my parents' lake is a happy place for me. But even to this day I am sometimes afraid of sharks when I swim in the lake, because Mom told my brother and I when we were very little that there were freshwater sharks in our lake, so that we wouldn't go play in the lake when she wasn't watching us and drown. It was a scare tactic. But I still think of it when I'm swimming out pretty deep in the lake and am still scared, even though rationally I know there can't be a shark in there.*

Now, as Patti filled in this background information, it seemed that we were dealing with an introject—a psychological construct (in this case a cautionary fear) that was instilled into her earlier in life and is now being identified as foreign and untrue. I asked Patti if we could use this as our working hypothesis—this dream shark was a personification of the shark-fear her mother had instilled in her as a child. She felt that this was resonant and true, and she added: "I think my husband is there in the dream because we're pregnant now, and it's time to confront that memory. I don't want it anymore and I don't want to pass it on to my baby." This made sense to me; I have noticed that there is often a kind of "psychic housecleaning" that occurs when a woman is pregnant or wants to get pregnant, as if she want to purge herself of old baggage and trans-generational taints before she brings a new life into the world.

I asked Patti if she wanted to confront the shark fear right now. She said yes, so I asked her to go back into the dream, to re-enter the feeling of running from the shark in fear, but then to catch herself, to realize that this is something that can now be confronted, and to turn and face the shark. She did this very readily, and immediately the frightening aspect of the shark changed: "I'm facing the shark now. He's taking on the persona of a British chap, with an accent, walking upright on his fins. He's saying that he's a figment of my imagination, a part of me, and I don't need to be afraid of him any more."

I asked: is he a positive part of you, or just an old fear that you don't need to have any more? I framed this question because I wanted to make sure that we were on the right track psychodynamically. Specifically, I wanted to make sure that the shark was not appearing as a shadow figure (a true part of self that is disowned, unknown, or repressed now approaching the dream ego seeking acceptance and integration). The shark does display two key attributes of shadow figures: it frightens and pursues the dream ego, and it shifts into something more positive once confronted.

Patti's answer was clear and unambiguous: "I don't think he feels positive. I think he's just the old fear of having sharks chase me. He's representing my own imagination. It's not serving me any good." Now we could confidently continue along the path of working with the shark as an introject. I asked her if she would like to test whether this imaginal exercise had indeed changed the power of shark-fear introject in her psyche; would she like to venture back into the lake with the "friendly" shark and swim with him?

> *All right. That's a bit scary, but I'll try it. I'm in the deep water now… he's physically vanished but I can feel his spirit. Now that I'm in the water his voice is almost protecting me. I feel now that I can fully relax in the water with no part of my mind on the alert. Now the water can be a truly healing place for me.*

I asked Patti to hold onto this wonderful feeling of full relaxation in the water with no trace of fear, and to revisit it in her imagination a few more times over the next few days. This will give the new post-introject feeling state a chance to be solidified and anchored in her feeling body. Then, the next time she has an opportunity to swim in a freshwater lake, she can test it again and continue the imaginal work if more needs to be done.

Patti's shark is what I would call a half-out introject: she has already removed the foreign construct from her psyche in the sense that she no longer believes it to be true in her rational thinking mind, yet the old irrational fear can still pursue her whenever she swims in deep fresh water. So she still needed to do some work with the introject to ensure that the shark was expelled and transformed once and for all.

And what about Patti's act of bravado in tearing up another shark in an attempt to intimidate the pursuing shark? This probably refers to some unsuccessful attempt she made in the past to overcome her fear of sharks, possibly the use of an affirmation technique (e.g., saying to herself "I will have absolutely NO fear of sharks when I enter the water"). Affirmations attempt to change the feeling body through opposition and bravado. In my experience, dreamwork is usually more effective than affirmation when dealing with embodied fears because it presents an accurate and current scenario the dreamer can use to practice facing his or her fears (rather than simply affirming that the fears do not exist). I think there is a great kernel of wisdom in the old adage about "facing our fears."

There are many kinds of introjects; this one is a fear introject—a discreet and specific unit of thought and association that the dreamer's mother intentionally instilled into her daughter's brain for a specific reason. This was probably well-intentioned but it created long-term negative consequences for Patti. Other types of introjects are instilled for other specific reasons, most commonly to promote desired behaviors and inhibit undesired behaviors in children. The nature of the human brain and the way it works makes it very susceptible to being introjected in this way, it is one of our primary modes of "learning" for better or worse. To cite another shark example from popular culture, how many people took in a shark-fear introject from watching the movie *Jaws*? Many viewers left the theater with their brains quite literally altered. After watching the movie, they carried a fear circuit that had not been there before; a new fear had been spliced into their minds that in many cases would remain active for the rest of their lives.

Psychodynamics of the introject motif

Introjection happens in the area of overlap between internal and external. Something was internalized but not fully assimilated. We have seen that many dream figures can be seen to have both an inner and an outer aspect (as was discussed in chapter 12) and this is especially true of introject motifs—they are both self and not-self, both inner and outer.

I think of introjection in four phases depending on how far into a person's psyche the foreign content has come: 1. threatening or recent; 2. inside; 3. being expelled; and 4. outside. The characteristic dream imagery is different for each of these phases. In Heidi's *Snakes and Globes* dream, the snakes were in phase 4 and the globes in phase 3. Patti's shark was in phase 2 at the time she had the dream and she managed to move it out into phase 4 with some focused imaginal work. In Yolanda's dream of *The Mechanical Scorpion* in chapter 14, the scorpion was in phase 4 but Yolanda was fearful it would return to phase 3.

How does introjection originally happen? As children we are bombarded with input from all sides—from our parents, siblings, peers, teachers, media, society, church, etc. If our young and impressionable minds find this incoming material compatible, we will digest and assimilate it readily. These ideas will become building blocks for our developing psyches. But what happens (to use a metaphor of digestion) when we find the incoming material indigestible? We will try to resist it, and vomit it back out. If this resistance is not allowed by our parents or teachers and the "force-feeding" continues then an introject problem will develop (phase 1).

The introject remains inside us, becoming a part of our personality and sense of self, yet not truly a part of self in the deepest sense. We human beings have a remarkable ability to tolerate introjects, often finding a way to live with them for decades, or even a lifetime (phase 2). But when the psyche has grown and matured to a certain point, it may suddenly feel it can no longer tolerate these constructs and will attempt to push them out (phase 3). This is when "expelling" introject motifs will start to appear in the dreams. The imagery used to depict these phenomena is often borrowed from humanity's primordial and visceral reactions against parasites, vermin, foreign bodies, and contagion. If we are able to fully expel the introject, another type of dream will appear. In these dreams there may be a sense of purging and enormous relief, which depict the psyche's jubilation at having succeeded in ridding itself of the unwanted psychic content (phase 4).

If you have a dream with an introject motif, your psyche is asking for help in recognizing and ultimately expelling something undesired. The appearance of this kind of motif suggests that you are ready, or almost ready to undertake a purging process. If the introject is not hopelessly entangled within your psychic fabric, it can be removed without causing too much damage. Unfortunately, some introjects have wormed their way in so deeply that they have become a fixed feature of the architecture of the psyche. To attempt removal in these cases might cause more damage than good—you may have to learn to live with the introject.

In my experience, dreams of foreign objects inside your body usually refer to something psychological, but they could also be pointing to something physical. Always consider this possibility before you move to the psychological realm—is the dream giving you information about an old wound, a walled-off area of infection, or some foreign object your body now wants to push out?

Distinctive features of an introject motif

Phase 1—threatening to come inside

- something attaching to, hooking or sticking onto, or entering your body

- something trying to get in your ear

- being shot

- being raped

- a figure who forces or implants something into your body

Phase 2—inside

- figures that harm, control, and threaten the dream ego

- a harshly critical figure or inner voice

- neurotic moral conflicts between a belief system and a desire

- strong feelings of "should" or "should not"

- pregnancy by rape

Phase 3—trying to expel an introject

- bugs, burrowing insects, vermin, parasites, worms, maggots

- implants, microchips, bits of foreign matter in the body that can't be taken out

- pockets of pus and infection

- eggs laid in the body

- frantically trying to get something out of the body that should not be in the body

- vomiting, pulling something out of the body, the mouth, nose, ears, anus

- feelings of horror, revulsion, and morbid fascination

Phase 4—expelled introject

- great relief at being rid of something or killing something

- wondering; did I get all of it out?

- concern that there may be more still in there

- purging feeling

- victorious feeling

Dreamworking suggestions for an introject motif

- *First, make sure you are dealing with an introject*
  If you suspect an introject, you must first be sure that it is something truly negative and undesirable. Ask yourself (or the dreamer): "Does this thing seem to be a part of you, or something from the outside that has got into you?" Or: "Do you think there might be something good about these bugs, or are you quite sure you want to be rid of them?"

- *Be the Part*

  Imagine that you are the foreign thing. If it is a true introject you may be able to role play it, but you will have trouble identifying with it or feeling anything potentially positive about it. If you are certain that you want to be rid of the thing after imaginally being it, it is probably an introject. Now you can go ahead and support the purging effort. Don't worry about making an irreversible mistake; if you feel that you want it back after you have imagined expelling it that's fine, you can imagine bringing it back into your body.

- *Use of the creative imagination to expel the introject*

  Re-enter the dream. Allow yourself to feel the feeling of the foreign thing inside you. Now imagine that it is coming out. Visualize it being completely purged. If it leaves a wound or an opening behind, visualize cleaning that wound and sealing it. You may want to dispose of the now externalized thing, kill it, bury it, contain it, or flush it away. Now feel what it is like to be completely rid of this foreign thing.

Further examples of this motif

Sliding Snake Wound, chapter 12

The Family Rapture, chapter 12

Spoons Push Their Way Out, chapter 13

The Mechanical Scorpion, chapter 14

Bag of Bugs on a Timer, chapter 15

The Hungry Ghost, chapter 19

Flying Bugs With Microchips, chapter 29

CHAPTER 23

Self-discovery Motifs

Essential message: "You are discovering more of yourself. Keep it up!"

Asking for: you to invest more energy and intention into self-discovery; to venture into new areas.

Have you ever dreamed of finding a new part of your house you didn't know was there? Perhaps you discovered a whole new suite of rooms, or came across a flight of stairs leading down to a whole new level. Perhaps you have dreamed of being taken by a guide figure who took you to a place where you learned or found something. This kind of motif is depicting you in the act of self-exploration, you are discovering new aspects and potentials in yourself that you never knew about. These motifs exhibit a classical positive feedback pattern, occurring more often at times when we are active in exploring our own psyches, and thus enticing and encouraging us to go on and find out even more about ourselves. Often these motifs are accompanied by a feeling tone of wonderment, surprise, and newness ("Wow! Look at this beautiful room!"). Quite often the sense of discovery is coupled with some problem that holds back further exploration—perhaps you feel this new house does not belong to you? Do you feel as if you are trespassing and may get into trouble? Do you get distracted and caught up in another issue? Do you encounter something frightening in the cellar?

Jasmine, 39 years old, was starting to do some dreamwork with me, finding it mystifying but interesting. She had a dream with very powerful and memorable imagery that featured a strange and exotic name—*Helikos:*

> *While traveling with my family I discover that I have a house. I'd forgotten that I had it. It is really disturbing to me that I have forgotten. The house is called "Helikos." It seems to be somewhere in the East. There are elements suggestive of Greek orthodox, or Kazakhstan, somewhere like that. The house belongs to me. It is a multi-terraced house on top of a hill looking over a crater surrounded by other houses. I have tenants who run a successful bar from the lower level, and I think: "why don't I operate this myself?" I see a city with a church in a valley. The culture is very foreign to me. I am given the gold papers to the house in a traditional ceremony. I was presented with the rolled-up papers in an urn. There is a very exotic feeling; the people are Asian looking. What really bugs me is that I had forgotten about this house.*

The element of realizing that she owns a house points toward a self-discovery motif. There is a strong feeling of claiming her birthright (or forgetting to claim it) in Jasmine's dream. The dream seems to be saying that Jasmine is now being presented with an opportunity to re-connect with herself after a long period of forgetting about herself in some critical way. There is a strongly accentuated invitation to take possession of what is hers; her dreammaker is taking great pains to signal how important this is, with a ceremony, golden ownership papers, and an urn. I was very aware that I wanted Jasmine to understand how important and auspicious this dream was. Would she remember it, work with it, and respond to it? Or would it slip away into the land of big-but-sadly-forgotten dreams?

The dream seemed to ask for a twofold response, one part to support the dynamic event that is trying to happen (re-claiming her house) and one to address the stuckness that may be blocking this from happening (forgetting that she has a house). For the first part, I invited Jasmine to go back into the dream and imagine accepting the ownership papers and urn, and then proceeding to enter her house and fully explore it. This she was able to do.

Second, to address the forgetting problem (which could easily happen again), I asked Jasmine: "In what way have you forgotten about yourself?" There were a few interesting clues in the dream—one clue is that she re-discovers the house while traveling with her family. This suggests that she may re-find some critical aspect of herself by turning toward her past, her childhood (she grew up in eastern Europe), revisiting her cultural and ancestral roots in some way. Another possible clue in the dream was her allowing other people to set up their business inside her house. This may be a metaphor of letting other people use her in some way. Jasmine was able to make important connections with both these elements.

At the time we worked with this dream, Jasmine could make no association with the name *Helikos* or the Eastern elements of the setting. Other than the very general observations that her original homeland lies to the east, and that she may feel "foreign" to herself because she has not been fully inhabiting herself for so long, we could not make any more specific connections. Often such insights will arrive months or even years later; this type of dream can reach far into the future, hinting at things that the dreamer does not yet know about herself.

Here's another example. This time the dreamer, a 36-year-old woman named Nathalie, makes an exciting discovery but it takes place in a house that she feels does not belong to her. She titled the dream *Discovering Unpublished Dr. Seuss:*

We are in someone else's basement (I don't know who 'we' is). The light is dim and it feels crowded. We snuck in to find shelter. The door opens and in comes a thick package of books, as if thrown away. I open them up. They are written by Dr. Seuss! Are they unpublished? They are books I've never seen. Some are color proofs with comments in his handwriting. Then the owner of the house comes in. He is surprised and angry to see us. I assure him that we're just leaving. I take the books. Even though I don't think he wants the books, I use my body to block his sight of them as I carry them out. I feel a little guilty, but I really want them. When we leave, it's like all we have is a car, no house.

The discovery of something new and exciting in a basement indicates a self-discovery motif; Nathalie is discovering something new and exciting about herself. It is likely to be something creative and very valuable to be depicted as a Dr. Seuss manuscript. The fact it has not been published yet suggests some unused potential that has not been brought out into the world yet. But there's a problem—Nathalie feels she is trespassing in someone else's basement. Does Nathalie feel that she does not have the right to explore in her own unconscious? We need to know what this man (the house owner) represents for her. It is helpful to use the Inner/Outer orientation here; if he is an inner part, it would mean that some part of Nathalie does not believe she has the right to be doing this exploring and discovering. If he is an outer figure, he could be standing for someone in Nathalie's life who is angry about her recent efforts of self-discovery and wants her to stop. If he is a depiction of an introject (straddling inner and outer) it could mean that Nathalie is running up against an old belief system wherein it is bad to explore the unconscious.

Can Nathalie take possession of this new region of herself and the treasure she has found there? At these moments I almost always urge the dreamer to proceed (at least imaginally) as if the house, all its rooms, and all its contents are indeed hers, even if she feels in the dream that they do not belong to her.

Again, the response would be twofold, one for the dynamic part and one for the stuckness. To support the dynamic discovery, I suggested to Nathalie that she imagine re-entering her dream house as the rightful owner. Then she could imagine exploring the books more fully without the interruption of the angry owner appearing. I was hoping her feeling would shift from: "I don't think this is mine … maybe I shouldn't be here," to "Wow! This place belongs to me! And look at this manuscript."

But it seemed that the stuckness represented by the house owner was preventing this. He seemed to hold a lot of power. To explore further I asked Nathalie to be the man who owns the house. As him, she felt angry and uncaring: "I just want these intruders out of my house." His only interest in the Dr. Seuss manuscript was that it might be worth some money. This role-playing experience led to Nathalie making an emotionally resonant connection—there was a part of her that was capable of throwing away something of great value like this manuscript, "something related to the whimsy and magic of childhood, as well as ecological and social values." I encouraged Nathalie to work with the house owner as an introject, a part of her that had been socialized and trained to place high value on work ethic, career, and financial stability. Perhaps the dream was asking for a shift in priority, showing her that this part was now too strong and was interfering with some very important new developments in the basement regions.

Psychodynamics of the self-discovery motif

If you sense that you've had a dream of this type ask yourself: "What have I recently found out about myself? How can I support this new development?" You may need to do a little self-coaching with the goal of investing energy into this process, being appreciative and engaged by it. The fact that these dreams so often couple the excitement of discovery together with a problem of some kind suggests that active self-exploration brings with it a taboo against knowing ourselves more deeply. Jasmine's curious tendency to forget about her house is an aspect of this taboo, so is Nathalie's angry house owner who wants to put a stop to the exploration. Whatever stuck point comes up for you, don't let it stop the whole process.

And what if you dreamed of venturing into a basement only to find that there is something frightening living down there? Would this deter you from further exploration? Could this mean that there is something in your unconscious you are afraid to encounter? It might mean that, and perhaps for good reason. But stay curious. Find a way to keep looking. You probably wouldn't want to live your life with a feeling that you had never opened up a large and unknown part of your own house.

When you start to explore your dream life, you will typically be rewarded with several self-discovery dreams. Expect dreams of new rooms, basements, water, and shorelines. Your unconscious will appreciate your efforts to get more self-acquainted and will initiate a positive feedback cycle, i.e., "If you show interest, I'll show you more." Very commonly these dreams will have you exploring basements and cellars or venturing into large bodies of water—not surprising since basements and water are universal symbols of the unconscious.

Distinctive features of a self-discovery motif

- walking through a house (or other structure) and finding new areas

- unsure if the house belongs to you, feeling like a trespasser

- going up or downstairs, discovering new levels

- finding treasure or money

- something frightening in the basement

- venturing out on a voyage or trip

- diving and exploring underwater

- dream settings on shorelines and beaches

- meeting a guide figure, being taken somewhere or shown something

Dreamworking suggestions for a self-discovery motif

- *Re-enter the dreamscape with heightened awareness*
  Go back into your dream house (or whatever it is) and allow yourself to explore it freely. Imagine that it is fully yours, even if that was not the feeling in the dream. Take full possession of it. Notice and remember everything that you see and feel. Even small details could be very significant. Once this set of rooms has been explored and appreciated, another door may open and another area may appear.

- *If there is an obstacle, explore it*
  Often there will be some problem that prevents you from feeling that you can enter and explore the space. It is critical that you both get a clear sense of what this is. This will be a depiction of the obstacle(s) that are currently preventing you from moving toward greater self-knowledge. Keep the Inner/Outer orientation in mind—is the obstacle a part of you, or is it someone or something in your life that is holding you back? If you're not sure, use the Be the Part technique—try being the obstacle and interview yourself.

Further examples of this motif

The Young Man and the Old Man, chapter 11
The Hobbit Door, chapter 13

CHAPTER 24

Rebirth Motifs

Essential message: "You are in a period of profound change and creativity. You are re-inventing yourself, reconceiving yourself, rebirthing, yourself, or giving birth to something."

Asking for: you to identify where you currently are in the creative rebirth process and support that phase.

What happens in your dream life when you go through a period of major transition? If you observe your dreams closely, you will probably notice that the imagery becomes more intense and dramatic. You may also notice themes of conception, intrauterine life, birth, and babyhood appearing in your dreams more frequently. In my years of working with dreams, I have seen again and again that a person's dreams will tend to follow the template of human conception, gestation, and birth while they are in a period of transformation or heightened creativity. It is as if your dreams are showing you re-conceiving yourself, becoming a different person, and coming out into the world changed and new. I have seen that this dream template of rebirth happens particularly under the following circumstances:

- going through a professional program or other intensive educational experience

- becoming a parent

- a major move or major career change

- going through an intense period of self-discovery

- any experience that transforms your identity

- undertaking a major creative project

Here is an example of a birth template dream that contains imagery of conception. George, the dreamer, is a 27-year-old man who recently decided to undertake a complete re-training and career change. He called this dream *The Pin-Screw Mission*:

I'm walking around a property that is under construction. It's completely fenced in with a huge crane in the middle. I walk along the fence and peer in. I notice two or three circular vents inset into the ground, equally spaced. Perplexed, I return to the parking lot and sit down. Three men come over the big mound of dirt (I was thinking it was like a big mound of shit). They are in heated conversation. After some time they all drop to the ground ... they're exhausted and depressed ... just beside themselves. I turn to them and I say: "Do you need any help?'" One of them says: "Sure!" I get up and walk over, and he says: "You could bring back the pin that is behind the open door marked Randolph." *It is on his property. I agree to try. I walk over to his property. There are no open doors. There's a high-tech security system in place resembling something from* Star Trek *that's around the site. Here I am, and I want to enter the property. It has these metallic thresholds that have illuminated touch screens; very high-tech security card features. I transform into a bug, and hide under a sign right under one of the thresholds. At some point somebody walks through one of the thresholds using the card feature. I see a pinkish red light. I seize this chance and I zoom in. I pick up the pin, and I patiently wait for someone to use the door again, to zoom back. The whole thing took only a few seconds; I knew where it was, I knew how to get it. I had to move with urgency, and I had a very clear idea of how big it was and where it was. It was called a pin, but it was actually a screw; like an industrial screw, meant to bind things together."*

Dreamworker: What are the feeling tones?

In the beginning there is a kind of depression, a pathetic-ness. The other guys are slumped down, stuck… and then I come along. When I get into the game plan there's a burst of energy. I could be doing something that's fruitful, so I take the initiative and I go for it. When I arrive at the threshold, I'm trying to outwit the system. The threshold is presenting this barrier, and I feel that I can get past it. When I transform into the bug, there's an amazing sense of accuracy, agility, speed. When I got the pin— it was like Conan when he got the gauntlet. The achievement! He had what he came to find; being on a mission, and actually achieving it. Very fulfilling and satisfying!

In George's dream, several men are on a mission to get inside something and have given up and collapsed in exhaustion. Whenever multiple males are surrounding and hyper-focusing on one thing I always suspect a sperm and egg motif. After the change of scale, we now have a tiny bug trying to get past a threshold into a large compound—things are even more suggestive of a sperm and egg scenario. The imagery of pin/screw/ binding together is also very suggestive of sexual union; it's the coming together of genetic material, and the exhilarating sense of achievement at the end is just what we would expect a victorious sperm to feel.

Looking at the dream in this way was both intellectually and emotionally resonant for George. He felt it fit the imagery and the feelings in the dream, and it also fit with his current life situation. He had just said goodbye to his former profession and re-conceived himself as a bodywork therapist, it made sense to him that his dream life would contain imagery of conception.

Here's another example from nine months further along in the rebirth process. Ian, 37 years old, told me a very troubling dream he'd had three months earlier. He named this dream *Come Find Me:*

> *I'm going through a dark tunnel. It's very scary, there are attacking things in it. I make it through to the other side, but a fragment of me has been lost in the tunnel. I know it is back in there. I call out to it, hoping that it won't answer, that it has made it out the other side or something. I know if I hear it I would have to go back into the tunnel to find it. I don't want an answer, but I get an answer. It was in there. I call a second time just to make sure. It answers again and says: "Come find me." I know this means that I have to go back in. There are other people around, so I ask them for tips about what to do inside the tunnel. One person gives me a tip—he says that dark energies can pose as my family members, so don't be fooled. I know that if I can maintain a certain perspective in the tunnel I will be fine no matter what is coming after me, it won't be able to hurt me. I go in. A big ferocious dog lunges at me and grabs onto my arm. I try to hold my perspective so the dog won't be able to hurt me. I know that if I can stay in this perspective, I will be aware that the dog is just an illusion. I am able to get that perspective momentarily but am not able to stabilize it, so I have the experience of the dog biting into me… and I wake up trying to shake the dog off my arm.*

As we discussed the dream, Ian was able to connect it to a feeling he has had as long as he can remember, a feeling that he lost part of his soul: "A soul part of me is lost. A part of me got fragmented and lost. I'm willing to go back in and try to find it, even though there are dangerous things in there and I'm really scared." But when and how did this fragmentation happen? I was struck by the fact that the dream was set inside a tunnel;

this often correlates to the experience of being in the womb and specifically moving into the birth canal. I asked Ian what he thought of this. He replied that he was intrigued and would like to explore it further. We were nearing the end of our session so I invited Ian to come up with an imaginal response to the dream on his own.

At the beginning of our next session, Ian described his imaginal work:

I created a visualization of my ideal birth—I imagine a vessel. I touch it to wake it up. I invite the energies of joy and love and compassion and courage and wisdom to come into the vessel. I touch the vessel, like striking a tuning fork, to let it learn to vibrate at the same rate as my soul. Once it is in alignment with my soul, then I imagine myself inside it, about to be born. In this birth I shift through smoothly, instead of having a gap and a disconnection.

This was a wonderful piece of imaginal work, but it did not include a reunion with the lost part. I suggested to Ian that he add in that one piece, specifically visualizing reuniting with the lost part of himself before going into the new vessel. Here we are working with the dream as a personal spirit motif, depicting a traumatized and split off part of self that wants to be found and reunited. He included this and did the new visualization several more times. This work brought very good results—Ian soon began to feel more whole and fully himself, more energized and visibly happier.

We can never be certain whether this dream depicts events that actually occurred during Ian's birth. Nevertheless, the fact that it contains birth imagery means that it can be worked with as if it relates to his birth. It is a good example of a dream that couples rebirth imagery with personal spirit imagery, a common pairing since the birth process (even an ideal birth) is always potentially traumatic and can easily cause a rupturing event in the psyche. As a further dream response, Ian contacted his mother and asked about the details of his birth. According to his mother's recollection Ian's birth process uncomplicated and fairly rapid. We cannot know for sure when this part of Ian was fragmented and lost, but that lack of certainty should not stop us from responding to these kinds of dreams. The most important thing in Ian's case was to help support the conditions for him to find his lost part and reunite with it.

Psychodynamics of the rebirth motif

High impact events stay with us. We may not remember our conception or our birth as an adult would remember a particular event, but there is a way in which we do remember it. We remember it in our feeling bodies, not in words but in images, emotions, and sensations. Pre-verbal memories are difficult to describe and even difficult to think about conceptually, but they do affect us nevertheless. I would describe them as unconscious feeling matrices, and these appear in our dreams frequently. Often, it is the dream life that gives us the best access to this powerful realm of experience.

When you dream of your conception, you are at a critical watershed moment—after the point of conception there is no turning back unless you decide to abort the new development that is happening in you. Psychologically speaking, the whole process of transformation will now start to move forward whether you get cold feet or not, although it may be many months or even years before things are ready to be birthed. Your dream life will now tend to symbolize the change you are going through or the project you are working on as your "baby." Your baby needs to grow through the stages of development that all babies go through—implantation, growth and gestation, labor pains, birth, and the critical bonding and attachment period following birth. Sit back and watch the whole show unfold in your dreams.

If these high impact events were made even more affective because of some difficulty or trauma that occurred in your early life, this may become a focal point for chronic suffering and stuckness that needs to be addressed. For example, a person who had a very complicated and traumatic birth may experience great difficulty as she approaches her graduation from college.

For another person who was kept at the hospital in an incubator for three weeks following birth, it may be the critical period immediately after graduating that is most problematic. Admittedly these theories are somewhat speculative and hypothetical, but this is true of most things in the world of human psychology. We are in a realm that is hard to verify and almost impossible to prove. Keep an open mind about it and try it on when you have a dream with imagery that seems to put the spotlight on a particular stage of the procreative process. If you have an emotionally resonant reaction to a possible rebirth motif, this is enough to proceed and use this possibility as your working hypothesis. If there is such a thing as proof, it can be found in the results of doing dreamwork with these kinds of dreams. People like George and Ian consistently feel different, happier, less troubled, and less held back after working on their rebirth dreams.

And what about women who are actually pregnant—when they have dreams of birth and babies are they dreaming about their own birth template? Are they having accurate pre-glimpses of the being that is growing inside them? Are they tapping into universal fears and concerns that all expecting mothers experience? All these may be happening and it is often difficult to tell what is what. I recommend Eileen Stukane's book *The Dream Worlds of Pregnancy* to fill in a backdrop of what the "normal" dreams of pregnant women can encompass. Stukane writes in her foreword:

> *Pregnant women's dreams … are permeated with babies: tiny babies weighing five ounces and giant babies weighing thirty-five pounds, angelic and demonic babies, mature babies that walked and talked at birth, and dolls and animals that symbolized infants. When baby imagery was present, anxiety was usually present. Intense body awareness was another feature that set these pregnant women's dreams apart from the "normal."*[13]

---

13   Eileen Stukane, *The Dream Worlds of Pregnancy* (New York: Quill. 1985), 5.

And what about men? Men have their share of conception, birth, and baby dreams, although in my experience women have more. I suspect this may be because women possess the anatomical and physiological landscape from which such dreams borrow most of their imagery. The events of conception, implantation, gestation, labor, birth, and breast-feeding actually occur within a woman's body, so it is not surprising that a woman would dream of these experiences more frequently and intensely. But men recreate themselves too, and men can give birth to ideas, men can gestate great projects and nurture their creations. A man can be pregnant in a dream, just as a woman can dream of being a sperm.

Distinctive features of a rebirth motif

Over the years, I have come to recognize a characteristic set of dream motifs that I believe relates to the events and stages of human procreation. Baby imagery is the most common and readily recognized, but there are many other motifs that come before the baby in the sequence. If you familiarize yourself with these motifs, you will probably start to notice them appearing in your dreams, and the dreams of people you work with. Here's my suggestion—as you read through this chart, notice if any bells of recognition start to ring. Watch out for emotional resonance—if it happens, you may be onto something worth investigating further. You have probably had several of those motifs in your dreams over the years. You may want to reconsider an old dream from the perspective of the rebirth template, and if you do you may find some new insight. Going forward, you will be more sensitized to recognize these motifs in future dreams.

Table of Rebirth Stages and Corresponding Dream Imagery
(Traumatic or problematic variations are shaded with gray)

Stage of the process	Corresponding perinatal stage	Corresponding dream motifs
Considering a major change or creation	*Pre-conception*	Dreams of space travel, arriving at a new world
Waiting for a fertilizing input from someone; wanting to attract a partner." *"I want it to come to me!"*	*Egg energy*	Dreams of attracting, drawing others energy, positioning oneself to attract the other, being at the center
Active pursuit, single-minded striving toward the goal. *"I'm going to go check this out! I want this!"*	*Sperm energy*	Dreams of fish, of swimming toward something, trying to get into a building, of many men all striving to do one thing
Decision, committing to something, starting the process. *"I'm going to do this!"*	*Conception*	Dreams of reaching a goal, entering a building, with feeling tone of excitement and accomplishment
Finding and being accepted in a place, institution, relationship, community where the transition will occur	*Implantation*	Dreams of grabbing hold, sinking in, burrowing into a safe place

Stage of the process	Corresponding perinatal stage	Corresponding dream motifs
Not successful in finding a place where the transition will occur	*Threatened miscarriage or abortion attempt*	Dreams of being blown away, pulled away, washed away
Going through the process	*Gestation*	Dreams of being pregnant, of tiny babies and children, of being on large vehicles, trains, taken somewhere
Launching/presenting something before it is ready	*Premature delivery*	Dreams of tiny and immature babies
Feeling of a key figure being missing	*Loss of a twin VTS (Vanishing Twin Syndrome)*	Dreams of one dying and one remaining
Stuck in a poisonous and dysfunctional place, institution, relationship, community	*Toxic womb*	Dreams of being poisoned, unable to get away; of something unhealthy entering the body through a tube
Sense of ease, acceptance, belonging, and support in the place, institution, relationship, community	*Healthy womb*	Dreams of cosmic bliss, floating, union, divine connectedness

Stage of the process	Corresponding perinatal stage	Corresponding dream motifs
Sudden feeling of disaster during the process	*Problems with placenta or cord*	Dreams of trees suddenly becoming sick or damaged
Becoming aware of one's new identity as the transition progresses (*"Oh! I am now a parent; a doctor, a husband, an artist…"*)	*Incarnation (consciousness developing in a body)*	Dreams of coming down to earth or onto a vessel from a great height
Difficulty accepting the transition into the new identity	*Traumatic incarnation*	Dreams of catastrophic falls, plane crashes
Nearing the end of the transition	*Labor*	Dreams of large vehicles in constrained spaces; body in a tight space; cannot turn and maneuver
Crisis near end of the transition	*Cord around neck*	Dreams of strangulation, suffocation, hanging, choking
Difficulties in the last phase of transition	*Hard contractions with no movement into birth canal*	Dreams of being pushed, crushed, squeezed, caught, wedged, buried, suffocated

Stage of the process	Corresponding perinatal stage	Corresponding dream motifs
Paralyzed, unable to face the last tests of the transition	*Fear of engaging birth canal; possible forceps or C-section*	Dreams of being afraid to enter a passageway; needing help. Life and death crisis feeling tone.
Moving through the last phase	*Movement through birth canal, or surgical removal*	Dreams of moving through an obstacle
First experience of the new identity, new state, presenting one's creation	*Newly born*	Dreams of dramatic changes of state, of environment
Difficulties with new identity, new state	*Post-natal trauma, shock*	Dreams of sick or traumatized babies
Needing support in the new identity, new state	*Bonding and attachment*	Dreams of nurtured and contented babies
Difficulty finding support in the new identity, new state	*Problems with bonding and attachment*	Dreams of traumatized, lost, orphaned, abandoned babies and children (personal spirit)

Dreamworking suggestions for a rebirth motif

- *Recognize and highlight*

  If you recognize one of the rebirth template motifs, ask yourself how it may connect to your current life and to your perinatal experience. This recognition will help you consciously appreciate and prepare for the big changes that are coming as you move through the whole sequence. Be on the lookout for other birth template dream motifs further along in the progression.

- *Re-enter and explore*

  If the dream highlights a problem or a stuck point, consider what can be done about it. Stay within the terms given by the dream and seek a good solution there. Go back into your dream, to the point where the problem is holding things back. Try different imaginal solutions until you find one that feels right. Practice this one until you feel the blockage starting to shift. After doing this work in your creative imagination for a time, start to think about how this new development could be translated into your waking life, and how it might relate to your own early history.

Further examples of this motif

Into the Tunnel, chapter 13

CHAPTER 25

Inspiring Contact Motifs

Essential message: "Be amazed! Be inspired! You have something unique and remarkable within you!"

Asking for: you to support a full realization of the encounter that is happening.

Have you ever dreamed of an encounter with a remarkable animal? Or a fascinatingly powerful object? An enchantingly attractive person? An ancestral spirit? A divine being? These dream encounters are usually private and personal; they are *only* for you. These motifs carry the strongest potentials for positive change, making them of great importance. They have a strongly positive feeling tone, leaving you with a sense that you have been touched deeply. Their soulful quality makes them readily recognizable. They engender feelings of wonderment, numinousness, strong attraction, longing, and specialness. They leave you with a feeling that you have received something of great importance that is somehow a part of your identity. If you have such a dream—don't let it slip away from you!

Here is an example of an inspiring contact dream—*Big Cat on the Tarmac*. The dreamer is a 31-year-old woman named Gina:

> *I am with a big group of people heading for a plane to return from a trip. We're on the tarmac. I turn around and see a big wild cat. I am very excited. It is so rare to see such an animal. I try to get everyone else's attention—"Wait! Don't get on the plane yet ... look at this cat!" But they don't seem to be interested. I try to take a picture of it, but it was too big to fit into the viewfinder, so I keep trying to move back. It looks like a female lion without a mane, but it has these red markings around the head and neck. They look like ancient geometric Aztec or Mayan markings. I wake up feeling excited and grateful to have been the one to see it.*

As so often happens in this type of dream, the other people who are present do not notice the big cat; the encounter is intended only for Gina. This uniquely personal quality is a hallmark of the inspiring contact motif. Is it a good idea to try to photograph the special being (as people often try to do in these dreams)? On the one hand it shows that Gina recognizes the amazing specialness of the experience and wants to be able to capture and remember it. But on the other hand, it interferes with the immediacy of the meeting. I will typically use the Good Thing/Bad Thing orientation at these times so I asked her: "Do you think it's a good thing that you are trying to get a picture of the big cat, or would it be better to put away the camera and walk toward her?" In this and in most other cases I have experienced, Gina wished she had not tried to use the camera. This sets up a natural imaginal response: "Imagine that you put away the camera and just look directly at the big cat ... how does it feel? Would you like to move closer?"

Here's another example. At 42 years old, Susan was contemplating a career change. Ideally, she wants to be a practicing dreamworker, but she was having some trouble seeing how she could manifest this transition logistically and financially. She had a dream called *The Tiny Burrowing Owls*:

> *I'm in a neighborhood in the west end of the city I live in, it's an area I love. The ocean is lapping up against a city street. There's lots of sand, and there's an opening in the sand. I crouch down to look at the opening. I see all these tiny little owls flying in and out of the opening! I'm watching them, fascinated. Someone (a disembodied voice) says: "Follow the owls and find the gold." I look at the opening, it's too small for me to fit inside. I can't follow the owls ... I wake up.*

I asked Susan what she had made of the dream so far. She answered: "The owls are nocturnal, like little dreamers or dreamworkers that can pass through the realms of nighttime and daytime, through this reality and the other reality." And what about the gold? "I imagined that I was the gold. I became a liquid golden person, very powerful and magical, able to transform everything I touched."

Here we see the Dynamic/Stuck dyad again; the owls and the gold are very dynamic, but there is a stuck point right at the end of the dream—Susan feels she cannot follow the direction the voice gave her as she is "too big" to enter the opening and follow the owls. She connected this to a lack of focus on her goal of becoming a dreamworker: "I'm too big. My focus is too wide. I'm doing too much. I should be narrowing down my intention onto what I really want to be doing. If I did that I could probably fit inside the opening."

This is a dream that in some cultures would be recognized as a shamanic dream, a naming dream, or a power animal dream. It can be seen as a critical life event that confers on the dreamer an identity, a role, and a calling. It is saying to Susan: "You are one of the Burrowing Owl Clan. Your role in the community is to pass back and forth through the opening between the two realms, inside and outside, nighttime and daytime, and bring the gold that can transform." This is a perfect job description for a dreamworker! Susan understood that the dream related to, among other things, her declared intention to become a dreamworker. Thus it became very critical that she address the blockage that was preventing her from moving ahead with that goal, the "bigness" that prevented her from entering the opening. Her response in the actual realm involved putting more focused energy into her dreamwork practice.

Psychodynamics of the inspiring contact motif

Dreams that feature a special encounter with a nature spirit have been highly valued by almost all human societies. The encounter is very often with an animal, but it can also be a plant, a flower, a tree, a celestial body, a pool or stream, a stone, a gem; indeed it can be anything from the natural world. It could also be something from the spirit realm—an ancestral spirit, an angel, a fairy, a divine being of some kind. The common element is the feeling of receiving something special and unique. If it is something from the world of nature, you may feel as though you have been offered a special connection with that species or substance. You may now feel an identification, a sense of shared power, a totemic alliance.

Why would your unconscious take the trouble to select one particular thing, surround it with an enormously positive feeling tone, and send it to you in a dream? Let's say, hypothetically, that you had a beautiful dream about a birch tree. What might it be asking you for? Could your dreammaker be suggesting that you should spend more time with trees, especially the birch? Could your dreammaker be recommending that you literally take some substance or energy of the birch tree into your body (an extract, a tea, a remedy)? Are you being introduced to one of your totems, allies, nature spirits, guides, or helpers in the guise of a birch tree? Is your dreammaker drawing on symbolic, cultural, transpersonal, or archetypal associations with the birch tree and using them to deliver a message to you? Are you receiving a blessing from the divine realm?

The answer is—all are possible. In any of these scenarios it is a good idea to respond by spending some quality time with a birch tree. Nourish the insight that is trying to happen. Create the conditions for deeper understanding. Notice the sense of energy, wonderment, and optimism that comes with such dreams. This kind of dream always has a sense of being inarguably meaningful on its own terms; you don't need to justify its importance to anyone else. It shows you a bridge between your current position and where your inner self would like you to go. The bridge is being offered to you… will you cross?

Such dreams may be trying to tell you that you have a special affinity with certain species or substances in nature. This is an idea that perhaps we do not give enough attention to in modern Western culture. You may find that you don't receive much support or recognition from those around when you share your inspiring contact dream. Don't let that discourage you. You are experiencing something as old as humanity itself—an encounter with something that is uniquely yours.

Distinctive features of an inspiring contact motif

- an encounter with a remarkable animal, nature spirit, angel, or ancestral spirit

- often you are the only one to experience a remarkable encounter (if there are other people present in the dream they do not seem to be aware or interested)

- an encounter with a teacher or a teaching

- finding gifts, treasure, and money

- a spiritual or religious experience, a sense of receiving a blessing

- visiting a soul place (often accompanied by a feeling of great familiarity or déja-vu)

- a divinely erotic or loving encounter

Dreamworking suggestions for an inspiring contact motif

- *Connecting the dream image to what is currently inspiring in your life*

  These motifs are showing you that you're being given something of value. But what is it? You need to know what it is so you can receive it fully and make good use of it. In Carlo's dream of *The Chameleon Concierge and the Wonderful Room of Gifts* discussed in chapter 12, what were the gifts referring to? Do they refer to a recent insight? A teaching? Renewed health? An increase of energy? A valuable connection? A spiritual breakthrough? A bit of good luck? An opening in the way? An inspiring idea? A new friendship? It can be anything; Carlo will know but he may need a bit of help arriving at the answer.

- *Responding with something special to match the specialness of the dream*

  What can be gained from this kind of encounter depends on how you receive it and respond to it. If you have forgotten all about it the next day, then not much has been gained. If, on the other hand, you receive it with a sense of honor and appreciation, the spirit of your dream may remain with you as an ally for the rest of your life. Ritual and creative responses are both well suited to this kind of motif. How about painting a birch tree? Putting some birch bark on your altar? A photo of a birch grove on your computer screen? Visiting a forest?

- *If there is a block, investigate it*

  Susan's inner voice told her to "follow the owls and find the gold." She had the energy, willingness, and desire to follow her owls, but there was a block—she was too big to fit into the opening. It is usually a good idea to respond to the block imaginally at first—re-enter the dreamscape and find a solution that works within the scenario given by the dream. Practice this for a while, this imaginal work will probably help you understand how the blockage manifests in your waking world, and what you may be able to do about it.

Further examples of this motif

Three Wolves in the Water, Introduction

The Big Loon, chapter 3

The Big Grasshopper, chapter 6

The Crow With the Glowing Eyes, chapter 7

The Archbishop's Car, chapter 10

The Chameleon Concierge and the Wonderful Room of Gifts, chapter 12

The Traveling Minstrel Grasshopper Show, chapter 14

The Colorful Toad, chapter 14

The Crystal Prayer Wheel, chapter 14

CHAPTER 26

Positive Feedback Motifs

Essential message: "You have just accomplished something very positive. Be aware of it, support it, encourage it, keep doing it!"

Asking for: you to invest more awareness and energy into the positive trend that is already happening.

Ingrid's daughter Carly is sixteen years old now, starting to move out into the big wide world in the way teenagers do. Ingrid, like most mothers of teenage girls, is trying to find the right balance between healthy guidance and anxious over-protectiveness. Ingrid's dream, *Ritual on the Beach,* seems to speak to this issue:

> *There is an elaborate and stunningly beautiful ritual being held on a beach. There are about a hundred people there. Carly and I are watching from a distance. The water comes up and everyone is running and laughing. The swell sweeps them away into the water. I look around and Carly is now gone! I'm so, so sad and worried about her. I'm looking for her.*

Then I see her swimming with beautiful fish at the bottom of the ocean. She's enjoying herself. It calms me, but I don't know what to do about it because I'm not there with her.

Ingrid has recently experienced waves of realization that her daughter is growing up and moving away from her. She has recognized that the process will be painful and at times frightening, but she is making an effort to allow it to happen in its own time and rhythm. By combining two contrasting elements (fear of loss and beautiful celebration), Ingrid's dreammaker is reassuring her, commending her for her efforts, and encouraging her to keep them up.

Here's another example. Olive had been on an antidepressant medication for several years, but recently had decided to wean off it because although it did help stabilize her moods she didn't like the way it flattened and distanced her emotions. Now that she was off the medication, she had occasional doubts about her decision, was the trade-off worth it overall? During this period of second-guessing her choice, Olive had a very short dream she called *The Suitcase*:

I'm in a vast ocean. I'm aware of all these images of things, many things, submerged under the water. I'm on the surface, I can sense these images but not clearly, they're deep down in the water. Then an antique style suitcase, reddish brown with an ivory handle, floats up to the surface. It pops up out of the water! I wake up.

When I asked Olive if she thought it was a good thing that this suitcase had come up to the surface she wasn't sure. We decided to investigate further. I asked her to re-enter the dreamscape. There she was, floating in a vast ocean with an old suitcase. What did she want to do? "I want to swim to shore and open it. I'm wondering what's inside." We visualized doing that. She got it to shore and opened it. "I feel angry. Anger and rage are coming out." I asked Olive if this might be a good development—anger that had been submerged for a long time finally allowed to come out? She thought this was certainly possible, and agreed to continue the imaginal suitcase work on her own.

In her next session, Olive reported that the suitcase work had been very productive:

I now know that the suitcase is something that was submerged by all the medication I was taking. It was able to bob up to the surface after I stopped taking the drug. The anger and rage didn't last long. What came after that was an old familiar feeling I remember from when I was a child. Hard to describe it, it's like a sense of the divine, that there are things divine in the world. That got submerged for awhile, but it's good to have it back.

One effect of Olive's work on the suitcase dream was that she felt it confirmed that she had made a good decision to come off her antidepressant. The metaphor of important things being submerged and out of reach made sense to her. She wanted to get more of these submerged parts back, open them up and look at them again. The dream even warned her about the Pandora's box effect that often happens after a long and "successful" suppression of the emotional life. When you first open the lid, watch out! But even though she had to deal with the stored-up rage and anger, Olive felt the dream gave her good advice, encouragement, and a sense of validation about her choice.

Psychodynamics of the positive feedback motif

Have you ever had a dream that starts out with a familiar sense of being frustrated and held back by a problem, but for whatever reason you are able to overcome the problem this time? These are wonderful dreams. They are pointing out that you have been stuck in some limiting pattern for a long time and have recently managed to get unstuck. Now you need to figure out exactly when and how you managed to do that in waking life.

Once you know what it is you're being commended for, you can reinforce and build on that achievement.

A lot of the feedback given in dreams is negative and critical feedback, as for example in ego check motifs. But not all! Dreams will also send you positive feedback and encouragement. This is particularly true if you are the type to downplay and undervalue your own achievements; your dreammaker will try to compensate for this hyper-modest attitude by blowing your own dream horn for you. It notices when you accomplish something significant and will send a dream to affirm and applaud. It is widely accepted that praise, reward, and positive feedback are powerful motivators for children, but not just for children; we all respond favorably, asleep and awake. These dreams typically have very positive feeling tones and leave behind no residue of frustration or stuckness. If there is a stuckness, it occurs in the early part of the dream and is then overcome.

Distinctive features of a positive feedback motif

- overcoming a fear, an obstacle, a stuckness, or a challenging problem.

- often refer back to former repeating dreams of stuckness, but this time you succeed!

- being congratulated, rewarded, celebrated, applauded, encouraged.

Dreamworking suggestions for a positive feedback motif
Recognizing and underscoring your recent accomplishment
Your dream appears to be saying that there has been a significant recent achievement—but what is it? Most often it will be something that you've *already* accomplished but occasionally these dreams will reach slightly into the future and herald something that is on the verge of happening. In either case, you need to know what it is so you can do more of it.

Connect through recognizing a pattern

If you're having trouble connecting the dream to your life, try a setup that reiterates the pattern in the dream, then ask yourself: "Where does that pattern exist in my life?" For example, with Olivia's suitcase dream we can ask: "In the dream you sense that many things have been submerged and out of reach, but one thing has recently popped up to the surface. Is there anything in your life that would fit that pattern?"

Further examples of this motif

Three Wolves in the Water, Introduction
The First Woman to Run for President, chapter 2
Blowing on the Fire, chapter 5
The Chameleon Concierge and the Wonderful Room of Gifts, chapter 12
Going Feet First, chapter 14

CHAPTER 27

Rogue Part Motifs

Essential message: "A part of your psyche has broken away from the whole; it is now acting autonomously and harming you."

Asking for: you to be aware of how the rogue part functions, so there can be a reduction in the harm it causes.

Some people encounter truly harmful and dangerous figures in their dreams. There is more than an expectation or fear of harm (as in the shadow motif), there is actual harm done in the dream: attacking, hurting, threatening, restraining, controlling, insulting, criticizing, even killing. If you have a dream with a dangerous figure in it, you need to carefully differentiate what type of figure it is before doing any work with the dream. We will be looking closely at this critical aspect of dreamworking in chapter 31. Many of these truly harmful characters are rogue figures—parts of self that have "broken away" and are capable of acting in a way that is harmful to the whole person. They are not interested in healing, wholeness, cooperation, growth, or change. They have their own autonomy and their own agenda, and often this agenda is dangerously at odds with the best interests of the whole person.

This is the dream of a 21-year-old woman named Meghan. As she told me her recurring dream of *The Huge Warship*, she was almost unable to speak, her fear was so strong:

> *It is a very fearful dream. It feels like there is some kind of war or disaster going on. I am running and hiding under whatever I can find, usually cars. Somehow, there is this huge military ship passing by with sweeping radar lights. Sometimes there is someone else who I'm trying to hide and protect as well, but I think a lot of the time it's just me. I'm hiding under cars usually… and then this ship comes."* (Long pause, Meghan is crying.)

Dreamworker: What kind of ship?

> *A great… big… armed… boat… with radar lights.*

DW: And how do you know about the radar lights?

> *The radar lights are there… sweeping… because I'm running from them…*

DW: You're running from them because…?

> *Because they feel dangerous… I'll be in danger if I get caught… that's where the fear is, I guess… I have to stay out of their sight somehow.* (long pause… at this point Meghan is barely able to stop herself from breaking down).

DW: And do you manage to stay out of their sight?

> *Usually I wake up just as I am being found.*

DW: Can you describe the feeling you have when you wake up?

> *Panicky… heart racing.*

What does the huge warship represent? It is important to consider the Inner/Outer question right from the outset. Is this an inner warship (an aspect of Meghan that intimidates and traumatizes her) or an outer warship (someone or something in her life that intimidates and traumatizes her)? As we worked with the dream in session, Meghan was able to make a partially resonant connection between the warship and her relationship with her mother. She felt that her mother's emotional needs were too intrusive and she was not allowed enough psychic space and privacy as she grew up (this was indeed still the case in their current relationship). Meghan was forced to hide from her mother's too intense need for emotional connection. This fit the feeling tone of the sweeping radar lights; it felt resonant. By this time Meghan was emotionally exhausted from the impact of the dream so we wrapped up the session.

However, that was not the end of it. The dream had been recorded on videotape and at our next session I suggested we watch it together. Meghan considered it for a moment and said: "I can only watch it if you go out of the room. I will be judging myself so intensely, and it will be worse if you're in the room." I left the room and waited outside for a few minutes while she watched the segment. As I waited, another possible connection regarding the huge warship began to resonate for me—was the huge warship a depiction of her inner judge and critic?

When I went back in the room, we discussed this possible connection and it was powerfully resonant, more resonant even than the previous connection she had made with her mother. Because Meghan was feeling stronger in this session, I was able to ask her to "be" the warship. As she did this she was able to identify with the warship as an aspect of herself that she is always trying to hide from, an intensely self-critical part of her that is always on the lookout for something to pick on.

Meghan still felt that the warship also related to the way she felt and still sometimes feels around her mother. We agreed that probably both connections were true—she has internalized what was originally an external problem and now carries around her own inner version of it. Indeed most of the self-judging and self-critical phrases that she now turns against herself were originally introjected from her mother; phrases about her physical appearance, her weight, her eating, her use of makeup, her style of dress, her mannerisms, and her way of speaking. Many of these were taken in verbatim and now live their own autonomous life inside Meghan—forming into a huge warship of critical self-scrutiny and self-judgment.

The warship is now so powerful, so autonomous, and so self-harming that I would describe it as a *rogue part* of Meghan. It is a part of her, but it is a part that has no interest in getting along with any other part of her. She cannot stop it or contain it, she can only hide from it in terror.

Here's an example of a dream that contains two very important motifs— a personal spirit motif (the abandoned forgotten child) and a rogue self-care motif (the violent foster father who won't allow the dreamer to connect with his child). *Yuri/Ari* is the dream of a 35-year-old man named Arnold:

> *I hide my brother—or my son—in a school. I say, "stay here, hide in this corner." I hide him in a place where no one will find him, under a staircase. I forget to come back for him for a couple of hours. He is traumatized. He is crying, he won't stop crying. He is young; he has to be about three years old. So I grab him. Then there is a break in the dream—it is years later—I'm going to pick him up at a foster home, because he is being abused there. I get into a big fight with the people who are there with him. For some reason I remember his name—it was either Yuri or Ari. When I go to pick him up at the foster home, I have a big fight with the foster parents, a violent confrontation. They won't let me take him. The little boy says, "who are you?' I say, "I'm your brother, or your father. You'll be safe with me." But the foster parent won't let him go. We get in a fight. I get kicked in the groin by the guy. I wake up in pain, feeling as if I had been kicked in the groin.*

To translate this story from the metaphorical language of the dream, Arnold lost a part of himself as a result of a trauma in the past. He is now becoming aware of this loss and wants to do something about it, but another part of him (a rogue part) will not allow him access. The dream is warning Arnold (and any kind of therapist who might try to help him) that if he wants to get his personal spirit back he will be facing a long hard battle with the internalized foster care system that he himself created.

Here is another example. Helen, a 45-year-old cancer survivor, connected the ominous cloaked figure in her dream with her disease. She called this dream *Followed By a Cloaked Man*:

> *I am walking in a downtown area and I am going to have dinner with my husband. As I walk through the area, somehow I get to another area that is a bit different. There is a dirt path and the houses are farther away from the path. It looks a bit like a construction area. As I walk, I feel that somebody is walking behind me but very close to me. So, I turn around to make room for that person to pass by and get in front of me. As I turn around, the person who is behind me also starts to turn around the other direction and starts walking the other direction. It's a man wearing a cloak and I am scared.*

The dream gave Helen important information about the status of her disease state. It indicated that she could not defeat the disease or get clear away from it, but she could cause it to retreat by turning to face it when it got too close. This was encouraging to her because it suggested that she had the power to force her cancer into remission by proactively confronting it.

Psychodynamics of the rogue part motif

I have found that rogue figures can often be identified with one of the following groups and reflect the original psychodynamic problems that gave rise to them:

1. *Rogue self-care figures*—arising from a self-care system created by the dreamer to cope with unbearable pain following trauma. These systems are usually created in childhood, but can also come into existence following trauma in adulthood, as in PTSD (post-traumatic stress disorder). We all have self-care systems, but if they become too powerful, autonomous, and self-harming they can appear in dreams as rogue figures that harm the dream ego (like the violent foster father in Arnold's *Yuri/Ari* dream). The fairy tale *Rapunzel* and the Disney version *Tangled* are about a rogue self-care system. The mother, wanting to protect and care for her daughter, becomes obsessed with isolating her daughter from the outside world and all other human contact. This can be seen as both a depiction of parental over-protectiveness gone rogue, but it also applies to an internalized self-protection system gone rogue. Either of these can become dangerous and destructive, though they both originate from a well-intentioned desire to protect and soothe.

2. *Rogue introject figures*—originating from an introject—an idea or belief system that was forced into the dreamer's psyche, usually in childhood. If that construct becomes very powerful and self-harming, it can appear in a dream as a dangerous and harming figure (like the huge warship in Meghan's dream).

3. *Rogue disease figures*—depictions of physical or mental disease states that live within the dreamer but are not self-limiting and seem to have their own "agenda," like the cloaked man in Helen's dream. I have found that the most common disease states to appear as harmful figures in dreams are: cancer, auto-immune diseases, conditions of unstable brain chemistry such as bipolar disorder, obsessive-compulsive disorder (OCD), drug addiction, suicidal ideation, eating disorders, body image disorders, brain injury, and parasitic infection.

Rogue parts are involved in many behaviors that make us feel temporarily better (feel-good fantasies, comforting habits, addictions, comfort eating, drug use, etc.). The combination of soothing yourself with a habitual behavior then abusing yourself for not being able to curb that very behavior is highly characteristic of a rogue dynamic.

The rogue part has usually been around for as long as the person can remember. Its origins are often lost in the forgotten suffering of early childhood. It is associated with chronic, intractable problems and repetitive behaviors. It tends to remain very static unless it is directly challenged. If it is challenged, it may retaliate by triggering a relapse, a renewed intensity of self-abuse, some form of self-sabotage, or some kind of "accident" or injury. Often a person will feel hesitant or afraid to confront or provoke such a rogue part, as Meghan was with her huge warship. She sensed how powerful the warship was in her psyche. She felt like she was confronting a dangerous bully, and she was quite naturally afraid of retaliation. As a psychotherapist, I have learned from experience that when *I* feel threatened or intimidated while working with a client there is usually a rogue part lurking nearby trying to sabotage the healing process.

The work of Jungian psychoanalyst Donald Kalsched is very helpful in understanding the complex psychodynamics of rogue figures. I highly recommend his two remarkable books that focus on this subject. [14, 15]

Distinctive features of a rogue part motif

- dream figures that actually attack and harm the dream ego

- dream figures that seem truly evil, malicious, and demonic

---

14 Donald Kalsched, *The Inner World of Trauma: Archetypal Defenses of the Personal Spirit* (London: Routledge, 1996).

15 Donald Kalsched, *Trauma and the Soul–A Psychospiritual Approach to Human Development and Its Interruption*(London and New York: Routledge, 2013).

- dream figures that criticize harshly and generate a feeling of self-hatred

- dream figures that block access to a child

- dream figures that block communication

- dream figures that evoke a feeling of comforting fantasy

- dream figures that offer or force the use of a drug or substance

- dream figures that threaten and intimidate

Dreamworking suggestions for a rogue part motif
Harm reduction through understanding how the system works

In my experience, rogue parts are the hardest figures in the psyche to work with. They appear to have no interest in any kind of personal growth work; in fact, they typically sabotage it. Thus the goal is usually a very modest one when dealing with a rogue dynamic—simply to reduce the harm the rogue is causing. Watching your dreams will reveal the presence of the rogue part, if there is one, and give some idea of how it operates in your psyche. If you are bewildered by your own self-sabotaging behavior, you may get great relief when you begin to understand some of the inner reasons for it. You will be able to anticipate when your relapses and self-sabotages are likely to occur, and you may be able to avoid or mitigate some of them.

Can rogue figures be healed or redeemed? Can a rogue part evolve into a benign and useful part of the psyche? Can it be gradually and incrementally weakened until it no longer generates self-harming behavior? Can a rogue be persuaded that healing, growth, and change are good for all parts of the self ? I believe all these are possible, but the work usually goes very slowly and is typically fraught with setbacks and relapses.

Further examples of this motif

Sliding Snake Wound, chapter 12
The Mechanical Scorpion, chapter 14
Can't Find the Spider, chapter 18

CHAPTER 28

Dreambody Motifs

Essential message: "Your dreambody has its own abilities, its own desires and needs."

Asking for: you to be attentive and supportive of what your dreaming body does and wants to do.

By "dreambody," I simply mean your body as it is within a dream. In dreams you can do things that are fully felt and experienced in your dreambody while your physical body lies asleep in bed. These experiences are real while they are happening, only becoming "unreal" when your ego wakes up and reestablishes its own perspective. In dreams you can escape from many of the constraints that apply in waking life, including gravity, morality, pain, injury, fatigue, ageing, the limitations imposed by time and space, and many of the limitations we impose upon ourselves.

There is a very powerful scene in the film *Avatar* in which the protagonist Jake awakes to find himself in a new body. In his old material body he was a paraplegic confined to a wheelchair, but in his new avatar body he is physically vigorous and powerful. He revels in his newfound body by running ecstatically, savoring the pure joy of movement that is now possible. This is the experience of finding yourself in your dreambody. You are free, strong, unencumbered! What will you do?

What does *your* dreambody like to do? When you become lucidly aware in a dream, what's the first thing you think of? If you're like most people you want to fly. Finding an attractive person to have sex with is also a popular choice. This is no coincidence—flying and sex are two things that the human dreambody loves to engage in. There is a group of universal dream motifs that arise directly from the unfettered desires and activities of our dreambodies. First up is flying!

Flying motifs

Over a decade ago, I had a dream in which the joy of flying was coupled with other important motifs. Here is *Finding the Key That is Special and Not Special:*

> *I am in a temple. My son Otis is there. There are some Tibetan-looking monks around, clad in traditional wine-colored robes. I pair up with one of the monks who is going to teach me an important movement. I go behind him and hold him, my front to his back. We start to do the hopping movement together, moving in unison. We start to get more and more flow and energy with each hopping movement, until we have built up enough energy to lift off the ground. Now we are airborne. We move upwards with a motion that is somewhere between floating and flying, and we move around inside the vast interior of the temple. Very exciting! Suddenly I become aware that there is something important in one of the carved alcoves that form the ceiling of the temple. I feel certain that if I reach behind me into a particular spot there will be something there. I fly/float up toward the spot. Sure enough, when I reach in with my hand there is an old-fashioned key with something attached to it. I take*

it and we float down to the floor to show it to the other monks. I feel it is important but I'm not sure how important. The monks do not seem terribly impressed. They react as if it is just another piece of the ongoing work, special but not special.

The quality of motion in this dream is quite different from my usual flying dreams in which I just jump up in the air and rocket around like Superman. This was something that I had to learn and practice, getting better and better until I generated enough lift to get off the ground. But once up in the air that wonderful feeling of freedom was strongly present. This helped me get some orientation with the dream—it was asking me to work at something with monk-like dedication and practice, something that will soon lead to a sense of freedom from limitation followed by an important discovery. And, after bringing that discovery back, the dream is telling me that I will have to continue the ongoing work and dedicated practice. I connected this key to the practice of dreamwork. Dreamwork *is* like a key, and it is something that is both special and not special. It is special because of the remarkable insights and growth it can bring; and not special because you still have to do the hard work; it is just one of many different daily practices that we may decide to include in our lives.

Psychodynamics of the dreambody motif

The flying or floating dream is one of humanity's most common and best-loved dreams. These dreams usually have a very positive feeling tone that is due, in large part, to the simple joy of weightlessness, freedom, and ecstatic movement. Thus, these dreams provide us with a healthy and necessary respite from the rigors of existing in a material body, and they should be enjoyed and appreciated simply for that.

But the flying will often lead you to something more. After flying for a while, you may find that you have arrived somewhere new, discovered something important, or met an intriguing person. The high voltage excitement and joy of a flying dream often seems to couple itself with other dream motifs that have a similarly positive feeling tone—especially self-discovery motifs and inspiring contact motifs.

The temporary uncoupling of the soul from the body (or we could say the dreambody from the material body) is often performed as a deliberate practice with a particular intention such as in guided imagery, active imagination, the re-enter and explore technique described in this book, vision questing, shamanic journeying, and experimental drug use. If you are interested in developing the skill of uncoupling your two bodies from each other and exploring what can happen, there would be no better place to begin than practicing with your own dream life, where this uncoupling and recoupling happens spontaneously and naturally every night.

Having trouble with your flying?

Flying dreams are usually very positive, but what about the negative ones? For example, what do we make of a person who repeatedly dreams of making a great effort to flap her wings and get off the ground but cannot quite do it? We can ask: is the dreambody's frustration a depiction of some problem in the dreamer's waking life—a depression? A heaviness? A failure of the imagination? A physical illness? A key lack of opportunity in life? A feeling of being trapped? Inability to get some important creative project off the ground? Perhaps. Or perhaps her dreambody just needs to practice flying and get better at it. Whatever the problem, is it can be addressed directly within the dreamscape by enlisting the creative power of imagination. If you have dreams like this, re-enter one of them and ask yourself: how would I like this frustrated flight scenario to change? You can try various things until you find something that feels right. Now visualize this new action actually happening for an extended time, let yourself experience it as fully as you can. Let yourself feel an imagined version of the deep satisfaction and pleasure that can come from dream flight. By doing this you will be supporting your dreambody in doing something it wants to do but can't. After practicing this a few times ask yourself: is this flying problem appearing as a metaphor for some problem in my waking life? Or is it just my dreambody trying to get airborne?

Falling and crashing motifs

What if your dream is not of controlled and joyful flying, but of falling from a great height and crashing to earth? In my experience, we are dealing with something different here, not simply the needs and desires of the dreambody. I believe that these motifs are saying something about the status of the dreamer's embodiment, the process of coming into and dwelling within the physical body. Thus these dream motifs are saying something about the complex relationship between the ego consciousness, the physical body, and the dreambody.

As the fetus grows in the womb, a new consciousness starts to become aware that it is existing within a material body. In human symbolism and in dreams (I wonder which came first?), this process is often depicted as the dreamer's awareness "coming down" into the body. Thus, dream motifs that refer to the incarnation process involve dramatic descent, falling from a great height often in a plane or spacecraft, and crashing to earth.

A normal, healthy embodiment may be depicted in a dream as a plane crash or a fall to earth, but with no subsequent trauma or suffering. I have had many people report dreams of crash landing a plane in which the dreamer and other people on board were momentarily frightened and shaken, but nobody was killed and the dream action continued. As Patricia Garfield describes in her book *Creative Dreaming*—the Senoi peoples would tell their children: "Falling is one of the best dreams you can have. The earth spirits love you; they are calling to you. Let yourself fall gently and land gently. Go and find the wonderful things that are waiting for you there." [16]

---

16   Patricia Garfield, *Creative Dreaming* (New York: Simon and Schuster, 1995), 103.

However, if your early experience in your body was traumatic, this will be reflected in your dream life. The falling and crashing to earth dreams will be more fearful and will be followed by other dream motifs of injury, suffering, trauma, isolation, hospitalization, etc. What are such dreams asking for? They may be asking for an old trauma to be recognized and addressed.

Embodiment is not just a singular event that happened in the distant past—it is an ongoing process that some of us have not fully accomplished even into adulthood. While your consciousness inhabits your material body, it is subject to all the laws and restrictions of the material realm such as discomfort, pain, gravity, trauma, illness, ageing, self-consciousness, and boredom. If at any time the experience of being embodied is too painful and difficult for you to bear, you may leave your material body and disincarnate as a self-protective adaptation. This results in a state that is variously described as outside yourself, spaced out, out of your body, always daydreaming, in shock, dissociated, and so on. People with an incomplete or problematic embodiment will have difficulty living comfortably and fully in their bodies, and will need to escape frequently, often through the use of a state-changing substance. In the case of a subject whose dreams repeatedly contain embodiment motifs, the practitioner must ask of him- or herself—why is it so hard for this person to be in their own body? Is there a known or unknown trauma that makes it unbearably painful? This line of inquiry must be followed. Be on the lookout for the dream motifs that signal deep unresolved trauma, especially personal spirit motifs and rogue self-care system motifs.

The difficulty may have begun very early in life, often in the intrauterine environment. Was the womb not welcoming in some way? Was the child not wanted? Was a child of a different sex wanted? Was the mother herself unwell or in distress? Was either parent not accepting of the pregnancy? Was there an abortion attempt? A hope of miscarriage? Or, slightly later, was there a medical crisis around the birth? Was there a disruption of bonding and attachment immediately after the birth or a later failure for other reasons? All of these are common and can be depicted in the dream life as a traumatic embodiment motif. Because these events occurred at a very early pre-verbal phase of life, they do not appear in dreams involving ideas, names, or words. Traumatic embodiment dreams are typically full of action and intense feeling, but no words.

Here is an example of a traumatic embodiment dream. Peter was 17 years old when he had this dream of *Falling to Earth*. As a newborn he contracted meningitis and was separated from his mother while being treated in the hospital.

I am falling in an airplane. I am tracking this debris that has fallen off a rollercoaster. I am flying around with the debris and I hearing in my headphones that I am supposed to be tracking the debris. The debris starts falling faster, so I turn off the engines of the jet and start falling with the debris. It is still falling faster than I am falling, so I eject myself from the plane. I remember looking down and putting my feet together to make myself more streamlined so I keep falling and falling. I lose track of the debris. Fifty to a hundred feet from the ground, I see myself falling. As I am coming down to the ground, my parachute still isn't open. That part happens slowly and yet really quickly all at the same time. I hit the ground and remember an impact came up through my feet, up through my neck, almost like an accordion effect... sort of like a cartoon... like if you could visualize wavelengths going through my body... like if you drop something and it hits the ground, and you slow down the video of it and you can see the impact. Everything goes black... Then I am in this other place, a swampy area. Things don't feel real. It feels like I have died somehow. Time is almost standing still, or going really, really slowly. I am with this older lady and an older guy (the woman is older, maybe in her sixties, the guy is probably in his thirties). He is bald; she has this gray curly hair. Supposedly we are in this swamp for rehab, because he has broken his leg and I have injured myself in the fall (even though I didn't feel or look injured). We are supposed to walk around in this swamp to strengthen our bodies. I say, "There's no way, it's way too thick, we're not going to be able to move... we'll sink." The guy says, "Don't worry—the more you practice the stronger you'll get; your body will become stronger, and it's a good way of healing yourself." I say "Okay" and the last thing I remember is taking a couple of steps.

Along with the embodiment theme of falling to earth, we can see several indicators of an unresolved trauma in Peter's dream, especially the dissociative witnessing himself from a distance and the ejecting himself from his plane. The experience is too much to be felt from within the body—it can only be seen as if it were a cartoon or video. The impact and its aftermath are too much to bear. There is a break in the continuity of personal history from this point, depicted as everything going black followed by a new reality where everything feels different.

The second part of the dream gives us important information about what Peter must do to heal the trauma, his "rehab." The healing will involve very hard work and getting help from others, even then it will be slow going. Peter is daunted by the difficulty of the rehab—he seems to feel that it is too difficult, too effort-full, too far beyond his abilities. There is a subtle background feeling here that is commonly present in embodiment dreams—a feeling that it is too hard to be in a physical body; the pain is too much, the gravity is too strong, the struggle is too much to bear. Therefore, let's cope by doing something that helps us, at least partially, to escape from our material bodies. Meanwhile, the older man is undaunted and encouraging. He cites one of the laws of neuroplasticity and human healing—the more you practice the stronger you get.

Amazing ability motifs

What does it mean when you dream of being able to do something perfectly that you cannot actually do in waking life? If I have a dream of being able to speak fluent Spanish (a dream I have had several times, also with French and Italian and even Latin), is the dream pointing out something or asking for something? Does it mean I can learn to speak fluent Spanish (probably true), or that I should do so? (Less clear.) Or is my soul just having fun and reveling in the experience of speaking fluent Spanish, because it can? It seems that in dreams we can be freed from the laws (or perceived laws) that govern our abilities, just as we can be freed from the laws of gravity.

I, and I think most people, have enjoyed several variants of this kind of dream. My personal versions having involved speaking other languages, being able to play different musical instruments with great skill and enjoyment, being able to sing with breathtaking beauty in very high registers (I can sing, but not like that!) and being able to play various sports with remarkable skill and power. The common feature of all these dreams is thrilling enjoyment—they are all great fun! As with other dreams that feature the unencumbered dreambody doing its thing, it often seems that nothing in particular is being communicated and nothing is being asked for.

Sometimes it seems as if these dreams are giving us an intra-psychic pep talk. Their feeling tone is so exciting that they can shift anyone's negative mindset, if only for a few moments. Could they be, in some cases, the dreammaker's attempt to compensate for feelings of discouragement, limitation, boredom, and depression? An attempt to cheer us up and inspire us? I have also wondered if such dreams may be trying to draw our attention to the creative powers of the imagination—pointing out that if we can *dream* about being able to do something then we can also *imagine* doing that thing. Visualizing ourselves doing new things can bring great benefits, benefits that we are only just beginning to comprehend.

Distinctive features of dreambody motifs

- flying, floating, soaring, hovering

- any superhuman physical action—fast running, jumping, leaping

- feelings of joyful and deeply satisfying physicality

- frustrating attempts to get off the ground, take off, fly
- looking down from a great height, often in a plane or spacecraft
- falling to earth from a great height, crashing, plane crashes
- coming down into a ship or other vessel
- spectacular impact from a spectacular fall
- falling combined with injury or impact
- doing something amazingly well, with supernatural ability

CHAPTER 29

Somatic Motifs

Essential Message: "This is your material body here. You're close to being awake and I'm coming into your dream."

Asking for: awareness of the material body and what it is experiencing.

Your sleeping body will often contribute raw material to the dream you're having. The fact that you have a full bladder may appear in your dream, or the smell of breakfast being made downstairs, the light coming in the window, the beginnings of a headache, sexual arousal, some stiffness or discomfort—this kind of input from your body and from the environment via your sense organs is somatic input. This kind of input does not necessarily affect your dreambody (your body as it is in a dream) because your dreambody can uncouple itself completely from all these material and environmental conditions. But as you approach the waking state, your material body comes back online, you once again become subject to all the facts and constraints of material existence, any of which may appear in your dream.

Should you ignore these dreams, or assign them a lesser degree of importance because they include a straightforward somatic component? Should you dismiss your toilet-seeking dreams with the rationale that of course you were dreaming about trying to find a toilet—your bladder was full and you needed to pee? It depends. What if your toilet dream contains other interesting elements that cannot be accounted for by the full bladder? In my experience, when we look closely at these dreams they often *do* contain something else of interest.

Often these somatic elements do not seem to be fully "of the dream." They may have a quality of intruding into the dream from our bodies and from the environment we are sleeping in, like people who stumble onto a stage and are somehow integrated into a play. Sometimes this intrusion wakes us up. But other times we remain asleep and the play goes on—it could go either way. This drama is usually played out in the liminal (shoreline) zone where we are close to waking but still asleep—the richest and most common time for good dream recall.

I think it is important to recognize that somatic intrusion creates dream material that is often distinguishable from the purely internal creations of the dreammaker. Since the two types of material can coexist within the same dream, we need to be good at making the distinction. I perform a mental operation that goes something like this: "Well, it makes sense that this somatic element is here in the dream because of X-Y-Z, but this other element seems to be present purely as a spontaneous internal creation of the dreammaker." In this way, I am giving relatively more importance to the non-somatic elements of the dream—the elements that have truly been generated by the dreammaker, as opposed to integrated and adapted by the dreammaker.

To take this matter further, I have noticed that certain kinds of somatic intrusion tend to influence the dream in characteristic ways and make it more likely that the dreammaker will generate certain motifs. For example, if you have a full bladder you will very commonly dream of needing to pee. But how will your bladder-y drama unfold? If you pee successfully and not much else happens then we have a purely somatic dream—universal but not very interesting. But what if, after much seeking, you still cannot find a private place to urinate? Now we have an element that may be carrying an important message from your dreammaker about a critical lack of privacy in some aspect of your life. In many dreams the somatic element, once it has found its way into the dream, acts as an attractor that tends to draw out and organize a certain kind of subject matter from the infinite storehouse that is available to the dreammaker. Let's take a look at some of the common somatic dream motifs and consider some of the other motifs that are often associated with them.

Surrounding environment motifs

The environment that surrounds you as you sleep will often find its way into your dream via your sense organs. Light, sounds, smell, warmth, cold, touch—any of these can be conscripted into the dreamscape. This happens most often just before waking, as your dreaming brain is transitioning into your waking brain. Very commonly it is the somatic intrusion that will rouse you and gives you the link that allows you to remember the dream.

Kevin dreamed that a bug was trying to fly into his ear. He woke himself and his wife up frantically trying to get the bug off of him. There may indeed have been something actually touching him near his ear, and it was probably this somatic intrusion that not only woke him up (thus allowing him to remember the dream) but acted as an attractor for a possible introject motif. Here is Kevin describing the dream, *Flying Bugs With Microchips*:

> *I dream about these flying bugs with microchips. They are trying to land in my ear and plant these microchips in my ear. My wife wakes me up; I was moving around and mumbling something to her. I say, "I have to kill these*

bugs!" She says, "I've already killed it for you." I reply, "You did?... You can't!... How?" I am just waking up. I think it is real. I am confused. I look around in the bed for a bug. I still think there may have been a real bug touching me, or something touching me.

If not for the presence of the microchips and the bugs' intention to get inside the ear, we would probably take this as a simple somatic dream—a light touch provoking a reflexive response to having an insect on one's body. By itself this is a simple somatic intrusion, but the bugs are trying to implant microchips inside him. There may be some very important content here piggybacking along with the simple somatic element. Whenever something tries to get into your ear there is a red flag raised for a possible introject—the bugs can be a metaphor for some unwanted content that he has recently heard and he is trying not to let in. It is all the more likely to refer to an introject because of the microchips, a common dream metaphor for programmed information and ideas.

Full bladder motifs

Have you ever dreamed of an overflowing toilet? You're not alone. The full bladder (or full bowel) dream is surely one of the most common dream motifs worldwide, and it has many variants. In many of these, the full bladder or bowel acts as a somatic attractor for a number of other dream motifs. Most common among these is the shadow dream. If you are doing shadow work of integrating repressed and disowned parts of yourself, you may be feeling the need to discharge energy and emotion in new ways, ways that you have not allowed yourself previously. You may have had an emotional outburst that you feel guilty about. This can appear in your dream as a horrible shitty mess from an overflowing toilet. Do you have to clean up this mess now?

Or, if your emotional body is backlogged with congested energy that needs to be discharged, you may dream about a clogged or malfunctioning toilet. If you find a toilet but feel it is too dirty to use, this may be pointing to a brain field motif that generates an exaggerated fear of germs and contagion. If a lack of privacy is your problem, you may have a dream like Carrie's *Can't Find a Private Bathroom to Use!* discussed in chapter 3. If you're having trouble finding a healthy way to discharge the emotions that you need to let go of, you may have a dream of being unable to find a toilet at all. So before you dismiss your toilet dream just ask yourself—might there be something interesting here?

Hunger and thirst motifs

Your sleeping body, not having eaten all night, might be getting hungry by the time you're experiencing an early morning dream. Hunger and food motifs are common in dreams (more common than thirst motifs in my experience) and they often seem to have the quality of somatic intrusions, stumbling up into your dream from your hungering body.

Frank had a very long and very tense dream in which he was an armed security guard searching a large building for robbers who had broken in. Then, in the last scene of the dream, he found himself in a completely different setting, out for a drink and relaxing with a big stack of freshly baked cookies. As he hungrily peeled off the top cookie from the stack and was about to sink his teeth into it . . . he woke up. We got a lot out of this dream, working with it primarily as a shadow motif that depicted the tension between the newly emerging aspects of self (the robbers) that had "broken in" to his personality and activated his change-resistant superego (the security guard). It is very possible that we would never have had the opportunity to work with this dream if not for the intrusion of the cookies that coaxed him into the waking state.

A hunger or thirst motif can also be internally generated by the dream-maker and used as an important metaphor in a dream. I have several clients who have had repeated dreams of banquets and tables piled high with mouth-watering foods, yet for some reason they cannot partake. Why not? These dreamers may indeed be hungry when they have this dream, but there may also be some key content in their inability to partake that should be addressed. Could there be something the dreamer's soul is hungering for that has not been fulfilled? In these cases the hunger or thirst can act as an attractor rather than just an intruder.

Illness motifs

If you are sick, or experiencing some pain or discomfort, this may find its way into your dream, sometimes metaphorically and sometimes quite literally. A fever might appear in your dreamscape as a fire or an overheating machine. A headache may be depicted as an injury to the head or a problem with the roof of your house. The mucus congestion of a common cold might appear in your dream as a disgusting substance in your mouth, even excrement. A localized pain may appear as an animal biting a part of your body. Menstruation, even when normal and healthy, is often accompanied by dreams of blood, wounds, collapse, and soiling of clothes or furniture. Sleep apnea commonly appears with variations on the theme of being deep underwater and swimming desperately up to the surface to get air. In general the dreams of a sick person tend to be distressing, repetitive, fatiguing, and long lasting. Commonly the suffering dreamer will partially wake, then fall right back into the very same dream over and over again. This illustrates that when the somatic input into the dream is very strong, as it is in acute illness, it can temporarily hijack and organize most or all of the dreaming function.

More serious diseases, including chronic diseases and the early stages of life-threatening diseases, may also be represented in dreams. When a person moves toward manifesting a serious disease, the inner healer function of the unconscious becomes very active, and it will attempt to send feedback and warning about the dangerous conditions that are developing. Much of this feedback comes through the dream channel, provided that it is open and taken seriously. Health warning dreams (also referred to as prodromal, healing, diagnostic, or prognostic dreams) have been much studied and described in the literature. You will find further references in the Recommended Resources section.

Here is an example of how dreams can bring us important information about our health and about the early conditions (or pre-conditions) of a disease. Holly, age 27, had a dream she named *Stopped at the Airport*:

> *I'm at the airport trying to get to my flight. A security guy is suspicious of me. He pulls me aside because I have a tiny button with spikes on it. I yell at him that I need to get on my flight, but it's clear I'm not going anywhere. He suspects me of having a concealed weapon. I'm going to be detained.*

Dreams of travel difficulties are very common, the unusual part here is the tiny button with spikes on it—what could that possibly refer to? It has that quality of oddness often seen in dreams, as if a spotlight is being shone on one specific detail. It also had the quality of being a possible introject because of the spikes. Was the dream calling attention to something that has attached itself to her, or might soon attach itself? Introjects in dreams usually refer to foreign psychic contents, but they can refer to physical objects as well. There was something about this spiky object that made me suspect it might have a physical aspect, so I asked Holly if she had an intra-uterine device (IUD). She replied that she did currently have one, and had been wondering if she should get it removed. The spontaneous feeling of resonant connection that happened at this point made it clear that we were on the right track.

As an imaginal response, I suggested that Holly visualize the device being removed from her body, and then experience a state of being without it. This could help her make a good decision in the actual realm about whether or not to have it removed, since she was very ambivalent about it. The IUD had worked well for her, it seemed to be well tolerated and she was not experiencing any overt symptoms from it. Yet she did not like the feeling of it being inside her body, and she often worried that it might damage her future fertility.

Two months later Holly had another dream that contained a similar image, *Shot with a Gold Disc*:

> *I'm trying to trap a master manipulator and expose her so everyone will see what she is. She is Lady Gaga. Nate (from the television series* Gossip Girl*) is on my side, as are two other people. Lady Gaga somehow grows stronger and is able to control people's minds. She tells Nate to shoot me with a golden gun that fires out little gold discs; each disc has seven needles sticking out on one side. He shoots me on my right side, just above the pelvic bone. The person beside tells me I will never get away.*

A second dream featuring a small metal object with sharp points on it! Both Holly and I noted the escalation of urgency in this second dream— the ominous theme of manipulation and mind control, and the fact that the object has now been violently forced into her pelvic area. This kind of escalation is often seen with ego check dreams, and particularly dreams that are delivering health warnings; subsequent dream messages have a similar theme, but it is expressed with higher stakes and greater intensity. Holly needed no further convincing, she decided to have the IUD removed as soon as possible.

Health warnings can come to us in many different ways, all of which are important. The dream channel is critical because it can bring us very early stage information, reporting on subtle disturbances that would not necessarily show up in medical testing and imaging, and might not yet be producing any symptoms. Holly's IUD was not yet on the medical radar, but it was creating a pre-symptomatic blip on her dream radar.

Paralysis motifs

Have you ever had the experience of thinking that you're awake and lying in your bed, but you're unable to move or make a sound? Very often the people who have this experience are not sure whether it involves true dreaming or not. Certainly they are convinced that they are fully awake during the experience itself and often find it terrifying. Sometimes it is accompanied by the proximity of threatening and frightening figures; and it typically takes place in the actual surroundings where you are sleeping (which contributes to the sensation that it is really happening in waking life). It is believed that this phenomenon has given rise to much of humanity's folklore concerning nightmares, hags, and incubi (terrifying demons that sit on the sleeper's chest and prevent them from moving or calling out).

In recent years, this condition has been given the name "sleep paralysis." Sleep research indicates that it is probably caused by a dysfunction of the reticular activating system, the part of the brainstem that is responsible for regulating the transitions between the sleep state and the waking state. In rapid eye movement (REM) sleep, most of the muscles in your body must be paralyzed, otherwise your body would be constantly enacting the movement of your dreaming body (have you ever seen a dog having a dream of chasing something?). When you transition back to wakefulness, this normal muscle paralyzing switch must be turned off again; if it gets stuck in the paralyzed position, your brain can be awake (or near awake) but your body cannot move.

This somatic experience, while originating in a bodily dysfunction, can act as an attractor for dream material (which arguably can be called "hallucinatory material" in this context). Usually, since the dreamer suddenly finds herself in the fearful state of being unable to move and speak, the kind of material that appears is negative and frightening, although this need not always be the case.

Here is an example from the experience of a 35-year-old woman named Brianne who suffered from this condition. On her first consultation with me, Brianne said, "I have had nightmares consistently since I was 14 or 15. Lately they have intensified so I find myself afraid of sleep, and I'm exhausted by it. My dreams don't reflect the positivity of my life. They're often more like visions. They're very intense and real. Often they are 3-D human forms that float into my bedroom. I'm frozen and I can't speak. I feel like I'm haunted!" Brianne later reported a version of this dream that she had recently experienced, *Two Ghosts Come Into My Bedroom*:

I am asleep in my current bedroom. The room is orderly and I am okay. The door is closed. I am aware of two figures, genderless ghosts, looming outside the door. Somehow, without moving my body, I check that the door to my room is locked so they cannot enter. I am frozen. The ghosts move the door despite it being closed. They move about my bedroom wreaking havoc everywhere, turning things over, going into things, and destroying things. I cannot move or stop them.

I suggested that Brianne work with the dreams using the creative power of her imagination to shift the outcome. She can revisit one of the recent frightening dreams, but introduce an element of conscious awareness such as, "Oh, I'm having one of the frozen dreams again." She can also bring an ally figure into the dreamscape to be with her and to help hold the awareness that she is in a dream-like state and can to some degree influence what happens.

A month later at her next visit, an interesting shift was underway—Brianne's dream content was becoming less frightening. In the one dream she described as a nightmare, her boyfriend was lurking outside the door, but she was able to call out and wake up. In another dream (not categorized as a nightmare because it was not fearful), a man's white dress shirt floated close to the bedroom ceiling and then morphed into a man folded into a fetal position. The imagery seemed friendly and almost comical in comparison to what she was used to experiencing. Over the next few months this positive shift continued. On one visit Brianne reported a dream that still contained the familiar pattern and elements (figures floating into her actual bedroom) but the content and the feeling tones had completely changed. She called this dream *The Glowing Female Buddha*:

I'm in my bedroom. I feel conscious. A luminous glowing female Buddha is floating above my bed. A very clear, very powerful presence. She seems to be full of energy. She floats above me and to the right, then she comes a bit toward me. I feel elated!

Three years later Brianne reported:

Thankfully, the significant improvement in my dreams and sleep pattern has held—the dreams are no longer problematic at all and almost never interfere with my sleep! Even when I have the odd frightening dream I'm able to find a way either to work with it while in the dream state or upon waking. I'm very thankful for the approach you presented, it definitely created a shift. I think in the "paralyzed" state, due to fear, it hadn't previously occurred to me that I could interact with or influence the dreams.

It appears that the key element in Brianne's ability to work with these dreams is simply *awareness*—the awareness that she is having a certain kind of experience and that it need not be terrifying. Many people do not experience full-blown sleep paralysis but they do have dreams that involve some degree of being unable to move freely or use their voice. Often they are able to move but their limbs are heavy or they feel as if they are running through quicksand. I suspect that the majority of these dreams involve the same mechanism as sleep paralysis, the dysfunction of the arousal circuits in the brainstem, but to a lesser degree. Often this somatic intrusion of semi-paralysis serves to wake up the dreamer and allow him or her to remember a dream that may have other important content. For more information about sleep paralysis, see the Recommended Resources section at the back of this book.

Falling and starting motifs

The transition between the sleep state and the waking state does not always go smoothly. The term "falling asleep" probably came into existence because so many of us experience a sensation of falling as we go through this transition (in either direction). Jerking, starting, twitching, kicking, and all manner of sudden shock-like movements may jar us awake if this transitioning process hits a glitch. In many cases we may manage to stay asleep but our bed-partner is disturbed by the commotion. Again, it is probably the stuttering of the arousal circuits in the reticular activating system of the brainstem responsible for most of these kicks and falls. As the REM stage muscle paralyzing switch is turned on or off, there is a complex sequence of electrical events that must take place to allow our physical body to engage or disengage from our dreaming body. It's not surprising that things sometimes go a bit roughly. If we interpret these events to be primarily somatic intrusions, we can put the focus on other dream content that may come along with them.

Of course, there are some dreams in which a falling motif may be extremely important in and of itself. Finding yourself up in a very high place with fear of falling, or actually falling from a height is a common element in ego check dreams, for example. How can you make the distinction between a fall that is produced by a somatic glitch and a fall that is the sign of a dangerously elevated ego position? Looking at the context and the other elements present in your dream will help you.

CHAPTER 30

Erotic Dreams

What about dreams of sexual attraction? What does it mean when you have a dream about an erotic attraction to someone other than your partner? Remember Iris's dream *Three Weeks Before the Wedding* in chapter 21? This is a universal dream type, yet it is something that can cause a huge amount of mischief and awkwardness among couples that share their dreams with each other. I expect that most commonly it simply has the effect of stopping the dreamer from sharing the dream (or causes them to report a censored version) for fear of causing hurt, anger, or misunderstanding. Many people are worried that their erotic dreams must signify something dire about their relationship: "Why am I always dreaming about having crushes on other men? Does it mean I'm with the wrong person?" I have even been told by a few people that the reason they do not keep a dream journal is that they fear their partner will snoop in it and find evidence of compromising erotic dreams. What a pity!

Psychodynamics of sexual and erotic dreams

In the most basic sense, I believe an erotic dream simply means you (or some part of you) wants something. The energy of desire is present. Thus a sexual element in a dream is not a motif in itself, it is an *energy* that can appear in almost any kind of dream or dream motif. We are attracted, drawn toward someone; we want to join with something. Sound simple? Sometimes it is simple and straightforward, but sometimes not. We may need to figure out which part of us is expressing the eroticized desire—Our body? Our dream-body? Our ego? Our inner child? Our shadow? I have found that erotic dreams are among the most difficult to get oriented in and to work with, for a number of reasons. Here are some of those reasons:

- Erotic energy is a powerful and hard-wired force that must find some expression in everyone.

- Erotic energy is repressed and denied more than any other kind of human energy.

- Erotic energy has been (and still is) maligned in most of the world's religious traditions.

- Many people feel neurotically conflicted about their erotic energies.

- Erotic impulses can be extremely destabilizing and threatening to committed relationships.

- Erotic energy is connected to the reproductive drive in all animals, including humans, and while humans have recently found ways to uncouple the connection in their conscious behaviors it remains very strongly present in the unconscious.

- Erotic energy is not *only* connected to reproductive drive in humans, it is connected to many other forms of desire and attraction (for example, the desire to be inspired, to learn, to emulate, to be cared for, to be protected—all these desires can be eroticized and all of them can appear as a sexual dream motif).

- The human dreambody enjoys freedom from limitation, including the limitations imposed by morality and the requirements of a committed relationship. It wants to be free to respond to many attractions and experience many erotic encounters. Most of these can (and probably should) only happen in the dream life. There isn't anything wrong with this as long as it is understood that it may just be the dreambody's desire rather than a life problem that needs to be acted upon.

- The material body is interested in sex and attraction for its own reasons. The somatic input that the body contributes is often clear, strong, and quite straightforward in dreams.

- Sexual somatic input is expressed differently in the dreams of men and women. In women, it is much more variable and synchronized to the hormonal cycle. For example, women will often have far more dreams of erotic attraction around their ovulation, often dreaming of attraction to many different men. This does not mean they are less satisfied with their partner all of a sudden, it may just mean they are having an "egg dream" and they wanted to be pursued and surrounded by many sperm/suitors.

- The human ego is also interested in sex and attraction and it brings a different agenda into the mix; the ego often has a lot invested in needing to feel attractive and being able to attract others. The ego's desires in sexual dreams are quite different than the soul's desires and the body's desires; they usually involve a problematic stuckness that needs to be addressed. Ego desires are usually best handled as ego check motifs.

- The personal spirit (or inner child) can also get into the sexual dream game. Childlike needs, including the need to be protected, to be unconditionally cherished, to be constantly reassured, to be instantly gratified, to be praised, and to be parented can all be invested into an erotic attraction. If this is the case, there will be erotic dreams that point to the issue. This is always to some degree problematic and involves a stuckness that needs to be addressed.

- Erotic energies can also find their way into shadow motifs. At times, when a person's sexual persona is needing to expand and grow, they may dream of new, taboo, exciting, and perhaps threatening sexual scenarios.

- Erotic dream motifs can also be about inspiration—these are some of the most high voltage and positive dreams of all.

Erotic dreams featuring your own partner

Next time you have a sexual dream about you and your actual waking life partner, notice the feeling tone. If it has a positive feeling tone, you might handle it as a positive feedback motif, pointing out something about your partner that you really want and you have recently been able to connect with. Try to figure out what it might be so you can reinforce it. If it has a negative or repetitive feeling tone, you might handle it as a relationship field motif, pointing out that you are both stuck in a sexual or relational rut and perhaps you can work together to find a way out toward something new.

Erotic dreams with guilty awareness of your own partner

What if you dream that you are sexually attracted to another person, but then you remember that you should be loyal and monogamous with your own partner? This is a very common dream experience, and in most cases it is healthy, normal, and not problematic. It has to do with differing needs and desires arising from different parts of you. While you are fully in your dreambody, you will want to enjoy the experience, free from any sense of moral limitation. But then another part of you may come into the mix and bring the awareness that you are in a committed relationship and should act appropriately. This often happens late in the dream, when your waking sense of self is becoming stronger. The dreambody does not seem to care much for "shoulds," but they do matter to your waking self. It's a good thing that you can have both these things happening in the same dream, don't feel guilty! Don't apply your waking morality to your dreambody, this will put you in an unnecessary state of neurotic conflict.

Dreams of attraction to a person who is not attractive (in waking life)

Have you ever woken from a dream wondering "How on earth could I be attracted to that person?!" Dreams of strange attractions are very common and often contain a gem of insight. Again, it is important to notice the feeling tone. If the encounter comes with a negative, uncomfortable feeling it is usually pointing out something problematic. It may be posing the question: why are you investing your libido energy into this kind of situation when there is clearly something you don't like about it? On the other hand, if there is a positive feeling, the dream may be highlighting something desirable about that person, i.e., "I seem to like being close to this person ... I wonder why." You could try asking yourself, "If I could have one of the person's qualities for myself, what would I want?"

Dreams of attraction to old partners

Don't feel bad if you have dreams of your former partner. This is very common, and it does not usually mean (as many people worry) that you made the wrong choice and are now with the wrong person. Use the "what does the dream want?" question to find your bearings. Sometimes these dreams seem to be asking for more closure of the old relationship. If this is the case, you can re-enter the dream and imagine a final and decisive goodbye. If you feel some pain and regret while imagining this scenario, that's all right, just let yourself feel it. This need not mean you have made a terrible life mistake, it may simply mean that you are acknowledging the loss, honoring the past love, and moving on. Such dreams may have an ego check function, pointing out that you are *using* comparisons to past lovers to avoid fuller intimacy and commitment in your present situation. Sometimes these dreams have the repetitive quality of a limiting field motif. Your brain is stuck in an old loop that revolves around an old partner; in your waking life you *really* do not want to be with that person but your dreaming brain can't seem to let go. If this is the case, you can re-enter the dream, catch yourself in the old familiar place, realize that you can walk away from it, then do exactly that. Walk away from the old partner and go find your current partner, if that feels right. This is what Iris resolved to do in response to her dream *Three Weeks Before the Wedding*. Remember—this kind of brain training always requires a few repetitions to really take hold.

Dreamworking suggestions for erotic dreams

There are many reasons why people misinterpret, repress, or censor their erotic dreams. By the time they get to the dreamworker (if they ever do) they are often a Pandora's box of confusion. Yet some erotic dreams are very important and should be worked with. How to get oriented then? Since erotic energy is a universal and primordial life force, it can act as an attractor for almost any kind of dream motif.

1. *Consider the other elements in the dream*—this will help you get a sense of what the dream message is and what it may be asking for. These dreams certainly can be about sexual arousal plain and simple; but they can also be about much more than that. Is there an ego quality of wanting to feed your sense of self-worth? Does it have some of the intense neediness of the inner child? Does it feel like the pure physicality of the dreambody enjoying itself? Does it have a feeling of inspiration, of aspiring to be like some attractive person? Does it have a frustrating repetitive quality?

2. *Orient yourself with: what is the dream asking for?* As is so often the case in dreamwork, when things get complicated and you feel confused come back to your most direct tool: what is the dream asking you for? Remember to stay within the dream scenario until you figure out what it wants you to do. Don't translate to your life yet, that comes later. If you are making out with Johnny Depp but you are feeling guilty because you're aware of your husband, what should you do? Explore further? Go all the way? Stop it immediately? Change it somehow? You can explore different possibilities until you find one that feels right. Then practice it, rehearse it a few times. Experience it fully. Now, what would this be asking you for in your waking life?

CHAPTER 31

Frightening Dreams and Nightmares

Fear is an emotional energy that can be present in many different kinds of dream. Like erotic energy it is not a motif in itself, it can accompany almost any motif. Therefore, it is important not to think of nightmares as a *category* of dream. A nightmare is just a very scary dream; you still need to figure out what kind of dream motif you are dealing with. To look at it another way, how do you know that the scary figures that appear in dreams are truly dangerous or harmful? Often dream figures that at first appear to have harmful intent turn out to be very positive. How do we tell the difference? Sometimes it is not an easy distinction to make, but it is a very important distinction, because the aim of the dreamwork will be very different depending on whether the figure represented something positive that should be integrated or something negative that should be avoided.

Guidelines to help you distinguish between frightening dream figures

When you wake up from a scary dream you may still be reverberating with the fear. People often do not want to work with their nightmares because they do not want to re-experience the fear; this is especially true of children. The orientation that normally comes by asking what the dream wants may not work at first; the only answer that comes is an instinctual post-fright response—"it wants me to get away from that monster!"

So, here's a technique you can try after your next scary dream: pick the most frightening figure (or figures) in the dream and consider the following five questions. If you're not sure about the answer to one of the questions just leave it and move on to the next one:

- Is the figure inner or outer (a part of you or a depiction of something or someone in your life)?

- Does it actually cause harm in the dream? (Or is there just anticipation of harm?)

- Does it become more positive when you encounter it in your imagination? (Do a brief imaginal exercise of meeting the figure face to face.)

- What is going on psychodynamically?

- What action is needed in response to it?

By the time you have run through these questions, you will probably be somewhat calmer and less frightened, and your natural curiosity about what is going on in your dreaming mind will be engaged.

The big bad 8

Although it is true that the emotional energy of fear can appear alongside almost any dream motif, in my experience if you dream of a really scary figure it will almost always be one of the following eight types. Until you have determined which of these eight types you are dealing with, you will probably have difficulty connecting the dream to your life.

1. Shadow Figure

Inner or outer? *Inner*

Can it cause harm? *May feel frightening and threatening, but does not actually cause serious harm*

Become more positive when encountered? *Yes*

Psychodynamic? *A new part of your psyche is trying to be integrated*

Needed response action? *Encounter the shadow figure and eventually integrate it*

2. Ego Check Figure

Inner or outer? *Inner—usually appears as an external dream figure who behaves badly, but it is a depiction of some aspect of you*

Can it cause harm? *Yes, can harm other figures in the dream*

Become more positive when encountered? *Yes, if you are willing to own up to it*

Psychodynamic? *The unconscious is pointing out a problematic quality that you cannot see in yourself and have been projecting onto others*

Needed response action? *Recognize the negative part in yourself, take responsibility for it, and try to change it*

3. External Figure

Inner or outer? *Outer—someone or something in your life will often appear in a dream causing exaggerated harm to you, or their part may be played by another figure*

Can it cause harm? *Yes*

Become more positive when encountered? *No*

Psychodynamic? *Your dreammaker is trying to point out to you that you are in danger of harm, or are allowing yourself to be harmed*

Needed response action? *Handle as an ego check motif—recognize the message as a warning or a reality check, then do something about the situation*

4. Introject Figure

Inner or outer? *Inner, but not a true part of self*

Can it cause harm? *Yes—can be truly mean, hurtful, critical, and attacking*

Become more positive when encountered? *No*

Psychodynamic? *A depiction of something that was forced into your psyche in the past, and is now internalized (e.g., a negative inner voice or belief system)*

Needed response action? *To identify the introject as foreign and unwanted, then weaken or expel it, if possible*

5. Brain Field Figure

Inner or outer? *Inner*

Can it cause harm? *Yes*

Become more positive when encountered? *No*

Psychodynamic? *A depiction of a neural network in your brain that you cannot modulate or control, as in a bad habit, compulsion, addiction, obsession, irrational fear, phobia*

Needed response action? *Brain training—practice going back into the problematic scenario in the dream and finding a way out of it*

6. Rogue Self Care System Figure

Inner or outer? *Inner*

Can it cause harm? *Yes*

Become more positive when encountered? *No*

Psychodynamic? *Originally created in your psyche as a response to trauma, to protect you from harm, or to comfort and soothe unbearable pain. Strongly resistant to change or help. Provokes relapse and self-sabotage.*

Needed response action? *Become more aware of how your problematic self-care system works to minimize the damage it can do*

7. Disease Figure

Inner or outer? *Can be seen either way*

Can it cause harm? *Yes*

Become more positive when encountered? *Usually not*

Psychodynamic? *A depiction of your disease, usually a rogue disease that is not self-limiting and seems to have its own "agenda." Most commonly depicted in dreams are cancers, auto-immune diseases, conditions of unstable brain chemistry, brain injuries, and parasitic infections.*

Needed response action? *The dream may be giving you clues about the best way to manage your disease condition.*

8. Sleep Paralysis Figure

Inner or outer? *Inner*

Can it cause harm? *Usually not, it is only a presence in the bedroom*

Become positive when encountered? *Yes*

Psychodynamic? *Typically, the dreamer is convinced they are fully awake in their own bedroom, unable to move or make a sound. Then a figure may appear, often near the foot of the bed. Because of the somatic component of paralysis the experience often becomes terrifying, although it need not be.*

Needed response action? *Be aware of what is happening physiologically* (see chapter 29). *Practice re-entering the dreamscape with awareness of what is happening. Retrain yourself to allow it to be a positive experience rather than a frightening one.*

When can we do our own dreamwork, and when should we seek help?

If you are troubled by frightening dreams, pick one to work with and try approaching it using the method described in this chapter. You may be able to arrive at a satisfying connection that leads to a good response. If you are successful with this, you will notice your frightening dreams start to change. If not, if you get bogged down and feel you cannot connect the dream fully, or if you feel you need some guidance and the benefit of someone else's perspective, then it may be time to get some help. Either way, I encourage you to be proactive with your nightmares; go to confront them, don't let them keep coming to find you. I have met many people who have suffered decades of torment from their bad dreams and never found a way to work on them. You don't need to be one of those people.

What about children's nightmares? Should they be handled differently?

Many a parent has wondered what can be done about their child's nightmares. Children, especially young children, are often hesitant to talk about their dreams; perhaps they don't want to re-experience the fear in the re-telling. Likewise, parents are often hesitant to discuss the dream often because they simply don't know what to do or say. Health care practitioners may not have much to offer, either; thus the problem is often left unaddressed. My experience is this—the same wonderful and reliable tool that works to transform the scary dreams of adults can be used just as effectively for children—the imagination! The essential technique involves helping the child imagine a scary outcome changing into a less scary outcome. This can be done in a variety of ways, and a wonderful new book has appeared on the horizon recently that describes and illustrates many of those ways. If you are the parent of a child who is having frightening dreams and you're looking for some guidance and inspiration, I would recommend taking a look at *Sleep Monsters and Superheroes: Empowering Children through Creative Dreamplay*. You can find out more about it in the Recommended Resources section.

A Final Word About Dreamwork

Now we close the circle and return to our opening question, why should we pay attention to our dreams? I hope I have been able to provide evidence that dreams carry very important messages. I strongly believe that our quality of life, both individually and collectively, will improve if we learn to value these messages more, to receive them better, to strive toward understanding them, and to respond to them.

For me, the most exciting experiences in dreamwork are the moments of connection, the Aha! moments where a dreamer suddenly gets the message of the dream; these moments will always be thrilling. But, in the long term, the most rewarding and satisfying aspect of dreamwork is the witnessing of how people's lives are enriched over time by their dream insights. How George recognized and appreciated that he was re-conceiving himself in both his career and his identity after his dream of *The Pin-Screw Mission*. How the dream of *The Big Loon* helped Domenica recognize the urgency of her situation and the need to slow down and re-prioritize her life. How Candace, after working with her dream of *The Key and the Hook*, understood the double-edged quality of the charge she felt around her parents and took steps to protect herself from it. And, for me personally, how I feel my energy for this book is sustained and re-invigorated by the insights I gained from my dream of *Blowing on the Fire*.

Dreamwork has such great potential, but for its full potential to be realized it must be woven right into the fabric of our daily lives, and this requires some dedication and practice. It is well worth the investment of time and effort. It is one of the most transformative disciplines that human beings can engage in. I have felt it transform me and I have witnessed it transform so many of the people I work with. I hope you will let it transform you.

Appendix 1:
Useful phrases and questions
for each stage of dream facilitation

Clarifying questions

- Go back into the dream if you can and describe it as if you were in it again.

- Tell me the dream in the present tense if you can, as if it is happening now.

- Take me into the dream.

- What is the setting of the dream?

- Where does the dream take place?

- Can you describe the part where ... happened a bit more?

- What do you mean when you said ... ?

- What happened then?

- What was the feeling when ... ?

- What do you associate with ... ?

- What qualities does ... have?

- What are the first three things that come into your head when you think of ... ?

Orienting questions

- What have you made of the dream so far?

- What do you think the dream is asking for?

- Go back into the dream at the point where ... Now become aware that you can change the scenario, what do you want to happen?

- Do you intuitively feel that the ... is a part of you? Or is it referring to something in your life that is affecting you?

- Do you think it's a good thing that you ... ? Or a bad thing?

- Can you *be* the ... ? How does it feel?

- What is trying to happen in this dream? Why can't it happen? What is stopping it?

- What is the problem in this dream?

- What is the stuck point in this dream?

- If the dream features a body part, is anything going on in that part of your body?

- What does that part do? What is its job?

Connecting questions

- In this dream something is ... (point out the metaphor) ... Have you been feeling ... (same metaphor)?

- In the dream you feel ... and ... and ... Where do you feel (use the same two or three words) in your life?

- In the dream this pattern of events seems to happen ... (point out the pattern). Does this pattern seem familiar? Or, do you have this pattern anywhere in your life?

- Is it possible the dream is using a wordplay or pun on ... ?

- Do you know the figure of speech ... ? Is it possible your dream is using that?

Responding questions

- Near the end of the dream the problem seems to be that ... Do you agree? (If client agrees)—What can we do that will help change that?

- In our imaginal re-entry we changed the outcome by ... How can we translate that change into your waking life?

- Let's try to come up with a response. What can we do to ... ?

- How do you want this pattern to shift, if it can shift?

Appendix 2:
Distinctive features
of common dream motifs

Shadow Motifs

- somebody or something scary at the door that wants to come in

- being chased or followed by a scary figure

- a sense of danger and anticipated harm, but no harm is actually done

- trying to lock doors, flimsy or ineffectual locks

- trying to secure multiple entry points

- trying to call the police

- dream figures that are wild, spontaneous, uninhibited, outrageous, crude, hyper-sexual, sacrilegious

- being triggered or morally outraged by somebody in a dream

Ego Check Motifs

- a dream figure or the dream ego acting in a problematic way

- driving difficulty

- a famous or infamous figure in a dream

- the dream ego or another figure killing or harming a small and defenseless figure

- the dream ego or another figure is up precariously high or in danger of falling

Brain Field Motifs

- back at your old school, tested, unprepared, unqualified, late, in trouble, held back from graduation

- being locked in, imprisoned, restrained, having a binding contract, having no choice

- moving but not able to choose the direction, on a train, a track, in a force field or a maze , running through corridors or stairwells

- trying to communicate or make a connection but can't

- feeling triggered, overwhelmed by extreme surges of inappropriate emotion

Personal Spirit Motifs

- a figure who is dead, murdered, abused, badly injured, suffering, sick, or starving (it could be a baby, child, adult, animal, or plant)

- a feeling tone of loss, suffering, separation, grief

- an abandoned baby, child, or animal

- orphans, parents separated from their children

- suddenly realizing that you were supposed to be looking after a baby, child, or animal

- two lost children, one younger and one older

- fragmentation of something that should be whole

Family Field Motifs

- dream setting is in your childhood home or neighborhood

- dream features your parents, siblings, and other figures from your family of origin

- two or more generations of your family in the same dream

- feeling childlike, immature, over-sensitive, disempowered

- unquestioned assumptions and roles derived from the family of origin

Relationship Field Motifs

- dreams that feature you and your current partner in a problematic situation

- repetitive dreams of previous partners

- dreams that feature family of origin figures and your current partner

Introject Motifs

Phase 1—threatening to come inside

- something attaching to, hooking or sticking onto, or entering your body

- something trying to get in your ear

- being shot

- being raped

- a figure who forces or implants something into your body

Phase 2—inside

- figures that harm, control, and threaten the dream ego

- a harshly critical figure or inner voice

- neurotic moral conflicts between a belief system and a desire

- strong feelings of "should" or "should not"

- pregnancy by rape

Phase 3—trying to expel an introject

- bugs, burrowing insects, vermin, parasites, worms, maggots

- implants, microchips, bits of foreign matter in the body that can't be taken out

- pockets of pus and infection

- eggs laid in the body

- frantically trying to get something out of the body that should not be in the body

- vomiting, pulling something out of the body, the mouth, nose, ears, anus

- feelings of horror, revulsion, and morbid fascination

Phase 4—expelled introject

- great relief at being rid of something or killing something

- wondering, did I get all of it out?

- concern that there may be more still in there

- purging feeling

- victorious feeling

Self-discovery Motifs

- walking through a house (or other structure) and finding new areas

- unsure if the house belongs to you, feeling like a trespasser

- going up or downstairs, discovering new levels

- finding treasure or money

- something frightening in the basement

- venturing out on a voyage or trip

- diving and exploring underwater

- dream settings on shorelines and beaches

- meeting a guide figure, being taken somewhere or shown something

Rebirth Motifs

See chart in chapter 24

Inspiring Contact Motifs

- an encounter with a remarkable animal, nature spirit, angel, or ancestral spirit

- often you are the only one to experience a remarkable encounter (if there are other people present in the dream they do not seem to be aware or interested)

- an encounter with a teacher or a teaching

- finding gifts, treasure, and money

- a spiritual or religious experience, a sense of receiving a blessing

- visiting a soul place (often accompanied by a feeling of great familiarity or déja-vu)

- a divinely erotic or loving encounter

Positive Feedback Motifs

- overcoming a fear, an obstacle, a stuckness, or a challenging problem

- often refer back to former repeating dreams of stuckness, but this time you succeed!

- being congratulated, rewarded, celebrated, applauded, encouraged

Rogue Motifs

- dream figures that actually attack and harm the dream ego

- dream figures that seem truly evil, malicious, and demonic

- dream figures that criticize harshly and generate a feeling of self-hatred

- dream figures that block access to a child

- dream figures that block communication

- dream figures that evoke a feeling of comforting fantasy

- dream figures that offer or force the use of a drug or substance

- dream figures that threaten and intimidate

Dreambody Motifs

- flying, floating, soaring, hovering

- any superhuman physical action—fast running, jumping, leaping

- feelings of joyful and deeply satisfying physicality

- frustrating attempts to get off the ground, take off, fly

- looking down from a great height, often in a plane or spacecraft

- falling to earth from a great height, crashing, plane crashes

- coming down into a ship or other vessel

- spectacular impact from a spectacular fall

- falling combined with injury or impact

- doing something amazingly well, with supernatural ability

Somatic Motifs

- dreams of smells, sounds, light, heat, cold, touch, and so on, that upon waking are realized to be from the surrounding environment

- dreams of a full bladder or bowel, seeking a toilet, urinating, or passing stool or gas

- feeling hungry or thirsty in a dream

- dreams of pain or discomfort that upon waking are present in the material body

- dreams of something wrong in a precise body location (especially when repeated)

- not being able to move, or move only slowly and with great effort

- wanting to call out but being unable to make a sound

- startling, starting, stumbling, falling, jerking, and so on, that cause waking

- difficulty breathing, trying to get up to the surface for air, gasping for breath

Glossary

The following terms are defined as they are used within this book. These definitions may not correspond exactly to usages that might be found in medical texts, dictionaries, or other writings on dreams or psychology.

anchoring—doing something after initially recalling a dream to make sure it is securely fixed in the long-term memory.

associations—the qualities a dreamer associates with key figures and elements in his or her dream.

brain field—a type of limiting field that arises from a network of connections in the brain that have become strongly ingrained and self-perpetuating. Such fields may be positive or negative, functional or dysfunctional.

brain field dream motif—a dream motif that arises from and depicts a brain field.

catching—the practices and techniques associated with remembering a dream fully and clearly.

clarification—the practices and techniques associated with obtaining a clear and complete account of the dream, including the setting, the events, the feelings, and the associations for each key figure in the dream.

coherence—a quality observed in some dreams whereby they seem to have been created by an intelligent part of the psyche that has selected and organized the dream contents in an attempt to deliver a message.

double resonance—a phenomenon that occurs when both dreamer and dreamworker simultaneously sense the truth of the connection or insight that has just been made.

double resonance test—a reliable way to determine whether a good connection has been made between the dream and the dreamer's life using the double resonance phenomenon.

dreambody—the body as it is within a dream; also that part of the person that is not tied to the material body, that can "leave" the material body in dreams, in visions, in death, in out-of-body experiences, and as a result of certain drug effects.

dreammaker—a name for the part of the human mind that creates dreams.

dreamscape—the place, setting, figures, and situation that occurred in a dream.

dreamworker—someone who can consistently help other people better understand their dreams.

dream catching—*see* catching.

dream ego—the "I" of the dream; the ego as it appears in a dream.

dream incubation—the practice of asking your dreammaker for a dream that will shed light on a particular concern or question.

dream motif—a distinctive and recognizable pattern occurring within a dream.

dynamic—the tendency to change, grow, learn, and evolve.

dynamic dream motifs—dream motifs that arise from the natural tendency of the human psyche to grow and evolve.

dysfunctional repetitiveness—the tendency of certain dreams, or dream themes, to repeat themselves, not for any useful communicative purpose, but simply because they are generated by an old and redundant neural field.

ego—the self-aware part of us, our sense of who we are, including self-consciousness, the elements of how we identify ourselves (name, age, gender, etc.), and the traits and qualities we believe ourselves to have.

ego check motifs—dream motifs that provide reflection and feedback to the ego consciousness.

embodiment—the process of consciousness arising, developing, and existing within the physical body.

escape field—a potential neural field that could be, with practice, developed adjacent to a problematic neural field, providing an escape route; i.e., a way to move out of the influence of the problematic field toward a more free state.

family field—a limiting field that originated in childhood within the family of origin, giving rise to pervasive distortions of the way one perceives, feels, and reacts to the world.

family field dream motif—a dream motif that arises from and depicts a family field.

feeling tones—the feelings and emotions that the dreamer (dream ego) experiences in a dream. These are not necessarily the same as the feelings, thoughts, or insights he or she may have about the dream later, when awake.

field—in physics, the region in which a particular condition prevails. As applied to the human brain—a pattern of potential brain activity that, once established, has the potential to be repeatedly activated.

functional repetitiveness—the tendency of certain dreams (or dream themes) to repeat themselves until the dreamer gets the message they are trying to deliver.

guarded—a characteristic of some self-care systems whereby they vigorously resist change, even potentially beneficial change.

incubation—*see* dream incubation.

inspiring contact dream motif—dream motifs that have a quality of specialness, uniqueness, and numinous importance. Often feature totem animals, nature spirits, ancestral spirits, teachers, guides, special places, and divinely attractive people.

introject—a construct forced into the psyche from the outside, never fully accepted and integrated as a true part of self, but yet occupying a deep-seated place in the individual's sense of self. A rogue introject is an introject that has become sufficiently autonomous and powerful that it causes significant harm to the whole person.

limiting field—a field effect that exists both within the dreamer's brain and his or her surroundings, and that has the effect of limiting and distorting perceptions, emotional reactions, and freedom of choice. *See also* brain field, family field, field, neural field, relationship field.

limiting field motifs—dream motifs that arise from and depict a limiting field.

lucid dreaming—the type of dreaming that occurs when the dream ego becomes aware that he or she is in a dream, and may subsequently become able to alter the content of the dream.

metaphor—something that stands for something else; is representative, analogous, or symbolic of something else. Many dream figures are not literally what they seem but are appearing as a metaphor for something in the dreamer or in the dreamer's life. For example, a rundown old car in a dream may be a metaphor for the dreamer's tired old body.

metaphor resistance—the resistance that many literal-minded people have to perceiving metaphor, including those metaphors that appear in their own dreams.

motif—*see* dream motif.

neural field—a neural network; a grouping of neurons in the brain that are organized to fire together, resulting in a certain event (cognition, feeling, awareness, memory, movement, and so on). *See also* brain field, family field, field, limiting field, relationship field.

numinous—having a strong religious or spiritual quality; indicating or suggesting the presence of a divinity; inspiring awe and wonderment, and carrying with it an unquestionable sense of importance.

oddness—the quality that some dream elements have that causes them to stand out and demand our notice.

orientation—the techniques and practices associated with getting one's bearings within a dreamscape.

part—a figure appearing in a dream that plays the role of one facet of the dreamer's personality, or the role of someone or something in the dreamer's life.

personal spirit—that aspect of a person that needs to be whole, to have a firm sense of self and an unbroken continuum of personal history.

personal spirit motifs—dream motifs that depict the drama of the personal spirit trying to re-establish a good connection with the ego consciousness.

positive re-frame—a technique that helps a client consider a seemingly negative element in a more positive light.

positive shadow shift—a characteristic shift from negative feeling tone (usually fear) to positive feeling tone that occurs immediately after confronting or meeting a shadow figure.

re-entering—a practice of revisiting a dream in your imagination.

re-enter and explore—the technique of re-entering the dreamscape and exploring different possible action scenarios that could move things in a desired new direction.

relationship field—a limiting field that includes key fields in the dreamer's brain, his or her partner's corresponding brain fields, and the shared field created by the way these two mesh with each other.

relationship field motif—a dream motif that arises from and depicts a relationship field.

responding—doing something specific in response to a dream, or an insight that came from working with a dream.

rogue part—a part of the psyche that has broken away from the whole and is capable of acting autonomously and causing harm to the whole person.

rogue part motifs—dream motifs that depict a rogue part.

rogue self-care system—a self-care system that has to some degree become autonomous, uncontrollable, and self-harming.

self-care system—a system of strategies and responses that help us cope with negative feeling states, stress, and difficult aspects of life.

self-discovery motifs—dream motifs that depict us in the act of exploring ourselves and finding out new information.

self sabotage—the tendency to resist psychodynamic change by causing relapse, dissociation, self-critical thinking, and discouragement; most typical of rogue parts of the psyche and especially rogue self care systems.

shadow—1. parts of the total potential personality that were repressed during the process of socialization; 2. parts of the potential personality that are disowned and disliked because they are contaminated with bad associations and experiences from the past; 3. parts of the total potential personality that have not yet fully emerged.

shadow motifs—dream motifs that depict and arise from the shadow. These figures typically appear to be threatening and negative at first, but on closer examination turn out to be emerging positive aspects of the dreamer's own self.

somatic—to do with the material body.

somatic attractor—a motif that arises from the body (e.g., hunger), becomes integrated into a dream, and subsequently attracts and organizes certain characteristic subject matter to appear in the dream.

somatic motif—a dream motif that arises from the body and its sense organs.

stuckness—resistance to specific dynamic changes that are trying to happen in the psyche.

stuck motifs—dream motifs that arise from and depict resistance to dynamic changes that are trying to happen in the psyche.

superego—the part of the personality that is concerned with conscience, appropriate behavior, and morality. The superego tends to be change-resistant and often appears in dreams as a police officer or security guard.

totem—a nature being that has particular relevance and specialness for a person. Most totems that appear in dreams are animals, but they can also be plant species, rocks, bodies of water, or any other element of the natural world.

unconscious, the—everything in ourselves that we are not usually conscious of.

universality—the quality of some dreams whereby they seem to be one individual dreamer's version of a larger type that is common and familiar to all of humanity. A universal dream motif is one that has this familiar quality (for example, the motif of an abandoned baby).

Recommended Resources

Chapter 1

Dream research

In their excellent collection *Dream Research: Contributions to Clinical Practice* (Routledge, 2015) editors Milton Kramer and Myron Glucksman have gathered together findings from twenty-two different dream researchers. In this book you can find fascinating articles on gender differences in dreams, the effectiveness of dream incubation, the treatment of post-traumatic nightmares, lucid dreams, and much more.

Chapter 2

The nature of dreaming

Dream researcher Ernest Hartmann's book *The Nature and Functions of Dreaming* (Oxford University Press, 2011) directly addresses the big dream questions—What are dreams? How are they made? Do they have a function? He writes about the function of dreaming:

This making of broad connections guided by emotion has an adaptive function, which we conceptualize as "weaving in" new material—taking new experiences and gradually connecting them, integrating them into existing memory systems. This primary function occurs whether or not a dream is remembered. When a dream is remembered the broad connections can also be adaptive in increasing self-knowledge and producing new insights and creations. (page 5)

Extraordinary dreams

Extraordinary Dreams and How to Work With Them (SUNY Press, 2002). Stanley Krippner, Fariba Bogzaran, and Andre Percia de Carvalho will give you a fascinating survey of many exceptional types of dreams. The authors discuss out-of-body dreams, visitation dreams, telepathic dreams, precognitive dreams, and other types of dreams that do seem to have the quality of "communications from the outside."

Lucid dreams

Lucid dreaming is quite rare, but it is to some degree a skill that can be practiced and cultivated. I believe that it could have great potential as a tool for those who wish to develop a deep relationship with their unconscious mind. However, it is an advanced and complex practice and is not the subject of this book—readers are referred to Robert Waggoner's excellent book *Lucid Dreaming: Gateway to the Inner Self* (Moment Point Press, 2009) if they would like to explore this field further. Waggoner makes the case that lucid dreaming is a powerful tool that can be used to explore the nature of dreaming itself, and to explore the contents of the unconscious.

End of life dreams

Jeanne Van Bronkhorst's beautiful book *Dreams at the Threshold* (Llewellyn Publications, 2015) explores end of life dreams and their potential value in helping and enriching the transition toward death, not only for the dying person but also for loved ones and caregivers.

Precognitive dreams

Can we dream about something that hasn't happened yet? Does our dreaming mind have access to the future? Are there really such things as precognitive dreams, prophetic dreams, and predictive dreams? Carlyle Smith's *Heads Up Dreaming* (Turning Stone Press, 2014) explores this fascinating aspect of dreaming.

Cross-cultural perspectives on dreaming

The question of where dreams come from has been deeply considered in many of the world's religions and philosophical traditions. A good survey of the differing perspectives and models can be found in Kelly Bulkeley's *Dreaming in the World's Religions: A Comparative History* (New York University Press, 2008). A fascinating cross-cultural and transdisciplinary exploration of the nature of dreaming can be found in *Sleeping, Dreaming, and Dying: An Exploration of Consciousness with the Dalai Lama* (Wisdom Publications, 1997). The Tibetan Buddhist model of consciousness and dreaming is compared with the model that is rooted in Western neuroscience.

Chapter 4

Reading list for a crash course in dreams

If you are interested in the world of dreams but feel you are lacking in the background knowledge, I would recommend reading the following four books:

- *Our Dreaming Mind* (Ballantine Books, 1994) by Robert Van de Castle—a remarkably thorough survey of the entire field of dreams and how they have been understood, studied, researched, and used in practice. Start with this one and you will have a good backdrop in place.

- *The Universal Dream Key* (Harper San Francisco, 2001) by Patricia Garfield—discusses common dream themes and their possible meanings. You will likely find all of these themes very familiar; these types of dreams are the ones we all have. Garfield does a good job of demonstrating how dream metaphors can be connected to people's lives in a way that is not reductionist or simplistic.

- *Extraordinary Dreams and How to Work With Them* (SUNY Press, 2002) by Stanley Krippner, Fariba Bogzaran, and Andre Percia de Carvalho—this book will help round out your knowledge of the many different types of dream experience people can have, focusing more on the rare but fascinating types of dreams such as telepathic and precognitive dreams.

- *Memories, Dreams, Reflections* (Vintage Books, 1965) by Carl Jung—this fascinating autobiographical book will immerse you in the psyche of a man who took dreams very seriously, both his own and those of his patients. If you don't have a real sense of what it means to work with your dreams, this book will give you a taste of what that can look like. Jung's influence on modern dreamwork (and modern psychology) is so pervasive, even among people who have no idea who he was or what he did, that any serious student of dreams should at least acquaint themselves with his writing. This book is a good place to start because it is beautifully written and more accessible than much of his other scholarly and alchemical writing.

Chapter 9
A brief survey of some other dreamworking methods

The method presented in this book borrows and adapts from many sources. Here are some of the dreamworking methods that I have been inspired and influenced by:

- *The Jungian method*—if there is such a thing as "the Jungian method" for me it has been most inspiringly exemplified by the work of Marie Louise von Franz. She has written many fine books but if I could recommend just one Von Franz experience I would choose *The Way of the Dream: Conversations on Jungian Dream Interpretation.* This series of film interviews, produced and directed by Fraser Boa, will immerse the viewer into the world of dreams and the richness of the Jungian method of archetypal amplification.

- *Gestalt therapy*—Fritz Perls's method of dreamworking, with its emphasis on having the dreamer directly experience the dream through playing a part of it, has influenced many dreamworkers including myself. I do not agree with Perls's assertion that *every* part of a dream is a part of the dreamer that has been disowned and projected onto others, but that is often the case and often enough that we must always consider it. Asking the dreamer to be a part of his or her dream, a technique championed by Perls, has become a core component in many styles of dreamworking. Perls's book *Gestalt Therapy Verbatim* (Real People Press, 1969) contains several transcripts of his dreamwork sessions.

- *General*—In their excellent recently-published collection, editors Jacquie Lewis and Stanley Krippner have gathered together and presented fourteen different modern dreamworking methods. These methods share a lot in common yet exhibit an amazing variety of approach, technique, and style. This is a very rich resource! *Working With Dreams and PTSD Nightmares: 14 Approaches for Psychotherapists and Counselors*, edited by Jacquie Lewis and Stanley Krippner. Santa Barbara: Praeger, 2016.

- *The Montague Ullman method*—Ullman developed a four-step dreamworking method that is intended primarily for group dream sharing. It emphasizes what he calls the "safety factor" (to ensure that the dreamer maintains control and ownership of the process) and the "discovery factor" (which comes from the input of others in the group). In step one, a volunteer relates a dream to the group and the group members can ask clarifying questions. In step two, members of the group offer their comments and insights prefaced with the phrase: "If it were my dream…" In step three, the dream is given back to the dreamer, who now has the chance to respond to any comments that were made if he or she wishes to. Step four happens at the beginning of the next group session when the dreamer is invited to share any further reflections or insights he may have had about the dream. The method has been widely used and adapted; more detail can be found in Ullman's book *Working With Dreams* (Jeremy P. Tarcher, 1979).

- *The Robert Johnson method*—Johnson is a Jungian therapist who has written several popular books on various aspects of Jungian psychology. His book *Inner Work: Using Dreams and Active Imagination for Personal Growth* (Harper San Francisco, 1986) presents a four-part method that is primarily designed for a person to use with his or her own dreams. Step one involves making associations with each important figure and element in the dream. Step two involves connecting these figures and elements to specific dynamics in the dreamer's inner life. Step three entails making an interpretation that ties together all these meanings; and step four involves doing rituals to make the dream concrete and physical in some way.

- *The Hill cognitive-experiential dream model*—Clara Hill is
  a researcher in the Psychology department at the University
  of Maryland. Hill has developed a three-stage model of
  working with dreams that is well-suited for use in ongoing
  psychotherapy. In the exploration stage, the therapist guides
  the client through an examination of the images, thoughts,
  and emotions in the dream. In the insight stage, the therapist
  and client work together to construct an understanding of
  the dream. Finally, in the action stage, the therapist supports
  the client in considering waking life changes based on the
  insights from the dream. This method is presented in a
  book edited by Hill: *Dreamwork in Therapy, Facilitating
  Exploration, Insight and Action* (American Psychological
  Association, 2010).

Chapter 10

Dream incubation

Gayle Delaney's *Living Your Dreams* (Harper and Row, 1988) has in-depth
information on dream incubation techniques.

Dierdre Barret's *The Committee of Sleep: How Artists, Scientists, and
Athletes Use Dreams for Creative Problem-Solving—and How You Can Too*
(Crown/Random House: 2001) cites many instances of dreams being
used in the service of creativity and problem solving.

Chapter 12

Motif recognition

If you'd like to give yourself a quick crash course in dream motif recognition, here are two good resources:

- Fraser Boa's ten-hour movie series *The Way of the Dream*
  showcases the remarkable dream interpretation skills of Marie

Louise von Franz. This series takes the viewer on a guided tour through the Jungian archetypes of the human psyche and how they can appear in dreams. Background knowledge of Jungian archetypal psychology is very helpful to have in dream facilitation, even if the practitioner is not adhering strictly to the Jungian model or using classical Jungian terminology ("shadow," "anima" and "animus," "Self," and so on). Von Franz was extremely knowledgeable in the realms of mythology, culture, fairy tale, and religion and is able to relate this material to dream motifs in a fascinating way.

- Patricia Garfield's book *The Universal Dream Key—The 12 Most Common Dream Themes Around the World* (Harper San Francisco, 2001) provides a good survey of common dream types. Everything discussed in this book is truly universal; we *all* have our own versions of these universal dream types.

- *Be the Part technique*—Kenneth Meyer's excellent chapter on gestalt dreamwork will provide a good background on dreamworking methods that involve enacting a part of the dream. For many people enactment is the easiest and most instinctual way to approach a dream, they would rather experience it than try to talk about it. See: Kenneth Meyer, "Gestalt Dreamwork," in *Working With Dreams and PTSD Nightmares: 14 Approaches for Psychotherapists and Counselors*, edited by Jacquie Lewis and Stanley Krippner, 66. (Santa Barbara: Praeger, 2016.)

Chapter 19

Trauma and dreams

Bessel Van der Kolk's *The Body Keeps the Score* (Viking, 2014) gives an excellent overview of the psychology of trauma and therapeutic strategies for healing trauma and includes many powerful case studies. Deirdre Barrett's *Trauma and Dreams* (Harvard University Press, 1996) focuses on the dream lives of people who have suffered different kinds of trauma, including incest, rape, war trauma, burn trauma, and divorce. Donald Kalsched's two remarkable books: *The Inner World of Trauma: Archetypal Defenses of the Human Spirit* (Routledge, 1996), and *Trauma and the Soul—A Psycho-Spiritual Approach to Human Development and Its Interruption* (Routledge, 2013) describe a Jungian psychoanalytical approach to the healing of trauma, including many fascinating case examples featuring dreamwork.

Chapter 29

Somatic dreams, prognostic dreams, and health warning dreams

Chapter 13, "Somatic Contributions to Dreams" in Robert Van De Castle's *Our Dreaming Mind* (Ballantine Books, 1994) surveys the subject of prodromal dreams, dreams associated with healing, and dreams during the menstrual cycle. Patricia Garfield's *The Healing Power of Dreams* (Simon and Schuster, 1991) explores the kinds of dreams that give us information about what is going on in our bodies. *Healing Dreams* (Riverhead Books, 2000) by Marc Ian Barasch makes a compelling argument for the importance of dreams as health warnings and healing potentials.

Sleep paralysis

Psychologist and dreamworker Fariba Bogzaran has developed a five-step model for working with sleep paralysis. The goal of the method is to transform what is usually a very negative experience into a more positive one through holding and identifying the state as it happens and developing the ability to change it through practice. This method is described in *Extraordinary Dreams and How to Work With Them* (SUNY Press, 2002), 49. Shelley Adler's book *Sleep Paralysis: Night-mares, Nocebos, and the Mind-Body Connection* (Rutgers University Press, 2011) will give you a good overview of the whole phenomenon of sleep paralysis.

Chapter 31

Children's Nightmares

Editors Clare Johnson and Jean Campbell have assembled an extremely valuable resource for parents and care providers of children who suffer from frightening dreams. Their book, *Sleep Monsters and Superheroes: Empowering Children through Creative Dreamplay* (Santa Barbara, CA: Praeger, 2016), provides a variety of practical approaches to try. The volume is a collection of contributions from many expert authors, and it is full of verbatim transcripts of dreams and dreamworking sessions (as any good dreamwork book should be!). It covers a wide range of ages, from very the young to the teenaged.

Bibliography

Adler, Shelley. *Sleep Paralysis: Night-mares, Nocebos, and the Mind-Body Connection.* New Brunswick, NJ: Rutgers University Press, 2011.

Barasch, Marc Ian. *Healing Dreams: Exploring the Dreams That Can Transform Your Life.* New York: Riverhead Books, 2000.

Barrett, Dierdre. *The Committee of Sleep: How Artists, Scientists, and Athletes Use Their Dreams for Creative Problem Solving—and How You Can Too.* New York: Crown Books/Random House, 2001.

Barrett, Dierdre, ed. *Trauma and Dreams.* Cambridge, MA: Harvard University Press, 1996.

Bly, Robert. *A Little Book on the Human Shadow.* New York: Harper Collins, 1988.

Bulkeley, Kelly. *Dreaming in the World's Religions.* New York and London: New York University Press, 2008.

Delaney, Gayle. *Living Your Dreams.* New York: Harper and Row, 1988.

Freud, Sigmund. *The Interpretation of Dreams.* New York: Avon Books, 1965.

Garfield, Patricia. *Creative Dreaming.* New York: Simon and Schuster, 1995.

———. *The Healing Power of Dreams.* New York: Simon and Schuster, 1991.

———. *The Universal Dream Key: The 12 Most Common Dream Themes Around the World.* San Francisco: Harper San Francisco, 2001.

Hartmann, Ernest. *The Nature and Functions of Dreaming.* New York: Oxford University Press, 2011.

Hill, Clara, ed. *Dream Work in Therapy: Facilitating Exploration, Insight, and Action.* Washington, D.C.: American Psychological Association, 2010.

Johnson, Clare, and Jean Campbell, eds. *Sleep Monsters and Superheroes: Empowering Children through Creative Dreamplay.* Santa Barbara, CA: Praeger, 2016.

Johnson, Robert. *Inner Work: Using Dreams and Active Imagination for Personal Growth.* San Francisco: Harper San Francisco, 1986.

Jung, Carl. *Memories, Dreams, Reflections.* New York: Vintage Books, 1965.

Kalsched, Donald. *The Inner World of Trauma: Archetypal Defenses of the Personal Spirit.* London: Routledge, 1996.

———. *Trauma and the Soul: A Psycho-spiritual Approach to Human Development and its Interruption.* London and New York: Routledge, 2013.

Krakow, Barry and Joseph Neidhardt. *Conquering Bad Dreams and Nightmares: A Guide to Understanding, Interpretation, and Cure.* New York: Berkley Books, 1992.

Kramer, Milton and Myron Glucksman (eds). *Dream Research: Contributions to Clinical Practice.* London and New York: Routledge, 2015.

Krippner, Stanley, Fariba Bogzaran, and Anthony Percia de Carvalho. *Extraordinary Dreams and How to Work With Them.* Albany, NY: SUNY Press, 2002.

Lewis, Jacqui, and Stanley Krippner, eds. *Working with Dreams and PTSD Nightmares: 14 Approaches for Psychotherapists and Counselors.* Santa Barbara, CA: Praeger, 2016.

Perls, Fritz. *Gestalt Therapy Verbatim.* Lafayette, CA: Real People Press, 1969.

Smith, Carlyle. *Heads Up Dreaming: How Your Dreams Can Predict Your Future and Change Your Life.* San Francisco: Turning Stone Press, 2014.

Stukane, Eileen. *The Dream Worlds of Pregnancy.* New York: Quill, 1985.

Ullman, Montague and Nan Zimmerman. *Working with Dreams.* Los Angeles: Jeremy P. Tarcher, 1979.

Van Bronkhorst, Jeanne. *Dreams at the Threshold.* Woodbury, MN: Llewellyn Publications, 2015.

Van de Castle, Robert. *Our Dreaming Mind.* New York: Ballantine Books, 1994.

Van der Kolk, Bessel. *The Body Keeps the Score.* New York: Viking, 2014.

Varela, Francisco. *Sleeping, Dreaming, and Dying: An Exploration of Consciousness With The Dalai Lama.* Boston: Wisdom Publications, 1997.

Von Franz, Marie Louise. *Puer Aeternus.* Boston: Sigo Press, 1981.

Von Franz, Marie Louise, Fraser Boa, and Marion Woodman. *The Way of the Dream: Conversations on Jungian Dream Interpretation with Dr. Marie-Louise Von Franz (with introductions and epilogues by Marion Woodman):* Windrose Films Ltd, 2008. Set of four DVDs available from the Marion Woodman Foundation: 212 Olive Street, Santa Cruz, CA. www.mwoodmanfoundation.org.

Waggoner, Robert. *Lucid Dreaming: Gateway to the Inner Self.* Needham, MA: Moment Point Press, 2009.

Index

His Dark Materials, 250

Hobbit Door, 176, 177, 287

homework, 9, 73, 78, 153, 160, 188–191

Huge Warship, 318–320, 322, 323

hypnosis, 23

I

idioms, 36, 44

illness motifs, 342

imagery rehearsal therapy (IRT), 197

imagination, 3, 4, 9, 23, 34, 50, 58, 72, 79, 89, 93, 94, 112–114, 131, 153, 181, 189, 191–193, 196, 197, 199, 222, 228, 244, 251, 259, 273, 274, 279, 301, 330, 335, 346, 358, 362, 382, 390

inner child, 141, 249, 350, 352, 355

inspiring contact motifs, 175, 215, 303, 330, 373

intention setting, 112, 113

Into the Tunnel, 179, 180, 292, 301

introject motifs, 146, 214, 269, 275, 276, 371

J

Jaws, 275

Jean Campbell, 394

Jeanne Van Bronkhorst, 386

Joseph Neidhardt, 197

Jungian model, 392

K

Kelly Bulkeley, 387

Key and the Hook, 206, 260, 363

Kidnapped!, 262

Knocking Out the Two Monkeys, 55, 236

L

language, 2, 21, 29, 34–36, 42, 44, 46, 50, 53, 64, 82, 132, 182, 184, 321

levels, 73, 87, 286, 373

limiting field motifs, 175, 380

Little Furry Creature, 232

lost, 8, 10, 21, 50, 51, 60, 77, 106, 108, 131, 134, 151, 161, 178, 205, 206, 249–251, 256, 292–294, 300, 321, 323, 371

lucid dreaming, 29, 30, 380, 386

what the dream is asking for, 72,
90, 94, 109, 208, 218

Y

Yogi Berra, 197

Young Man and the Old Man,
132, 191, 287

Yuri, 251, 252, 320, 322